John Scott

A Bibliography of Works Relating to Mary, Queen of Scots.

1544-1700

John Scott

A Bibliography of Works Relating to Mary, Queen of Scots. 1544-1700

ISBN/EAN: 9783337323998

Printed in Europe, USA, Canada, Australia, Japan

Cover: Foto ©Thomas Meinert / pixelio.de

More available books at **www.hansebooks.com**

A BIBLIOGRAPHY OF WORKS RELATING TO MARY QUEEN OF SCOTS · 1544-1700

BY JOHN SCOTT C.B.

PRINTED FOR THE
EDINBURGH BIBLIOGRAPHICAL SOCIETY
MDCCCXCVI

The Edinburgh Bibliographical Society.

A BIBLIOGRAPHY OF WORKS RELATING TO MARY QUEEN OF SCOTS: 1544-1700.

INTRODUCTION.

THE history of Mary Stuart Queen of Scots, of Scotland during her reign, and of the personages who figured during that period, in direct connection with the Queen, or who were brought into notice by their connection with the political events of the time, forms a mass of literature which the lapse of three hundred and fifty years has not sufficed to bring to a close. The books composing this mass are not to be found written in one language, or issuing solely from the presses of England and Scotland, but may be gleaned from almost every country in Europe, and, latterly, even from America.

While among the authors who have contributed to it are to be found men celebrated in the ranks of literature—as historians, poets, critics, dramatists, and novelists—many books are to be noted written by men little known in the world of letters, thus testifying to the world-wide interest which the history and misfortunes of the unfortunate Queen have called forth.

In the following pages an attempt has been made to enumerate the books printed between the date of Queen Mary's birth and the year 1700, which treat of the various branches of her history. Many of these books are commonly to be met with; others are of such rarity that they must be searched for in cabinets of the curious, or on the shelves of the choicer of the public libraries.

No systematic attempt, it would appear, has ever been made to catalogue or classify this heterogeneous mass of information. Some of the books which exist do not appear ever to have been noticed or quoted by modern authors. Although some lists have been prepared by various writers, all of them are more or less imperfect and unsatisfactory from a bibliographical point of view.

The first writer who devoted attention to the subject is Bishop Nicholson, in his *Scottish Historical Library*, published in 1702, where twenty-five printed books are quoted and partially described, in addition to a large number of manuscripts.

Watt, in the *Bibliotheca Britannica*, gives a fairly extended list; but, in accordance with the plan of his work, this partakes much of the character of an index.

The Crypt, a magazine published at Ringwood and at Winchester between the years 1827 and 1829, gives a list of 169 books published up till that date. The compilation of this list, from notes attached to some portions of it, seems to have given the editor infinite trouble. Much of the information is drawn from the catalogues of Thorpe and other booksellers, consequently the titles are, for the most part, abridged, and many errors have ensued. The description of the rarer books mentioned is drawn from reprinted editions, and some of them are noted in a manner altogether erroneous. The editor concludes his labours with the following note:—" Our bibliographical readers are probably not a little astonished to see this remarkable list so far extended as to comprise no less than 169 articles. We cannot promise that it is even yet concluded, and although every available source has been already explored, we do not despair that accidents may still occasionally add to our collection." The magazine ceased to be published after the issue of the number containing this note, and expectation was not from this source further gratified.

The list given in *The Crypt* probably formed the basis of the catalogue given in Lowndes' *Bibliographer's Manual* (Bohn's edition). The latter is, however, more comprehensive; but the additions having mainly been compiled from sale catalogues, it cannot, as a whole, be depended on either for correctness of title or name of author, and in the larger number of items no collation is given.

Brunet (*Manuel du Libraire*) notices a few of the rarer books, and refers the student to Lowndes.

Labanoff (*Collection des Lettres de Marie Stuart*) gives a list of books restricted to those which reproduce one or more of the Queen's letters, and few of the books mentioned come within the period embraced in the following enumeration.

Anderson, in his general preface to *Collections relating to the History of Mary Queen of Scotland* (1727) states that he has seen forty books in print professedly relating to the story of Queen Mary, and above sixty which occasionally, and sometimes very fully, touch upon her affairs. But beyond one or two books quoted in the preface, and the few rare books which he reprints, no systematic list is given by him.

The Catalogues of the Library of the British Museum and those of the Library of the Faculty of Advocates, and the Library of the Writers to the Signet, Edinburgh, contain valuable lists, including many of the rarer books which have been incorporated in the following Bibliography. It will be found, however, from the entries in the text that none of these magnificent collections are exhaustive, as, in common with all library catalogues, they necessarily contain only the books to be found on their respective shelves.

It has been considered most expedient to arrange the Bibliography in chronological order of publication, with full title and collation of each book, obtained in every case from a direct examination of one or more of the copies to be found in the libraries mentioned in the footnote following the collation of each book. Many of the books have been collated from copies in my own collection, which are distinguished by the mark *S*. Appended to the collation of each book is the dimensions in inches of the copies examined. Full sized photographic facsimiles of the titles of a number of the rarer books have also been added.

Bishop Nicholson (*Scottish Historical Library*), in his opening remarks on the literature connected with Queen Mary's reign, makes the following suggestions :—"Queen Mary of Scotland had a reign of so much action, and her sufferings, to the end of it, were of so extraordinary a nature, that 'tis no wonder that so many have attempted either the whole or part of her story, insomuch that we must be obliged to sort these numerous writers into several classes before we can be able to take a distinct view of the men and their labours." Even after the lapse of nearly two hundred years, the Bishop's advice appeared to be not unworthy of adoption. The various books have accordingly been classified after the following scheme, and a notification of the classes to which each belongs has been appended.

I. Books referring to the political state of Scotland during the early portion of Queen Mary's reign, including those especially treating of her proposed contract of marriage with Edward VI.; the French occupation of Scotland, and the English invasion.

viii   INTRODUCTION.

    II. Books referring to the personal history of the Queen while in France, and her marriage to the Dauphin.

    III. Books referring to her personal history, and the events of her reign, from the time of her return to Scotland until her flight into England.

    IV. Controversial books connected with the Queen's personal history, from her arrival in England until her death; the political state of Scotland during that period; the right of succession to the Crown of England; and her imprisonment and execution.

    V. Books dedicated to the Queen.

    VI. Books containing poems or sonnets addressed to the Queen.

    VII. Biographical monographs and memoirs of the Queen.

    VIII. Official documents issued during the Queen's reign; Acts of Parliament, Proclamations, &c., having special reference to her.

    IX. Dramas and Poems, having the Queen's history for their subject, or in which she is introduced as one of the *dramatis personæ*.

    X. Formal histories of the Queen's reign, and histories partially treating of it.

    XI. Books which refer incidentally to the history of the Queen.

My warmest acknowledgments are due to Mr J. T. Clark, Keeper of the Library of the Faculty of Advocates, Edinburgh, and to Mr T. G. Law Librarian of the Library of the Writers to the Signet, Edinburgh, for their attention in facilitating my examination of many of the books described.

Mr G. P. Johnston, the Secretary of the Edinburgh Bibliographical Society, and Mr William Cowan, a member of the Society, have rendered most valuable assistance in examining the copies from which the collations have been taken, and correcting the proofs.

To Mr H. G. Aldis, a member of the Society, who has most carefully prepared the Index, my best thanks are due.

JOHN SCOTT.

HALKSHILL, LARGS, AYRSHIRE,
    October 1896.

A BIBLIOGRAPHY OF WORKS RELATING TO MARY QUEEN OF SCOTS · 1544-1700

BY JOHN SCOTT C.B.

PRINTED FOR THE
EDINBURGH BIBLIOGRAPHICAL SOCIETY
MDCCCXCVI

BIBLIOGRAPHY.

1544

1. The late expedicion in Scotlande, made by the Kynges hyghnys armye, under the conduit of the ryght honorable the Erle of Hertforde, the yere of oure Lorde God 1544. Londini. Cum priuilegio ad imprimendum solum.

 8vo (5⅜ × 3½). 𝔅. 𝔏. A—D in fours. Catchwords, but no pagination. A1^a Title. A1^b—D4^b Text, beginning, The late expedition in Scotlande sent to the ryght honorable Lorde Russel, Lorde priuie seale, from the Kynges armye there by a frende of hys. (This sentence printed in italic.) Colophon at bottom of D4^b. Imprynted at London in Powls churchyarde by Reynolde Wolfe, at the synge of ye Brasen Serpent. Anno. 1544. Cum priuilegio ad imprimendum solum.

 A MS. note by Mr Grenville attached to his unique copy of this book, now in the British Museum, states, "This account of the Protector Somerset's expedition into Scotland while he was still Earl of Hertforde is perhaps the rarest of the Scotch Historical pieces, and was sold at the Roxburghe sale for 30 guineas; since that time I have not seen another copy."

 It is the first book having reference to Scottish history printed after the birth of Queen Mary, and gives an account of the expedition launched by Henry VIII. against Scotland with a view of enforcing the marriage treaty. The bad faith of the Scots is put forward by the Earl of Hertforde in the answer given by him to the Provost of Edinburgh when the latter declined to surrender the town. The expedition, it says, was intended (D1) "to proue whether the Scottes had yet learned by theyr importable losses lately chaunced to them to teder theyr owne weales by true and reasonable unytynge & adioynyng them selues to the Kynges maiesties louyng liege people." Grafton, in his Chronicle (see No. 59), has in many passages embodied the narrative of this book verbatim. The Tract was reprinted by J. Graham Dalyell in Fragments of Scotish History (Edinburgh, A. Constable, 1798, 4to); and with modernised spelling in Rare and Curious Collection of Historical Tracts and Pamphlets (No. 15. Edinburgh, E. & G. Goldsmid, 1886, 8vo).

Class I.   *B.M.*

1547

2. An Exhortacion to the Scottes, to conforme them selfes to the honorable, expediēt, and godly union, betwene the twoo Realmes of Englande and Scotlande.

 8vo (5 × 3⅜). 𝔅. 𝔏. a—h in eights. Without pagination. a1^a Title, enclosed in a woodcut border, with emblematical supporters, having the Royal Arms of England on a globe at top and Richard Grafton's Printer's Mark at bottom, verso blank. a2—a7 Dedication : To the right high and mightie prince, Edward, Duke of Somerset, &c., Gouernor of the persone of the Kynges Maiestie of Englande, and Protector of all his Realmes Dominions and Subiectes &c. : James Harryson Scottisheman wisheth healthe, honor, and felicite. a8^a blank. a8^b a woodcut of the Arms of England, borne by Angels, with the motto Dieu et mon Droit encircling a rose. b1—h8 An Exhortacion. Colophon at bottom of h8^b : Excussum Londini in ædibus Richardi Graftoni typis Impressoris. Anno salutis nostre, 1547.

 An extremely scarce tract, issued when the Protector Somerset was approaching the Scottish frontier prior to the battle of Pinkie.

 The Queen of Scotland is very frequently mentioned in reference to the marriage treaty.

A

The following MS. note by Mr Grenville is attached to his imperfect copy now in the British Museum: "I have not heard of any copy of the original Declaration being extant, except the present."

The accompanying facsimile (No. I.) of the title-page is taken from a very beautiful copy which has appeared since the date of Mr Grenville's note.

The tract has been reprinted, with an assumed title taken from Lowndes' Bibliography, in an appendix to the English Text Society's reprint of the Complaynt of Scotland, edited by Dr J. A. H. Murray (London, 1872, 8vo).

Class I.   *B.M. (wants title-page). S.*

1548

3. An Epitome of the Title that the Kynges Maiestie of Englande, hath to the souereigntie of Scotlande, continued vpon the auncient writers of both nacions from the beginnyng. M.D.XLVIII. Cvm priuilegio ad imprimendvm solvm.

    8vo (5¾ × 3½). 𝔅. 𝔏. a—h in eights. Without pagination. a1ª Title, verso blank. a2ª—a5ª To the most noble and excellent prince, Edward the VI. by the grace of GOD Kynge of Englande, &c.: your humble and obediēt subiecte Nicholas Bodrugan otherwise Adams, wissheth lōg life, and the same prosperous and happie. a5ᵇ—h6ᵇ The Kynges Title to Scotlande. h7ª Colophon: EXCVSVM LONDINI, IN AEDIBVS RICHARDI GRAFTONI, TYPOGRAPHI REGII. M.D.XLVIII. CVM PRIVILEGIO AD IMPRIMENDVM SOLVM. h7ᵇ—h8 blank.

    This and the following tract have been reprinted by the English Text Society in an Appendix to the Complaynt of Scotland, edited by Dr J. A. H. Murray.

(See Facsimile No. II.)

Class I.   *B.M. Adv. S.*

4. An Epistle or exhortation, to vnitie & peace sent frō the Lorde Protector & others the kynges moste honorable counsaill of England To the Nobilitie, Gentlemen, and Commons, and al others the inhabitauntes of the Realme of Scotlande.

    8vo (5¼ × 3⅜). 𝔅. 𝔏. A—B in eights + C⁴. Without pagination. A1 Title, enclosed within an elaborate woodcut border, surmounted by the Royal Arms of England, verso blank. A2—C4ª Edward by the grace of God Duke of Somersett, Erle of Hertford &c.: To the nobilitie . . . and all others the inhabitauntes of the realme of Scotlande: Gretyng and Peace. An Epistle. C4ᵇ Colophon: EXCVSVM LONDINI, IN AEDIBVS RICHARDI GRAFTONI, TYPOGRAPHI REGII. ANNO SALUTIS HUMANÆ. M.D.XLVIII. CVM PRIVILEGIO AD IMPRIMENDVM SOLVM.

    A very rare tract, issued after the battle of Pinkie, showing the advantages to Scotland of uniting the realms by the marriage of the sovereigns. A Latin edition is said by Lowndes to have been issued simultaneously with the title: Epistola exhortatoria ad pacem missa ab illustrissimo Principe Domino Proctectore Angliæ, ac caeteris Regiæ Maiestatis Consiliariis ad Nobilitatem ac plebem, universumq: populum Regni Scotiæ. Lond. per Reg. Wolfium, 1548.

(See Facsimile No. III.)

Class I.   *B.M. S.*

5. The Expedicion into Scotlāde of the most woorthely fortunate prince Edward, Duke of Soomerset, uncle unto our most noble souereign lord ȳ Kiges Maiestic Edward the. VI. Goouernour of hys hyghnes persone, and Protectour of his graces Realmes, dominions and subiectes: made in the first yere of his Maiesties most prosperous reign, and set out by way of diarie, by W. Patten Londoner. Vivat Victor.

    8vo (5½ × 3⅜). 𝔅. 𝔏. ✠ + a — c in eights + d² + A — P in eights. Without pagination. ✠1ª Title. ✠1ᵇ Felicitation, To the Right honorable Syr William Paget, Knyght of the Garter. ✠2—✠4ª Dedication. ✠4ᵇ—d2 A Preface seruing for muche parte, instead of argument for the

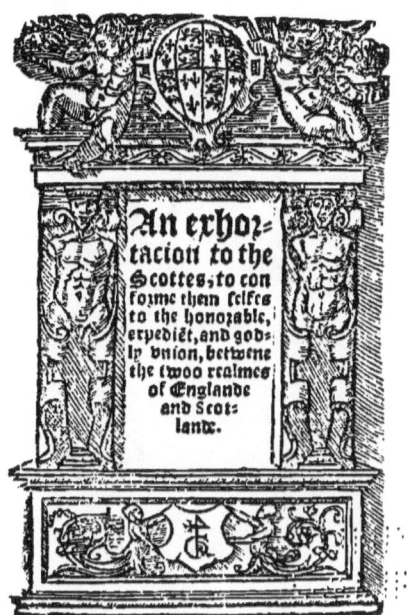

Edin. Bibl. Soc.—Queen Mary Literature. Facsimile No. 1.   See No. 3, page 2.

AN EPI=
tome of the title that the kynges Maiestie of Englande, hath to the souereigntie of Scotlande, continued vpon the aunci‑
ent writers
of both
na‑
tions, from
the beginnyng.

M.D.XLVIII.

CVM PRIVILEGIO
AD IMPRIMEN‑
DVM SOLVM

matter of the storie ensuing. A1 Certayn noble men, and other beyinge speciall officers in thys expedicion. A2—P1ᵃ The Story and proces of the journey. P1ᵇ—P7ᵃ Peroracion unto the gentle reder, with a shorte rehersall of the Actes doon. (At end) Out of the Parsonage of s. Mary hill in London this xxviii. of January 1548. P7ᵇ P8ᵃ Fautes escaped in the pryntinge, and to be correct as followeth. P8ᵇ Colophon: Imprinted in Londō, the last daie of June in the second yere of the reigne of our souereigne lorde King Edward the vi.: by Richard Grafton, printer to his most royall Maiestie, in the yere of our lord M.D.XLVIII. ¶ Cum priuilegio ad imprimendum solum.
Reprinted in Dalyell's Fragments of Scotish History, 1798.

Class I.   *B.M. Adv. Signet. S.*

1549

6. The Complaynt of Scotland vyth ane Exortatione to the Thre Estaits to be vigilante in the Deffens of their Public veil.

8vo ($4\frac{1}{4} \times 3\frac{1}{4}$).

Of this book, so interesting in connection with the early period of Queen Mary's reign, and so remarkable for its literary peculiarities in matter and in style, the authorship is uncertain and the place of printing a matter of debate.

Only four copies (those indicated below) are known to exist, in a more or less imperfect condition, and none of them now contains a title-page.

It is superfluous in this place to give any account or criticism of the matter of the book, or to insert a collation. The reprints, edited respectively by Dr Leyden (Edinburgh, 1801, 8vo) and by Dr J. A. H. Murray for the English Text Society (London, 1872, 8vo), enter fully into these subjects.

It suffices to notice that in the Dedication to Mary of Guise, addressed by the author as "The Excellent and Illustir Marie Quene of Scotlande, the margareit and perle of princesses," her daughter, Mary Queen of Scots, is mentioned in the following passage: "Ande als your grace heand absent fra your only young dochter, our nobil princes, and rycheteous heretour of Scotland : quha is presentlye veil tretit in the gouernance of hyr fadir of lau, the maist illustir potent prince of the maist fertil and pacebil realme," &c., &c.

Class I.   *B.M. (two copies). Adv. S.*

1555

7. The Copie of a letter sent in to Scotlande, of the ariuall and landynge, and moste noble marryage of the moste Illustre Prynce Philippe, Prynce of Spaine, to the most excellente Princes Marye Quene of England, solemnisated in the Citie of Winchester: and howe he was receyued and installed at Windsore, and of his triumphyng entries in the noble Citie of London. ¶ Wherunto, is added a brefe ouerture or openyng of the legacion of the most reuerende father in God Lorde Cardinall Poole from the Sea Apostolyke of Rome, with the substaunce of his oracyon to the Kyng and Queenes Magestic, for the reconcilement of the Realme of Englande to the unitie of the Catholyke churche. With the very coppe also of the Supplycatiō exhibited to their highnesses by the three Estates assembled in the parlamente. Wherin they representing the whole body of the Realme and dominions of the same, haue submitted theselues to the Popes Holinesse.

[Colophon: Imprinted at London in Fletestrete at the signe of the Sunne ouer agaynst the Conduit by John Waylande. Cum priuelegio per septenium.]

8vo ($5\frac{3}{4} \times 3\frac{3}{4}$). ❦. ℒ. A—F in eights. A1 Title, verso blank. A2—F6ᵃ A copy of a letter sent into Scotlande, To the ryghte reuerende & his very especial good lord, lord Robert Stuarde

Bishoppe of Cathenes, & priest of Dūbritane Colledge in Scotland, John Elder his humble oratour, wisheth health, and prosperous felicitie. F6ᵇ—F8ᵃ The copy of the Queenes Magesties letters patentes, ending with the Colophon printed above. F8ᵇ blank. Without pagination, but with catchwords on both sides.

This very rare book contains the first notice of Lord Darnley. John Elder, its author, a native of Caithness (see Laing's Works of John Knox, Vol. I. Appendix VI. p. 526) spent twelve years at the Universities of St Andrews, Aberdeen, and Glasgow. He fled to England probably in 1541, and about two years later addressed a letter to Henry VIII., containing a project for the Union of the Kingdoms " by a Pryinces whom your excellent Maiestie moost godly desyres for to be mariede with noble prince Edowarde, your Graces lawful begotten sonne & heare of the empyre of England." This letter is printed from the original MS. in the British Museum in Bannatyne Club Miscell., Vol. I. Probably through the influence of Robert Stuard, Bishop of Caithness (to whom this book is addressed), he was patronised by the Earl of Lennox, and was appointed tutor to the Lord Darnley. The Copie of a letter sent in to Scotlande was printed shortly after he had vacated that charge. Its concluding sentences, giving an account of his pupil's character and attainments, and presaging a happy future for so virtuous a gentleman, were sadly belied by the events of little more than ten years after, which have thrown so melancholy a halo round the memory of Henry the Lord Darnley. The passage is as follows :—" I haue also sent your lordship certaine verses and adages written with the hande of the Lord Henry Stuarde, lorde Dernley, your nephew, which he wrot this time tweluemoneth : I beinge with him then at Temple Newsome in Yorkshire. And what praise your Lordship may thinke him worthie, for this his towardnes in wrighting, being yet not fully IX. yeares of age, The like praise is he worthye (suerlye) in his towardnes in the latin tonge and the frenche, and in sundrye other vertuous qualities : whom also, God and nature hath endued with a good wit, ientilnes, beautie and fauour. So yf it may please God to lend him long life, he shall proue a witty, vertuous and an actiue well learned gentle man, Whose noble parentes are my singular good patrons. . . . From the citie of London this new yeares day and the first of yᵉ Kalenders of January 1555. By youre Reuerende Lordeships humble oratour Iohn Elder."

From a Memorandum among the Harleian MSS. (Printed for The Maitland Club—Selections illustrating the Reign of Mary Queen of Scots, p. 101) it appears that Elder was in France in 1561. The following extract, taken in connection with the passage quoted above, is curious :—" One Elder, a Scottisheman my acquentance, haitht been witht me ; he tould me he had letters from my lorde Obenze to my lorde of Levenax, my lord Dernelie as I think to my lady. Amonge otheres talkes he said my lorde Dernelie was muche spoken of in France, and that my lorde Obenze tould him the King of Naverne asked him in talkes of my lorde Dernelie, his stature age and upbringing. Elder said that he shew the quene of Scottes in France my Lord Dernelies hande, which he wrote being eight yeares of age ; he seameth to sew for his pencion, and yf he spede not thinketh he shalbe welcum to the Scottishe quene. I know the man, and haitht gone no fardar witht him as yett, yt . . . he confessed to me he had fyftie crownes in his departour from the Cardinall of Lorraine ; he haitht wytt to playe the aspye where he listeth."

Elder's letter is a book of very great rarity. A copy, which had formerly been Lord Oxford's, and thereafter successively in the libraries of West, Mason, Bindley, and Heber, was sold at Dr David Laing's sale to Mr B. Quaritch. This and the copies mentioned below seem to be all that are known.

Class I.   B.M. (three copies, one imperfect). S.

8.   In Dominicam Orationem Pia Meditatio, qua in Deum animus fidelis, mirum in modum excitatur.   Authore Patricio Cocburno, Scoto, etc. [Woodcut of Hercules and the Centaur.]

Ex Typographia Iohannis Scot, in Ciuitate Sancti Andreæ 15. Calendeis Octobris. 1555. Cum Priuilegio Regali.

8vo (5¼ × 3½). Sll. unsigned + *4+A—L in eights. 1 Title, verso blank. 2—ᵒ2ᵃ Epistola Nuncupatoria. Illvstrissimae Principi, Generis Nobilitate, atq; virtutum omnium splendore, clarissimae: MARIAE, Regni Scotorum Regenti dignissimae, Patricius Cocburnus, obedientium humillimus, & obsequentissimus, Gratiā, Salutem, & Pacem optat, A deo patre nostro, per IESVM Christum Dominum nostrum. *2ᵇ—4ᵃ In oratione pia, et fideli observanda. *4ᵇ Oratio Dominica. A—L8ᵃ The Text. L8ᵇ Typographvs pio lectori, followed by Colophon : Excudebat Ioannes Scott. 1555. C. P. R.   Each sheet is signed on first recto only, and these leaves have no catchwords. The leaves of Text A—K are numbered 2—80. Sheet L is without numeration.

The dedicatory epistle to Queen Mary of Guise is of considerable interest, from its references to that Queen's participation in the government of Scotland and her husband's career. It seems to be the first printed book which mentions Mary Queen of Scots by her name. The following is the passage (Epistola Nuncupatoria, leaf 3), "Agnouit nimirū tua satis prudētia, hāc tuā in nos collatā beneficentiā, in totam Remp. tuā redundare : cum ex hac tua academia, tranquillitate, & ocio sancto, tuo fruente beneficio (ut olim ex equo illo troiano armati milites irruerunt) prodituri sunt uiri, bonis literis ornati, atq ; omnium bonarum artium genere, instructi, & muniti : qui in Rep. tua moderanda, & administranda : in Christiana item religione, et fide propugnanda, & promouēda, tibi, tuaeq ; filiae MARIAE Reginae nostrae serenissimae, Reip. & Regno, vsui, & ornamento esse possunt."

Pia Meditatio, the second known book printed by John Scot at St Andrews, is of great rarity. Dickson and Edmond (Annals of Scottish Printing) only quote the copy from which the collation is taken, but another occurs in the Advocates' Library at Edinburgh. The author is named by Spottiswood (History of the Church of Scotland) as one of the foremost men in promoting the Reformation. He states that "Next to him (Sir David Lindsay of the Mount) shall be remembered Mr Patrick Cockburn, a gentleman of the house of Langton, in the Merse. This man having by his studies attained to great learning, lived a long time in the University of Paris, well esteemed . . . by the treatises yet extant which he wrote, it appeareth that he was a man of good learning, and a favourer of the truth. Seven years after issuing the Pia Meditatio, he was appointed to preach, in conjunction with others, in the unplanted kirks of the Merse, and afterwards became the first Protestant minister of Haddington."

Class I. *Adv. S.*

1556

9.   L'Histoire De La Gverre D'Escosse, Traitant comme le Royaume fut assailly, & en grād' partie occupé par les Anglois, & depuis rendu paisible à sa Reyne, & reduit en son ancien estat & dignité.

A Monseigneur Messire François de Montmorency, Cheualier de l'ordre, Capitaine de cinquante hommes d'armes, Gouuerneur de Paris, & de l'isle de France. Par Ian de Beaugué, gentilhomme François.

A Paris, pour Estienne Groulleau, libraire demeurant en la rue neufue nostre Dame, à l'image sainct Ian. 1556. Avec Privilege dv Roy.

8vo (6¼ × 4). a—p in eights. 119 numbered ll., with catchwords on verso. a1ᵃ Title. a1ᵇ Privilege to Gilles Corrozet, dated 1556. Acheué d'imprimer pour la premiere edition le douziesme dudit mois de Septembre audit an 1556. a2ᵃ—a3ᵇ Ode de Ian de Barot Baron de Taye, sur l'histoire du Seigneur de Beaugué. a3ᵇ—a6ᵇ Table des Chapitres. a7—a8 Dedicatory letter to F. de Montmorency, dated Paris, 10th September 1556, and signed Ian de Beaugué. b1—p7 Text, with colophon, Imprimé à Paris par Benoist Preuost, en la rue Freinentel, à l'enseigne de l'Estoille d'or. p8 blank. All the copies of the book bear the same colophon, but it was issued in identically the same form, with the exception of the imprint on the titles, as the copy of Groulleau, described above. A Paris, Pour Gilles Corrozet [the proprietor of the privilege] en la grand' salle du Palais, pres la chambre des Consultations, 1556, Avec Privilege dv Roy ; and also A Paris, pour Vincent Sartenas, tenant sa boutique au Palais, en la gallerie de la Chancellerie & en la rue Neufue nostre

Dame, a lenseigne sainct Ian l'Euangeliste 1556. Avec Priuilege dv Roy. The book in each variety of imprint is of considerable rarity, but the copies issued by Sartenas are more uncommon than the others.

L'Histoire de la Guerre d'Escosse is occupied by an account of the expedition sent to Scotland in 1548 by Henry II. of France, to assist Mary of Guise in repelling the occupation of the country by the English power, in reference to the renunciation of the marriage contract between Queen Mary and Edward VI. The author accompanied the Commander of the French force probably as one of his staff, and, as an eyewitness, has given, in the quaint French of the sixteenth century, many interesting details, not only of the events of the campaign, but of the incidents of the Scottish politics of the period. A reprint was made by the Maitland Club (Edimbourg, 1830, 4to), with a preface, which contains a curious error. It is stated, "Of the author M. De Beaugué, after a very careful search nothing can be discovered or even of his more distinguished friend M. de Desse, the commander of the expedition." As regards the latter, the statement has been made without care. André de Montalembert, Seigneur d'Esse, born in 1483, a most distinguished soldier who had won renown in Italy, Provence, and France, was specially selected for his valour and skill to conduct the Scottish expedition. After distinguishing himself there, he was recalled to France to receive still higher command against the English at Boulogne. Finally, in 1553, selected to conduct the defence of Thérouane against the army of the Emperor, he died fighting in the breach a few days before its capture. Brantome and other French biographers have amply described his life, but it has been left to the representative of his family, Comte de Montalembert, since the publication of the Maitland Club reprint of De Beaugué's work, to focus the information which is available. In a second reprint, A Bordeaux par G. Gounouilhou, 1862, 8vo (a copy on vellum, S.), "avec un avant-propos par Le Comte de Montalembert, ancien Pair de France, l'un des quarante de l'Académie Francaise," much interesting information is given. It may be interesting to note that F. de Montmorency, to whom De Beaugué dedicates his book, was the second in command at the defence of Thérouane, and that Ian de Barot, the author of the preliminary ode, was an officer in the Scottish expedition, and was with D'Esse on the fatal day at Thérouane.

An English translation of De Beaugué's book has the following title, The History of the Campagnes 1548 and 1549 being an exact Account of the Martial Expeditions performed in those days by the Scots and French on one side, and by the English and their Foreign Auxiliaries on the other. Done in French, under the Title of the Scots War, &c., by Monsieur Beaugue, a French Gentleman. Printed at Paris in the year 1556. With an introductory preface by the Translator. Printed in the year M.D.CC.VII. 8vo. The translator is Patrick Abercromby, author of the Martial Achievements of the Scottish Nation, who adds a long preface.

Class I.   *B.M.*   *Adv.*   *Signet.*   *S.*

1558

10.   Ioachimi Bellaii Andini Poematvm Libri qvatvor : qvibvs continentvr, Elegiæ. Varia Epigr. Amores. Tvmvli. [Printer's Mark of F. Morellus.]

Parisiis, Apud Federicum Morellum, in uico Bellouaco, ad vrbanam Morum. M.D.LVIII. Cvm privilegio regis.

4to (8¾ × 5¼). A—P in fours Q². 62 ll. numbered. A1 Title. Privilege on verso. A2ª Epistle to the Printer. A2ᵇ Dedication to Margaret, only sister of Henry II. A3—Q1ᵇ Elegies. Q2ª A poem in Greek and tables of errata. Q2ᵇ blank. On f. 30 In fvtvras nvptias Francisci Gall. Delphini, et Mariæ Stuartæ Scotorū Reginæ.

Class II.   *S.*

11.   Nvptiale Carmen Renati Gvillonii Mercvrium agentis, quo exhortatur Franciscū Valesium Galliarum Delphinū ad vxorem ducendam, Mariam vtpote Scotiæ reginam, quam tandem duxit anno. 1558. Aprilis die 24.

Addita svnt ab eodem Avtore aliquot Epigrammata, quorum aliqua pertinent ad historiam nostri temporis.

Parisiis. Apud Andream Wechelum. 1558.

<small>4to (8½ × 6). A in four. With pagination. A1 Title, verso blank. A2—A4 Nuptiale Carmen, &c.</small>

Class II.   *S.*

12. Epithalamivm Francisci Valesii, Illvstriss. Franciæ Delphini & Mariæ Stuartæ, sereniss. Scotorum Reginæ. Adr. Turnebo auctore. [Woodcut with Cupid in the centre, surrounded by entwined serpents.]

Parisiis, M.D.LVIII. Apud Guil. Morelium, in Græcis typographum Regium.

<small>8vo (6⅞ × 4⅜). A⁴+B². A1 Title, verso blank. A2—B2ᵇ Epithalamium. The Text is printed in italic letter.</small>

Class II.   *B.M.*   *S.*

13. In Francisci Illvstriss. Franciæ Delphini, et Mariæ Sereniss. Scotorvm Reginæ Nvptias, viri cvivsdam ampliss, carmen. [Morel's Printer's mark.]

Parisiis, Apud Federicum Morellum, in vico Bellouaco, ad urbanam Morum, 1558. Cvm Privilegio Regis.

<small>4to (8 × 5¾). Four leaves signed A. Without pagination or catchwords. A1 Title, verso blank. A2—A4 Text. The Text is printed in italic letter.</small>

Class II.   *B.M.*   *S.*

14. Chantz Royavlx svr les Triumphes du mariage du Roy Daulphin, & de la Royne Daulphine. Par Iacques de la Tapie d'Aurillac.

[Printer's mark, a portcullis with floreated border, and the motto, Evertit et Æquat. The initials of the printer, D. O. H., in the centre.]

A Paris. De l'Imprimerie d'Oliuier de Harsy, au clos Bruneau à l'enseigne de la corne de Cerf. 1558.

<small>8vo (6¼ × 4). A—D in fours, without pagination or catchwords. Sheet A is unsigned. A1ª Title. A1ᵇ Anagrammatization du nom d'illustre Princesse Marie d'Esteuart, Royne d'Escosse, & Daulphine de France.</small>

> As tu de meriarie,
> Et de sur art amie
> Dieu, mer, & hasard?
> Dame d'art seruie,
> Tard me sert, à vie
> Mettie ieu d'hazard.

At the top of this page is a printer's arabesque ornament with human figure in centre, and two compartments with the initials T F F and F F F. A2—D2 Text. The first and second chantz royaulx are addressed to François de Valois Roy d'Escosse & Daulphin de France. The third and fourth to Marie d'Esteuart Royne d'Escosse & Daulphine de France. The fifth to Cardinal Charles de Lorraine. The sixth du mesme à la divine bonté. D3ª Hvictain à la Royne Daulphine, with a repetition of the arabesque ornament at top of page. D3ᵇ Egregio Viro ac doctiss. D. D. Iacobo Betonio Glasciiensi Archiepiscopo observandiss. Scotiae Legato, I. Tapianus. Fourteen lines of Latin elegiacs. D4ª Observandissimo D. D. Roberto Reid. Orcadum Insularum Episcopo Scotiæ Legato, I. Tapianus. Fourteen lines of Latin elegiacs. D4ᵇ blank.

The Archbishop and Bishop formed part of the deputation sent from Scotland to attend Queen Mary's marriage. The book is of great rarity.

Class II.   *S.*

15. Discovrs dv Grand et Magnifiqve Trivmphe faict au mariage de tresnoble & magnifique Prince François de Vallois Roy-Dauphin, filz aisné du treschrestien Roy de France Henry II. du nom, & de treshaulte & vertueuse Princesse madame Marie d'Estreuart Roine d'Escosse. Avec Priuilege.

    A Paris par Annet Briere, en la rue des Porées, à l'enseigne sainct Sebastian. 1558.
       8vo ($6\frac{1}{4} \times 4\frac{1}{2}$). A—C in fours. A1 Title, privilege on verso. A2^a—C3^b Discours. C4 blank.
       A reprint of this very rare book was made by G. Gounouilhou, Bordeaux, 1863. A few copies only were issued, one in my collection being on vellum.

Class II.   *B.M.*

16. Le Discovrs Dv Grand et Magnifiqve Trivmphe faict au mariage de tresnoble & magnifique Prince François de Vallois Roy-Dauphin, filz aisné du treschrestien Roy de France Héry ij. de ce nom, & de treshaulte & vertueuse Princesse madame Marie d'Estreuart Royne d'Escosse.

    A Lyon, Par Jean Brotot. 1558.
       8vo ($6\frac{1}{2} \times 4\frac{1}{4}$). A—B in fours. A1 Title, verso blank. A2—B4 Discours.
       This edition, like No. 17, is a contemporary reprint, without privilege, of the Paris original (No. 15), and is of extreme rarity. The text of the Discours does not differ from the Paris edition, and it will be observed that it reproduces the unusual form of spelling Estreuart. It may be noted, as a strange omission in this account of the marriage, that no mention is made of the presence of the Scottish noblemen sent to represent their country at the ceremony.

Class II.   *S.*

17. Discours du Grand et Magnifique triumphe, fait au mariage de tresnoble & magnifique Prince François de Vallois Roy Dauphin fils aisné du treschrestien Roy de France Henry deuxiesme du nom, & tres haute & vertueuse Princesse, Madame Marie d'Estreuart Royne d'Escosse.

    A Rouen chez Iaspar de Remortier & Raulin Boulée, au Portail des Libraires. 1558.
       8vo ($5\frac{3}{4} \times 3\frac{1}{2}$). A^4 + B^2. A1 Title, verso blank. A2^a—B2^b Discours.
       Reprinted by William Bentham for the Roxburghe Club. London. G. Woodfal. 1818. 4to.
       It appears that Mr Bentham believed that this pirated Rouen version was the original and only edition.

Class II.   *B.M.*

18. Ioannis Mercerii Montacvtani Adolescentis Dialogus, in nobilissimi gallorum Delphini, & Illustrissimæ Scotorum Reginæ Nuptias. Eiusdem aliquot Epigrammata. Ad Nobillisimum clarissimúmque virum, Dominum Annam de la Chenal, Belleacum Abbatem, Regium Eleemosinarium, Cardinalisque Lotharingi Protonotarium.

    Parisiis, Apud Gabrielem Buon, in clauso Brunello, ad D. Claudii insigne. 1558.
       8vo ($6\frac{1}{4} \times 3\frac{7}{8}$). a—c in eights d^4. Without pagination. a1 Title, with a poem to the book on verso. a2^a Dedication. a2^b Diologi Personae (Nuntius, Apollo, and the nine Muses). a3—a8 Dialogus. b1—d3^b Epigrammata. d4^a Errata. d4^b blank.
       The various personages represented in the Dialogus refer frequently to the young Queen's mar-

DESCRIPTION DES ROYAVL-
MES D'ANGLE-
TERRE ET
D'ESCOSSE.

Composé par Maistre Estienne Perlin.

A PARIS,

Chez François Trepeau, demeurant rue Sainct Victor, deuant le Colleige du Cardinal le moyne.
1558.

riage, and extol the renewal of the ancient alliance with Scotland. Two of the Epigrams are addressed to the Dauphin as King of Scotland, while two others have his marriage to the Queen as their special subject.

Class II.   *B.M.*

19.   Ex Cvivsdam commentariis Historiarvm Nostri temporis, excepta Oratio, quam ipsa sponsalium die Regina Scotiæ ad Henricum regem habuit.

Parisiis Apud Andream Wechelum. 1558.

4to ($8\frac{1}{4} \times 5\frac{1}{4}$). A in four. A1ª Title. A1ᵇ—A4ᵇ Text, without catchwords. Pages 1-8 inclusive of title.

The text is concluded with the words, "Cætera in libris historiarum." No other copy of this very rare tract has been traced in this country, except a copy which was in Heber's possession. (Heber Sale Catalogue, Part VII., No. 4108.) It was probably the composition of Michel de l'Hospital, the Chancellor of France, and issued as a State paper at the time of Queen Mary's marriage to back up the pretensions of the Dauphin to be recognised as King of Scotland by the Scottish Ambassadors who attended the marriage.

The preamble contains many curious passages regarding the Queen before her departure from Scotland for France. In the speech to the King of France, Mary is made to place everything in his hands.

Class II.   *S.*

20.   The Appellation of Iohn Knoxe from the cruell and most iniust sentence pronounced against him by the false bishoppes and clergie of Scotland, with his supplication and exhortation to the nobilitie, estates, and cōmunaltie of the same realme.

Printed at Geneva M.D.LVIII.

8vo (5 × 3). A—K in eighths. 80 numbered leaves, with catchwords on verso. A1 Title, verso blank. A2—F6ᵇ The Appellation of John Knoxe. F7—H3¹ John Knoxe to the Commvnaltie. H3ᵇ—K5ª An Admonition to England and Scotland to call them to repentance, written by Antoni Gilby. K5ᵇ—K6ª John Knoxe to the Reader. K6ᵇ—K8¹ Psalme of David xcIIII., turned into metre by W. Kethe. K8ᵇ blank.

Queen Mary is specially named in reference to the Treaty of Edinburgh and her marriage with the Dauphin.

Class I.   *B.M. Adv. S.*

21.   The First blast of the Trumpet against the monstrvovs regiment of women. Veritas temporis filia. M.D.LVIII.

8vo ($5\frac{1}{4} \times 3\frac{3}{8}$). A—G in eighths. 56 numbered leaves. A1 Title, verso blank. A2—A8 The Preface. B1—G8 Text.

Class I. II.   *B.M. Adv. S.*

22.   Description des Royaulmes d'Angleterre et d'Escosse, composé par Maistre Estienne Perlin.

A Paris, chez Francois Trepau, demeurant rue Sainct Victor, deuant le Colleige du Cardinal le moyne. 1558.

8vo ($6\frac{1}{4} \times 4\frac{1}{4}$). A—E in eights. A1 Title, privilege on verso. A2ª—A3ᵇ Dedication to the Duchess de Berri. A4—E5 Text. E6—E8 Three blank leaves. Dedication and Text have the leaves numbered 2—37, with catchwords on verso.

This very curious book, which is of extreme rarity, contains several references to Queen Mary. A MS. note, by James Bindley, attached to my copy is as follows :—" Mem : a very scarce and curious Book. Reprinted by Mr Gough, as such in 4to in 1775, together with De la Serre's Entrée de la Reine Mère dans la Grande Bretagne &c. I never saw another copy of the original, except that mentioned by Mr Gough, sold at Mr West's Sale in 1773, April 23rd, No. 4195 of his Library Sale Catalogue, and purchased by Mr Martin of Worcestershire, while I was in the Room, at a considerable Price. J. B. 1793." The copy in the British Museum is probably that bought at West's sale.

In addition to the reprint mentioned in Bindley's note, a translation appeared in the *Antiquarian Repertory*, Vol. IV. This translation has been reproduced by Mr P. Hume Brown, in *Early Travellers in Scotland*. Edinburgh, 1891. 8vo.

Mr P. H. Brown assumes, in the introduction to his reprint of the translation, that the author was an ecclesiastic. But in another work (De variis morborum generibus opusculum, authore Stephano Perlino Parisiensi, Parisiis, 1558) the privilege describes Perlin as "nostre bien amé, maistre Estienne Perlin estudiant en la faculté de medicine en l'Université de Paris."

It seems probable that he had visited Scotland as a medical attaché to the French army of occupation during the regency of Mary of Guise, and that the date of his visit was earlier than 1551-1552 assigned to it in *Early Scottish Travellers*.

(*See Facsimile No. IV.*)

Class I.   B.M. S.

1559

23. Epitalamio di M. Gabriel Symeoni Fior. Sopra l'vtile della Pace, & la celebratione delle Nozze del Re Catolico & de l'Illustrissimo Duca de Sauoia. A i due primi Principi Christiani. [Emblematical Woodcut with mottos PRVDENTVM CONCORDIA REGVM and PAX ORBI TER RESTITVTVM].

Stampato in Parigi da Andrea Wechello, nella via di San Giouanni di Beauuois, all' insegna del Cauallo alato. M.D.LIX.

4to (8½ × 6). A⁴ + B². A1 Title, verso blank. A2 Dedication. A3—B2ª Epitalamio. B2ᵇ blank, with arabesque ornament in centre. 6 ll. without pagination.

The sixth stanza describes the marriage of the King Dauphin, by means of which he had taken possession of Scotland and increased the realm of France.

Class II.   S.

24. La Paix, faicte entre Treshaults & Trespuissants Princes Henry II. de ce nom, Treschrestien Roy de France, & Philippe Roy d'Espagne trescatholique, les Roy & Royne d'Escosse, Daulphin, & la Royne d'Angleterre.

A Lyon, chez Nicolas Edoard. 1559. Avec Privilege.

8vo (6 × 4). A in four. A1 Title, privilege on verso. A2 Account of the festivities at Lyons, 13th April 1559. A3—A4 Letters of Henry II. to the Governor of Lyons.

Class II.   S.

25. Entreprise dv Roy-Davlphin povr le Tovrnoy, sovbz le nom des Chevaliers advantevrevx. A la Royne, & aux Dames. par Ioach Dv Bellay Ang. [Printer's Mark.]

A Paris, de l'imprimerie de Federic Morel, Rue S. Ian de Beauuais, au franc Meurier. M.D.LVIIII. Avec Privilege dv Roy.

4to (8¾ × 6). A—C in fours + D². A1 Title, privilege on verso. A2—D1 Text. D2ª *L'imprimeur au Lecteur*, apologizing for having produced this Poem at a moment of national grief (the death of Henry) when it was in reality prepared for a time of festivity, presumably the Marriage of Queen Mary to the Dauphin.

Reference is made to Queen Mary several times, and one of the poems is specially addressed to her.

Class II.   B.M.

LES ORDRES TENVZ A LA RECEPTION ET

Entrée du Roy Treschrestien François II. & de la Roine, en la ville d'Orleans.

Description des arez triumphaux, magnificences, & theatres faictz en icelle ville pour ladicte reception & entrée.

A PARIS

Par Guillaume Nyuerd Imprimeur & Libraire, tenant sa boutique ioignant le pont aux Muniers vers le Chastellet.

AVEC PRIVILEGE.

26. Tvmvlvs Henrici Secvndi Gallorvm Regis Christianiss., per Ioach. Bellaium. Idem Gallice todidem uersibus expressum per eumdem. Accessit et eivsdem Elegia ad illustriss. Principem Carolum Card. Lotharingum. [Printer's Mark.]
Parisiis, Apud Federicum Morellum, in vico Bellouaco ad vrbanam Morum. M.D.LIX.
<small>4to (8¾ × 6). A—C in fours D2. Without pagination.
Queen Mary is alluded to twice in the poem as having joined Scotland to France.</small>
Class II. *B.M.*

27. Discovrs Moral de la Paix faicte entre treshaultz, tresexcellentz & trespuissans Princes, Henry (second du nom) treschrestien Roy de France, et Philippes Roy des Espaignes, et Françoys, & Marie Roy, & Royne d'Escosse, Daulphins de France, Et Elizabeth Royne d'Angleterre. [A quaint woodcut of a crowned Queen on the right, and two crowned kings embracing each other on the left.]
A Paris, Par Barbe Regnault rue Sainct Iacques, à l'enseigne de l'Elephant deuant les Mathurins. 1559. Auec Priuilege.
<small>8vo (6 × 4). A—B in fours. A1ᵃ Title. A1ᵇ Woodcut, with angels within a circle, having a black circular space in centre, surrounded by a square-lined border, with the hand of God in right corner. A2—B3ᵃ Discours moral in verse, with woodcut of a crowned king with sceptre within a square-lined border. B3ᵇ (in italic letter) Account of the publication of the Peace in Paris on the 17th April 1559, and of a Te Deum chanted in Nutre Dame, followed by a description of a Religious Procession and exhibition of the Relics of the true Cross of our Saviour Jesus Christ on the following day. B4 blank. The treaty of peace forming the subject of this book was the abortive one of Casteau Cambreses. (See No. 24.)</small>
Class II. *S.*

28. Les Triomphes faictz a l'entrée du Roy a Chenonceau le Dymanche dernier iour de Mars.
A Tours, par Guillaume Bourgeat. 1559.
<small>4to.
A copy of this tract, describing the festivities of the visit of Francis and Mary to Chenonceau, was, in 1857, in the possession of Mons. J. Tascherau of Paris, but it has not been further traced. The title given above is taken from a reprint of limited number, having an interesting introduction by Prince Augustus Galitzin. (Paris, J. Techener, 1857).
It was from the country surrounding Chenonceau in Touraine that Queen Mary drew the dowry which formed her means of support in the years of her captivity.</small>
Class II.

1560

29. Les Ordres Tenvz à la reception et Entrée du Roy Treschrestien Francois II. & de la Roine, en la ville d'Orleans. Description des arcz triumphaux, magnificences, & theatres faictz en icelle ville pour ladicte reception & entrée. [Woodcut with foliated border enclosing the Printer's initials, and having the Royal Arms as centre.]
A Paris par Guillaume Nyuerd Imprimeur & Libraire, tenant sa boutique ioignant le pont aux Muniers vers le Chastellet. Avec Privilege.
<small>8vo (6 × 3¾). A—D in fours. A1 Title. A2ᵃ—D3ᵇ L'Entree dv Roy, and de la Royne en la ville d'Orleans, faicte le 18 iour d'Octobre, 1560. 15 numbered leaves. D4ᵃ Privilege dated at Paris 22nd November 1560. D4ᵇ A crowned shield with fleurs-de-lys in centre, surrounded by the collar of the Order of the Cockle.</small>

This extremely rare pageant describes the festivities which took place on the entry into Orleans of Francis and Mary, on the 19th October 1560. The unfortunate king was destined never to leave the city, his death having occurred there on the 5th December 1560.

(*See Facsimile No. V.*)

Class II. S.

1561

30. Oraison fvnebre es Obseqves de tres Haute, tres Puissante, & tres Vertueuse Princesse, Marie par la grace de Dieu Royne douairiere d'Escoce. Prononcee à nostre Dame de Paris, le douxieme d'Aoust, mil cinq cens soixante

A Paris, de l'imprimerie de M. de Vascosan, Rue S. Jaques, à l'enseigne de la Fontaine M.D.LXI. Avec Privilege dv Roy.

8vo (7 × 4½). A—G in eights. A1 Title, verso blank. A2—B1ᵃ A la Royne Marie, Royne d'Escoce, Douairiere de France. Signed Claude D'Espence. B1ᵇ—F7ᵇ Oraison Fvnebre. F8 blank. G1ᵃ—G7ᵇ C'est le droit que Dieu fait à la vefue & orphelin. G8 blank. With pagination.

Class II. V. S.

31. Elegie sur le despart de la Royne Marie retournant à son Royaume d'Escosse. [Printer's mark, with the mottoes: Beati omnes qui timent Dominum, and, Initium sapientiae timor Domini.]

A Lyon par Benoist Rigaud. 1561.

8vo (6⅞ × 4). A in four. A1ᵃ Title, verso blank. A2 Repetition of above title and commencement of verses, which consist of 116 decasyllabic lines, ending on A4ᵃ. A4ᵇ blank. This little book is of extreme rarity, and the copy in the possession of the Earl of Rosebery is probably the only existing example.

The verses are by Ronsard, and, in an altered form, may be found in the collected editions of his works; but they appear not to have been printed separately, except in this form. Queen Mary sailed from France for Scotland on 14th August 1561, and this tract must have been issued very shortly after. It was reprinted (one copy on vellum, in my collection) at Bordeaux, in 1852, from the copy then in the possession of M. Techener.

Class III. IX. The Earl of Rosebery.

1562

32. Certane Tractatis for Reformatioun of Doctryne and maneris, set furth at the desyre ãd in ye name of ȳ afflictit Catholikis, of inferiour ordour of Clergie, and layit men in Scotland be Niniane Winzet, ane Catholike Preist borne in Renfrew Quilkis be name this leif turnit sall schaw. Murus aheneus, sana conscientia. Edinburgi, 21 Maij 1562. [The Hercules and Centaur device used by John Scot.]

4to (8 × 5⅞). A—E in fours. Sheet A is unsigned. The work ends on E3ᵇ with the woodcut, used by the printer, John Scot, of the Transfiguration, which is also to be found in Archbishop Hamilton's Catechism. It has been reprinted by the Scottish Text Society.

The first Tractate is an Exhortatioun to the maist excellent and gratius Souerane Marie Quene of Scottes, &c.

Class III. Edin. Univ.

1563

33. Vincentius Lirinensis of the Natioun of Gallis, for the antiquitie and veritie of the catholik fayth, aganis ye prophane nouationis of al hæreseis, A richt goldin buke

writtin in Latin about .XI.C. zeris passit, and neulie translatit in Scottis be Niniane Winzet a catholik Preist : Vt ædificenter muri Jerusalem. Psal. 50.
Antverpiae ex officina Ægidij Diest, 1. Decemb. 1563. Cum Gratia & Priuilegio.

    8vo (5½ × 3⅜). A⁸+a⁴+B—H in eights+1⁴. A1ᵃ Title, within an emblematical woodcut border, with the figures of two of the Apostles as supporters. A1ᵇ Shield with Royal Arms of Scotland. A2—a3 Dedication, To ye maist Catholik, noble and gratious souerane Marie Quene of Scottis, &c., dated from Antwerp the 2 December 1563. a4ᵃ Testimonies in Latin from Gennadius and from Tritemius. a4ᵇ To the Reidar. B1—13ᵃ Text, ending with Latin verses. 13ᵇ—14ᵃ In defence of yis auctor. 14ᵇ ¶ The faltis. From B1 leaves numbered 1-60, with catchwords on both sides. Reprinted by the Scottish Text Society.

Class V.   *Adv.*

34. La Harangve de Tresnoble et Tresuertueuse Dame, Madame Marie D'estuart, Royne d'Escosse, Douairiere de France, faite en l'assemblée des Estats de son Royaume, tenuz au mois de May dernier passe.

[Benoist Rigaud's Printer's mark, a woman with a palm leaf in her hand, with the mottoes, Virtus Phoenici similis and Vivit post fvnera virtvs.]

A Lyon, Par Benoist Rigaud. 1563.

    8vo (6 × 4). A in four. A1ᵃ Title. A1ᵇ—A4ᵇ Text, with catchwords, but without pagination.

    This extremely rare tract presents a curious example of the interest taken in France at this period in the details of Scottish national affairs. It is difficult to conceive how a translation of the Queen's Speech at the opening of Parliament in Edinburgh came to be printed within a few weeks at Lyons. No Scottish authority has produced the text of the Speech, which, as given in this tract, is couched in singularly moderate and patriotic terms, and without any special mention of the religious and other troubles which had recently assailed the Queen. The Parliament in question met on the 26th May 1563. Randolph, in a letter to Cecil on 3rd June, says:—" On which day the Queen came to it in her robes and crowned. . . . She made in English an oration publiquely there and was present at the condemnation of the two Earles Huntley and Sutherland." John Knox (History of the Reformation in Scotland, Laing's Edition, Vol. II. p. 381)—" Such styncken pryde of wemen as was sein at that Parliament, was never sein befoir in Scotland. Thre syndrie dayis the Quene raid to the Tolbuyth. The first day sche maid a payntet orisoun and thair mycht have bene hard among hir flatteraris ' Vox Dianæ !' The voce of a Goddess (for it could not be Dei), and not of a woman ! God save that sweat face ! Was thair ever oratour spack so properlie and so sweitlie !"

    A copy of this tract appears in Heber's Sale Catalogue, Part VII., No. 4108.

Class III.   *S.*

1564

35. Psalmorvm Dauidis paraphrasis poetica, nunc primùm edita, Authore Georgio Buchanano, Scoto, poetarum nostri saeculi facilè principe.

Eiusdem Dauidis Psalmi aliquot à Th. B. V. versi. Psalmi Aliquot in versus itē Graecos nuper à diuersis translati.

Apud Henricum Stephanum, & eius fratrem Robertū Stephanum, typographum Regium. Ex Privilegio Regis.

    8vo (7½ × 4½). *⁴+a—r in eights+s⁴+a—c in eights. *1 Title, verso blank. *2 Ad Mariam Illvstriss. Scotorvm Reginam, Georgii Buchanani epigramma. *3*4 Poems addressed to

Buchanan. a1—s3ᵃ (pp. 1–277) Text. Without catchwords. Emendanda at bottom of p. 277. s3ᵇ blank. s4 blank. a1—c7 Psalmi Aliquot in versus Graecos (pp. 1–46). c8 blank.

This is the *Editio Princeps* of Buchanan's Psalms, including his celebrated dedication to Queen Mary. It is without date, but was printed probably in 1564.

Class V.   *B.M. Adv. S.*

1565

36. The Actis and Constitutionis of Parliament made be the rycht excellent Princes Marie quene of Scottis.

    Colophon : Imprintit at Edinburgh be Robert Lekpreuik 1565.
    Folio. See Dickson and Edmond, *Annals*, p. 223.

Class VIII.

37. Allegations against the Svrmisid Title of the Quine of Scotts and the fauorers of the same.

    The above is printed close to the top of title-page. Beneath, a number of letters, almost entirely consonants, are scattered in an irregular figure. On verso of last leaf, letters making the following words are scattered over the page : Lucem debet aspicere qui de tenebris vvlt jvdicare. Excusum S. A. 7 Decembris 1565.

    4to (7¾ × 5¾). Printed in a rude italic type on very coarse paper. 16 ll. with pagination, and without signatures.

                            (*See Facsimiles Nos. VI. and VII.*)

Class IV.   *B.M. Adv.*

38. Henrici illvstrissimi Dvcis Albaniæ Comitis Rossiæ &c. et Mariæ Serenissimæ Scotorum Reginæ Epithalamium. Per Tho. Craigvm.

    Impressvm Edinbvrgi per Robertvm Lekprevik. Anno 1565.

    8vo (5¾ × 3¾). Aⁿ. A1 Title, verso blank. A2—A7ᵇ Text, without pagination, but with catchwords. A8 blank.

    The only known copy is in Edinburgh University Library. A reprint of twelve copies with a Latin Preface was issued by Dr David Laing in 1821, having the following separate Title : Thomae Craigi Epithalamium quo Henrici Darnleii et Mariæ Scotorum Reginæ Nuptias celebravit. Impressum Edinburgi. Anno M.D.LXV. Denuo Editum Anno M.D.CCC.XXI.

Class VI.   *Edin. Univ.*

39. Petri Bizzari varia opvscula, qvorvm indicem seqvens Pagina demonstrabit. Aldus [The Anchor and Dolphin] Venetiis, MDLXV.

    8vo (6 × 4). A—T in eights + V⁴. 156 ll. A1ᵃ Title. A1ᵇ Contents : De Optimo Principe. De Bello & pace. Pro Philosophia & eloquentia. Aemilij accusatio & defensio. Pro L. Virginio contra Ap. Claudium. Poemata uaria.

    De Optimo Principe is dedicated to Queen Elizabeth. De Bello et Pace with a separate Title, Ad Mariam Serenissimam Scotiae Reginam, followed by Sapphic verses in which her marriage to Darnley is referred to. At p. 123 another poem in honour of Queen Mary occurs. There are also poems addressed to Jacobus Stuardus Scotus (The Earl of Murray), George Buchanan, and Andrew Melvin.

Class V. VI.   *S.*

1566

40. Proditionis ab aliqvot Scotiæ Perdvellibvs adversvs Serenissimam suam Reginam non ita pridem perpetratæ breuis & simplex narratio ex amplissimi cuiusdam viri literis fideliter descripta. [Printer's ornament.]

ALLEGATIONS AGAINST THE SVRMISID TITLE OF THE QVINE OF SCOTTS AND THE fauorers of the same

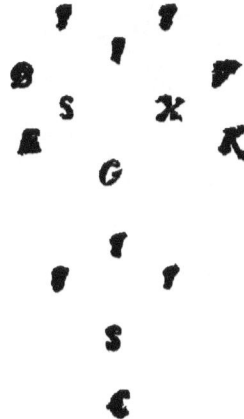

Edin. Bibl. Soc.—Queen Mary Literature. Facsimile No. VI. See No. 37, page 14.

order thiese things so: as vve maie enioie good peace & quyetnesse, vnto his honor, & vnto the glorie, of his boolye Name.

Excusum S A 7 Decembris
1565

Lovanii, Apud Rutgerum Velpiū Bibliop. Iurat. Sub Castro Angelico. An. 1566.

8vo (5⅛ × 3⅞). A—B in fours. Sheet A has no signatures. Sheet B is signed only on recto of first leaf, below the woodcut border. A1ᵃ Title, enclosed in a woodcut border. A1ᵇ—B4ᵃ Text, each page surrounded by a woodcut border. B4ᵇ Printer's mark, a warrior with a sword in his right hand embracing a woman holding a flower in her left hand, surrounded by an emblematical framed border with motto, Justicia et Pax.

The book, of which this number and the next are distinct editions, deals with the rebellion of the nobles which accompanied the murder of Rizzio. The death of Rizzio is described in the following words, which give an impression of his age very different from the popularly accepted one—" Primo impetu in oculis Regis et Reginæ quendam Secretarium, nomine Dauidem, hominē prope quinquagenarium, sexaginta vulneribus perfoderunt." There is nothing to indicate who is the author.

Mr Grenville's copy, now in the British Museum, has a MS. note in his writing as follows :— " I have not met with any other copy of this rare tract on Rizzio's murther except one in quarto with the same date but without place or printer's name—that other copy is also in my library."

Class III. *B.M.*

41. Proditionis ab aliqvot Scotiæ Perdvellibvs adversvs serenissimam suam Reginam non ita pridem perpetratæ breuis & simplex narratio ex amplissimi cuiusdam viri literis fideliter descripta. M.D.LXVI.

4to (8⅞ × 6). Aᵃ. A1 Title, verso blank. A2—A5ᵇ Text. The matter in this edition corresponds exactly with that of the 8vo (No. 40).

Class III. *B.M.*

42. A Sermon preached by Iohn Knox Minister of Christ Jesus in the Publique audience of the Church of Edenbrough, within the Realme of Scotland, vpon Sonday, the .19. of August 1565. For the which the said Iohn Knoxe was inhibite preaching for a season. 1. Timoth. 4. ¶ The time is come that men can not abyde the Sermon of veritie nor holsome doctrine. To this is adioyned an exhortation vnto all the faythfull within the sayde Realme, for the reliefe of suche as faythfully trauayle in the preaching of Gods worde. Written by the same Iohn Knoxe, at the commaundement of the ministerie aforesayd. Imprinted Anno. 1566.

8vo (5⅛ × 3⅞). Printed in roman letter with numbered leaves and catchwords. A⁴ + B² + A—G in eights+H⁴. A1 Title, verso blank. A2—B1ᵃ To the reader, dated at end, At Edingbrough the .19. of September 1565. B1ᵇ blank. B2 Isaias 26 Chap. verses 13-21. A1—G1 A Sermon preached by John Knoxe, 49 numbered leaves. G2—H4ᵃ The Exhortation, &c., 11 ll. with separate numeration. H4ᵇ blank.

Class III. *B.M. S.*

43. Georgii Bvchanani Scoti Poetæ eximij Franciscanus & fratres, quibus accessere varia eiusdem & aliorum Poemata quorum & titulos & nomina XVI. indicabit pagina. Eiusdem Psalmos seorsim non sine accessione excudit.

Basiliæ Ravracorvm Thomas Gvarinvs Nervivs.

8vo (6¼ × 4⅛). a+A—V+Aa—Ll+AA—II in eights. a1—8 Title and preliminary verses. A—V Buchanan's Tragedies, Epigrams, &c., pp. 1-319. V8ᵇ blank. Printed in italic letter with catchwords. Aa—Ll Silvæ of Turnebius, Hospitalius, and Auratus, pp. 1-176. AA—II pp. 143 Utenhovius Allusionum Lib. 1.

This book contains George Buchanan's Marriage Ode to Francis II. and Queen Mary, with many other poems in honour of the latter.

Class II. IX. *Adv. S.*

44. Kurtzer Ausszug und schlechte erzelung / eines Landuerreters stucks / wider die Künigin in Schottland / von etlichen abfalligen / mainaydigen / vund aussrürischen beschehen / vermerckt auss eines hoch ansehnlichen Herzens Schreiben / trewlich verteuischt. M.D.LXVI.

  4to (7¾ × 5¾). A and B in fours. A1 Title, verso blank. A2—B3ª Text. B3ᵇ—B4 blank.
  This tract refers specially to the murder of Rizzio.

Class III.   *B.M. S.*

45. The Acts And Constitutiounis of the Realme of Scotland maid in Parliamentis haldin be the rycht excellent, hie and mychtie Princeis Kingis Iames the First, Secund, thrid, Feird, Fyft, and in tyme of Marie now Quene of Scottis, viseit, correctit, and extractit furth of the Registers be the Lordis depute be hir Maiesteis speciall commissioun thairto. Anno Do. 1566.

  Colophon: Cvm Privilegio Ad Decennivm. ¶ Imprentit at Edinburgh be Robert Lekpreuik . . . the zeir of God ane thousand fyue hundreth thre scoir sax yeiris.
  Folio (11 × 7¾). ♃. ℥.
  The peculiarities of the various issues of this book have been so fully described by Dickson and Edmond (*Annals*, p. 226), it is considered unnecessary to repeat them.

Class VIII.   *B.M. Adv. S.*

46. An Oration against the Vnlawfull Insurrections of the Protestantes of our time, vnder pretence to Refourme Religion. ¶ Made and pronounced in Latin in the Schole of Artes at Louaine, the XIIII. of December Anno. 1565.

  ¶ By Peter Frarin of Andwerp M. of Arte, and Bacheler of both Lawes. And now translated into English with the aduise of the Author. [Fouler's device, a tree surrounded by birds, flanked by the letters I F and surrounded by the motto: Respicite volatilia coeli, et pullos corvorvm.]
  Antverpiae Ex officina Joannis Fouleri. M.D.LXVI.

  8vo (5¾ × 3¾). ♃. ℥. A—L in eights. A1 Title, verso blank. A2ª Quotations from Scripture in Latin. A2ᵇ Privilege in Latin to P. Frarin Bruxellae 14 Martii 1565. stilo Brabantæ. A3—A7 The Translator to the Gentle Reader, from Antwerp Maii 9. 1566. Signed Ihon Fouler. A8—K3ª Text. K3ᵇ blank. K4ª—L8ª The Table of this booke set out not by order of Alphabete or nũbre, but by expresse figure to the eye & sight of the Christian Reader, and of him also yᵗ cannot reade. L8ᵇ blank. Without pagination.

  This very rare book is one of the most curious works printed in England in the sixteenth century. Queen Mary is mentioned several times. One passage may be quoted (E6):—" It were to long to rehearse, how the noble Queene of Scotlãd that now raigneth, was driven a great while to liue like a poore priuat woman in her own realme, to obey her own subiectes, & to do no more than they gave her leave: yea, and in the meane tyme was euerie daye and euery houre in greate perill & danger of her life among them."

  The woodcuts forming part of the table mentioned in the collation are very curious; the doggerel verses attached are quaint. The following may serve as an example:—

    "Caluin in his chamber fiue yeares taught a Nonne
     Tyll she was great with Gospell and swolne with a Sonne.

  A copy of the original Latin work of Peter Frarin, from which this is translated, is in the British Museum.

Class IV.   *B.M.*

1567

47. Discours des Troubles nouuellement aduenus au Royaume d'Angleterre. Auec vne declaration, faicte par le Comte de Nortumberland & autres grands Seigneurs d'Angleterre.
A Paris. Pour Laurent du Coudret Imprimeur Jouxte la Copie de Jacques Blochet. Auec Priuilege.
    8vo (6¼ × 4). A—B in fours. B4 blank. Without pagination or catchwords.
Class III.   S.

48. ¶ The Complaynt of Scotland.
    Folio. Broadside (11⁷⁄₁₆ × 7¼). B. L.
    One of Robert Sempill's Poems on the murder of Lord Darnley. Without date, place, or printer's name, but printed by Robert Lekpreuik in 1567.
    Reprinted in the *Gentleman's Magazine* by Joseph Ritson, November 1791; in Scottish Ballads and Songs, edited by James Maidment (Edinburgh, 1859); and in The Sempill Ballates (T. G. Stevenson, Edinburgh, 1872).
Class IV.   *B.M.*   *Public Record Office.*

49. Heir followis ane proclamation That the Lordis of Secreit Counsall made the xxvj. day of Iunij 1567.
    [End] Imprentit at Edinburgh be Robert Lekpreuik Anno. Do. 1567.
    Broadside. Folio. B. L.
    This is a proclamation for the apprehension of the Earl of Bothwell.
Class VIII.   *Adv.*

50. ¶ Heir followis the Proclamatioun that the Nobilitie and Lordis made at the Croce of Edinburgh the xj. day of Iunij 1567, declaring the effect of thair assemblie in Armour [End] Subscriuit with our handis at the Cannagait the xj day of Iunij. Anno Do. 1567.
    ¶ Imprentit at Edinburgh be Robert Lekpreuik.
    Broadside. Folio. B. L.
Class VIII.   *Public Record Office.*

51. ¶ Heir followis ane act that the Lordis of Secreit counsall made in the Tolbuith of Edinburgh the xij. day of Iunij. 1567, declaring Iames Erle Bothwell to be the principall authour and murtherar of the Kingis grace of gude memorie and rauysing of the Quenis Maiestie.
    [End] ¶ Imprentit at Edinburgh be Robert Lekpreuik 1567.
    Broadside. Folio. B. L.
Class VIII.   *Public Record Office.*

52. Heir followis ane Ballat declaring the Nobill and gude inclinatioun of our King.
    [End] Imprentit at Edinburgh be Robert Lekpreuik, 1567.
    Broadside. Folio. B. L. Arranged in three columns.
    One of the Poems of Robert Sempill. Reprinted in The Sempill Ballates.
Class IX.   *Public Record Office.*

53. Heir followis the testament and tragedic of vmquhile King Henrie Stewart of gude memorie.
[End] Imprentit at Edinburgh be Robert Lekpreuik. Anno Do. 1567.
> Broadside (𝔅. 𝔏.) of sixteen twelve-line stanzas in three columns.
> One of the Poems of Robert Sempill. Reprinted in Scottish Poems of the Sixteenth Century, collected by John G. Dalyell (Edinburgh, 1801), and in The Sempill Ballates.

Class IX. *B..M.*

54. ¶ Heir followis ane Exhortatioun to the Lordis.
[End] Imprentit at Edinburgh be Robert Lekpreuik Anno Do 1567.
> Broadside. Folio. 𝔅. 𝔏.
> One of the Poems of Robert Sempill. Reprinted in The Sempill Ballates.

Class IX. *Public Record Office.*

55. ane deeclaratioun of the Lordis iust quarrell.
Finis ¶ Imprentit at Edinburgh be Robert Lekpreuik. Anno Do. 1567.
> Broadside. Folio (13¾ × 9¼).
> One of the Poems of Robert Sempill. Reprinted in Dalyell's Scottish Poems of the Sixteenth Century, and in The Sempill Ballates.

Class IX. *B..M. (2 copies).* *Public Record Office.*

1568

56. The Actis Of Parliament of the maist hie, maist excellent, and michtie Prince, and our Souerane Lord James the sext, be the grace of God, King of Scottis, begun and haldin at Edinburgh, the xv day of Decemb. The zeir of God, ane thousand, fyue hundreth LXVII. zeir. Be our said Souerane Lordis derrest cousing & Vncle Iames Erle of Murray, Lord Abirnethie, &c., Regët to our Souerane Lord, his Realme and Leigis. Togidder with the Prelatis, Erlis, Barronis, Commissioneris of Burrowis, specialie comperand in the said Parliament, as the thre estatis of this Realme. The saidis actis being oppinlie red, concludit and votit in the said Parliament, to remane as perpetuall lawis to the Subiectis of this Realme in all tymes cuming.
> Colophon: Imprentit at Edinburgh be Robert Lekpreuik, Prentar to the Kingis Maiestie, the vj. day of Aprill, the zeir of God ane thousand fyue hundreth thre scoir aucht zeiris.
> Folio (11 × 7¾). 𝔅. 𝔏. A—F in fours. A1 Title as above over large woodcut of the arms of Scotland, verso blank. A2—F3ᵃ The Actis of King James the Sext. F3ᵇ—F4ⁿ The Tabill and Colophon, verso blank. In addition to the Title there are 22 folios, numbered on recto, the first folio of text being unnumbered and the second being numbered 111.
> These Acts include that for the Retention of Queen Mary in Lochleven (ff. 15 and 16), The Act for appointing Murray as Regent, which repeals *in extenso* the Deed resigning the Crown forced from Queen Mary at Lochleven on 24th July 1567 (folio IV), and the Confession of Faith and Doctrine beleuit and professit be the Protestantis of the Realme of Scotland (folio V verso to IX recto).

Class VIII. *B..M. (two copies imperfect).* *Adv. S.*

57. ane proclamatioun anent the tressonable Conspiratouris and trublaris of the tranquillitie of the commoun welth now latelie assemblit aganis the Kings grace authoritie.

[End] At Glasgow the .vij. day of Maij. 1568. and of our Regne the first zeir.
¶ Imprentit at Edinburgh be Robert Lekpreuik Prentar to the Kingis Maiestie.
Broadside. Folio. 𝔅. 𝔏.
A proclamation issued by the Regent Murray immediately after the escape of Queen Mary from Lochleven Castle.

Class VIII.   *B.M.*   *Public Record Office* (2 copies).

1569

58. To the Quenes Maiesties poore deceiued Subiectes of the North Countrey, drawen into rebellion by the Earles of Northumberland and Westmerland. Written by Thomas Norton and newly perused and encreased. Seen and allowed according to the Queenes Iniunctions.

Colophon: Imprinted at London by Henrie Bynneman for Lucas Harrison. Anno Domini 1569. 8vo (5½ × 3¾). A—C in eights D4. Without pagination. Two other editions were issued in 1569.

Class III.   *B.M.*   *S.*

59. A Chronicle at large and meere History of the affayres of Englande and Kinges of the same, deduced from the Creation of the vvorlde vnto the first habitation of thys Islande: and so by contynuance vnto the first yere of the reigne of our most deere and souereigne Lady Queene Elizabeth: collected out of sundry Aucthors whose names are expressed in the next page of this leafe.

Anno Domini 1569. Cum Priuilegio.

Folio (11½ × 8). 𝔅. 𝔏. Six leaves + A—Q in sixes + R⁴ + A—Dddddd in sixes + Eeeeee³ + a—c in eights. 1 Title, in a woodcut border, containing in compartments portraits of Moses, Saul, David, William the Conqueror, Albanact, Henry the Eighth, Queen Elizabeth, and others. 1ᵇ The names of the authors that are alleged in this History. 2—3ᵃ Dedication to Sir William Cecill, signed Richard Grafton. 3ᵇ—6ᵃ To the Reader. 6ᵇ blank. A—R⁴ Text and Tables. A1ᵃ Second Title: The seconde Volume beginning at William the Conqueror, endeth with our moste dread and souereigne Lady Queene Elizabeth. Seene and alowed according to the order apointed. Cum priuilegio Regiæ Maiestatis. Anno 1568. A1ᵇ To the Reader. A—c5ᵃ Text and Tables. c5ᵇ Printer's mark: (a cask, with a tree growing through the bunghole, and the motto, Svscipite inuity verbvm Jaco. I) and colophon: Imprinted at London by Henry Denham, dwelling in Paternoster Rowe, for Richard Tottle and Humffrey Toye, Anno 1569, the last of March. Seene and allowed according to the order appointed ¶ Cum priuilegio ad imprimendum solum. c6—8 blank.

Pp. 1258-1279 are occupied almost entirely with an account of Scottish affairs at the end of the reign of James V. At p. 1269 the good treatment of the Scottish noblemen and gentlemen captured at Solway Moss is recounted. The rubrics of this passage are as follows:—The death of the Scottish King—The birth of Mary daughter to the King of Scottes—The first mocion of the mariage of the heyre of Scotland with prince Edward heire of England began of the Scottes. (See No. 1.)

George Buchanan, in his History (Edinburgh, 1582, folio), folio 170, has almost textually embodied this account of the dealing of Henry VIII. with the Scottish nobles. Grafton's Chronicle was also printed in several forms in 1568 and 1572, and reprinted London, 1809. 2 vols. 4to.

Class X.   *B.M. Adv.*

60. Theodori Bezæ Vizelii Poematum Editio Secunda, ab eo recognita, Item, Ex Georgio Bvchanano aliisque variis insignibus poetis excerpta carmina, presertimq; epigrammata.

Anno M.D.LXIX. Excudebat Henr. Steph. Ex cuius etiam epigrammatis Græcis & Latinis aliquot cæteris adiecta sunt.

8vo (6¼ × 4½). *+**+a–l+A—Q in eights. *1 Title, verso blank. *2—**8ᵃ verso blank, pp. 1–31, Dedication and prefatory verses in roman letter. a1—l7, pp. 1–174 Bezæ Poemata. 18 blank. A1—13ᵃ Buchanani Epigrammata, Franciscanus, &c. 13ᵇ—Q8ᵃ Aliorum Poemata, Q8ᵇ blank. Pagination irregular, the last four leaves are not numbered. The text is in italic letter.

The Poems of Beza include two referring to Francis II. Buchanan's Poems include his Ode on the Mariage of Queen Mary and Francis II., and his poem Adamas in cordis effigiem sculptus annuloque insertus quem Maria Scotorum Regina ad Elizibetham Anglorum Reginam misit anno 1564.

The first Edition of Beza's Poems was also printed by Henr. Stephanus, but it does not contain any of the poems relating to Queen Mary.

Class IX. *B.M. S.*

61. ¶ A discourse touching the pretended match betwene the Duke of Norfolke and the Queene of Scottes.

8vo (5¼ × 3½). a⁸. a1 blank. a2—a7 Text. a8 blank. Without printer's name or place.

This extremely rare tract has frequently been described as wanting title, but it is complete as above, never having had a title-page. The heading and chapter titles are in roman letter and the text in italic. A copy was sold in Laing's Sale, Part II. The copy now described was formerly in the possession of the Duke of Roxburghe.

Another edition in similar form, but of a different setting, is in the British Museum. Press mark G. 5926. (2a).

Reprinted in James Anderson's Collections relating to the History of Mary Queen of Scotland (Vol. I., pp. 21–32). Anderson attributes the anthorship "to one Sampson a preacher," but it is more probable that it was inspired by Cecil, as Anderson states that he "had seen a copy in MS. which was sent down to Mr Randolph, Ambassador in Scotland, before it was printed."

Class IV. *B.M. S.*

62. A defence of the honour of the right highe, mightye and noble Princesse Marie Queene of Scotlande and dowager of France, with a declaration aswell of her right, title and intereste to the succession of the crowne of Englande, as that the regimente of women ys conformable to the lawe of God and nature. [Printer's ornament.]

Imprinted at London in Flete strete, at the signe of Justice Royall against the Blacke bell, by Eusebius Dicæophile. Anno Dom. 1569.

8vo (5¼ × 3¾). †⁶+a—s in eights+t². Sign. P1 is a capital. †1 Title, verso blank. †2—†6ᵃ The Author to the Gentle Reader. †6ᵇ The Printer to the reader. a1—g2ᵃ A Defence of the Honevr of the ryght hyghe, ryght myghtye and noble Princesse Marie Quene of Scotlande, and Dowagere of France. The fyrste Booke. g2ᵇ—p5ᵃ The Seconde Booke Towchinge the right title and interest of the foresaid Ladie Marie Quene of Scotlande, to the Succession of the crowne of Englande. p5ᵇ—t2ᵇ The Thyrde Booke, where in ys declared that the regimente of whomen ys conformable to the lawe of God and nature. t2ᵇ Colophon. Imprinted at London in Flete strete at the signe of Iustice Royal, againste the Black bell, by Eusebius Dicæophile, anno D. 1569, and are to be solde in Paules church yearde, at the signes of Tyme & Truthe, by the Brasen Serpēt, in the shoppes of Ptolomé and Nicephore Lycosthenes brethren Germanes. Title and prefatory matter unnumbered. Text of the three Books 148 numbered leaves.

This is one of the rarest of the series of controversial books regarding Queen Mary. It was so rigorously suppressed that not more than two or three copies, in addition to that noted below, are now in existence.

A defence of the
honour of the right highe, mightye and noble Princesse Marie Quene of Scotlande and dowager of France, with a declaration aswell of her right, title & intereste to the succession of the crowne of Englande, as that the regimente of women ys conformable to the lawe of God and nature.

Imprinted at London in Flete strete, at the signe of Iustice Royall against the Blacke bell, by Eusebius Dicæophile. Anno Dom. 1569.

ANE
Tragedie in forme of ane Diallog betuix honour gude fame, and the Authour heirof in ane Trance.

Imprentit at Edinburgh be Robert Lekpreuik. An. Do. 1570.

That John Lesley, Bishop of Ross, was the author seems to be beyond doubt, although in style and form of expression he may have been assisted by Dr Good, "with whom the Bishop left a copy that he might turn into English any Scottish words in it, which was returned to the Bishop with some few notes by the Queen to be added thereto."

Notwithstanding the spurious imprints on the title and colophon, its place of printing is uncertain, but from a passage in a letter from Cecil to Sir Henry Norris, Queen Elizabeth's Ambassador in France (4th May 1870), which says, "Of late the Bishop of Ross caused one of his Servants secretly to procure the printing of a book in English, whereof before eight leaves could be finished, intelligence was had, &c." it would appear that, unlike the second edition (No. 73), it was actually produced in London. Anderson supports this opinion unreservedly, while Lowndes (Bibliog. Manual), possibly forming his opinion from the peculiarity of the type employed, asserts that it was printed abroad. The following note, inserted between the Preface and the first leaf of the text, does not throw much light on the disputed point: "The printer to the reader. I Require ād hartelie praye the (good and louinge reader) that yf in this praesent Booke thou finde any alligation not dewlye coted, or a poinct out of place, a lettre lackig, or other wise altered : as n for u, and such littill light faultes against orthographiae, thov wilt neither impute the same to the authour of this worthie Worke, nor yet captiouslye controule the errour: but rather of thy humanitie and gentilnes, amende that which is amisse with thy penne. For if thou diddist knowe with what difficulté the imprinting herof was atchiued, thou woldest rather curtouslye of frendlye fauer pardon many greate faultes, than curiouslye withe rigorouse censure to condemne one litle. Christe kepe the in his faithe and feare praesentlie and perpetuallye. Amen." It may be noticed, however, that the spelling of some of the words and the accent on the final vowel of the word difficulté foster the suspicion of a French origin.

The work is divided into three books, which, in distinction to the edition of 1571 (No. 73), have no sub-titles, but they are voluminously provided with marginal rubrics and quotations of authorities, not found in the latter.

Some portions of the book appear to have been prepared at an earlier period than the date of its publication, but its special object was to reply to the injurious reflections on the Queen of Scots' character contained in the tract (No. 61)—A discourse touching the pretended match betwene the Duke of Norfolke and the Queene of Scottes ; and as an answer to the work of John Hales, Clerk of the Hanaper : A Declaration of the Succession of the Crowne Imperial of Ingland, which was circulated in MS., and remained in that condition until printed in The Heredetary Right of the Crown of England asserted (Helkanah Bedford, London, 1713). Fol. (Appendix VIII., pp. xx-xlii.)

This edition of Bishop Lesley's work has not been reprinted.

(*See Facsimile No. VIII.*)

Class IV. S.

1570

63. Ane Tragedie in forme of ane Diallog betuix honour gude Fame, and the Authour heirof in ane Trance.

Imprentit at Edinburgh be Robert Lekpreuik. An. Do. 1570.

8vo. (6½ × 3¾). B. L. A in eight, without pagination, but with catchwords on verso. A1ᵃ Title, verso blank. A2—8 Text, ending with an Epitaphe " OBIIT XXIII. IANUARII. ANNO DO. M.D.LXIX. This is the date of the Regent Murray's murder.

The only known copy is in the Advocates' Library.

One of the Poems of Robert Sempill. Reprinted in Dalyell's Scottish Poems of the Sixteenth Century, and in The Sempill Ballates.

(*See Facsimile No. IX.*)

Class IV. Adv.

64. ¶ The Poysonit Schot.
[End] ☞ Imprentit at Edinburgh be Robert Lekpreuik. Anno Do. 1570.
Broadside. Folio (14½ × 10).
One of the Poems of Robert Sempill. Reprinted in The Sempill Ballates.
Class IV.   *B.M.*   *Library of the Society of Antiquaries of London.*

65. The Regents tragedie ending with ane exhortatoun.
☞ Finis Quod Robert Sempill ¶ Imprented at Edinburgh be Robert Lekpreuik. Anno Do. 1570.
Broadside. Folio. 𝔅. 𝔏.
One of the Poems of Robert Sempill. Reprinted in The Sempill Ballates.
The copy in the Record Office is of a different setting.
Class IV.   *B.M.*   *Library of the Society of Antiquaries of London.*   *Public Record Office.*

66. ¶ The spur to the Lordis.
[At end] ☞ Imprentit. Anno Do. 1570.
Broadside. Folio. Without place or name of printer, but in the type of Lekpreuik.
One of the Poems of Robert Sempill. Reprinted in The Sempill Ballates.
Class IV.   *Library of the Society of Antiquaries of London.*

67. Discovrs des Trovbles nouuellement advenuz au Royaume d'Angleterre au moys d'Octobre 1569.
Auec vne declaration faicte par le Comte de Nortumberland et autres grands Seigneurs d'Angleterre.
[Printer's mark, the sun with surrounding motto, Domini Laudabile Nomen I.H.S., with Maltese cross in centre.]
A Lyon par Michel Joue M.D.LXX. Avec Permission.
4to (6 × 4). A—C in fours. A1 Title, verso blank. A2—C1ᵃ Discours envoye de Londres. C1ᵇ blank. C2—C3ᵇ Copie d'une declaration faicte par le Comte de Nortumberland. C4 blank. Pp. 122, without catchwords.
This interesting little volume begins with an address to Queen Elizabeth, praying her to name a successor. Then follows the Right of the Prince of Scotland, the genealogies of the Countess of Hertford and the Duke of Norfolk, and an account of the coming of Mary Queen of Scots into England, with the names of those who accompanied her.
Class IV.   *B.M. S.*

1571

68. The Bishoppis lyfe and testament.
¶ Finis ☞ Quod Sempill ¶ Imprentit at Striuiling be Robert Lekpreuik Anno Do. M.D.LXXI.
Folio. Broadside. 𝔅. 𝔏.
One of the Poems of Robert Sempill. Reprinted in The Sempill Ballates.
Class IV.   *Library of the Society of Antiquaries of London.*

69. Salutem in Christo.
[At the end.] At London the XIII. of October 1571 Your louying Brother in Lawe R. G.
8vo (5⅔ × 3¼). Eight leaves. 𝔅. 𝔏. Without printer's name or place. The two first leaves

are blank. The Text commences as above at the top of the third leaf (signed A3) and ends as above on verso of A7. The last leaf is blank.

This curious tract has reference to the proposed marriage of Queen Mary to the Duke of Norfolk, and to the Duke's committal to the Tower.

Class IV. *B.M. S.*

70. Ane Admonitiovn direct to the trew Lordes maintenaris of Justice and obedience to the Kingis Grace. M. G. B.

Imprentit at Striveling be Robert Lekprevik. Anno. Do. M.D.LXXI.

8vo (5¼ × 3¾). A—B in eights. Printed in Roman letter. Catchwords on verso of leaves. Without pagination. A1 Title, verso blank. A2—B8 Text.

Two other editions appear to have been printed by Lekprevik in the same year. They are fully described in Dickson and Edmond's Annals, pp. 249, 250. A copy of one of these is in the library of Trinity College, Cambridge, and of the other in the Lambeth Library. There is in the Advocates' Library a second copy of the work, wanting title, which is probably the same edition as the Lambeth copy. In this the account of the third conspiracy is omitted, and the tenor of the narrative altered. See Vernacular Writings of George Buchanan (Scottish Text Society), 1892.

Class IV. *Adv.*

71. Ane Admonition direct to the trew Lordis mantenaris of the Kingis Graces Authoritie. M. G. B.

¶ Imprinted at London by John Daye, accordyng to the Scotish copie Printed at Striuelyng by Robert Lekpreuik. Anno Do. M.D.LXXI.

8vo (5¾ × 3¾). A—D in fours. Catchwords, but no pagination.

Class IV. *B.M. S.*

72. ¶ The effect of the declaratiō made in the Guildhall by M. Recorder of London concerning the late attemptes of the Quenes Maiesties euill, seditious and disobedient subiectes.

Imprinted at London by Iohn Daye dwelling ouer Aldersgate.

8vo (5½ × 3½). ❧. ❧. A—B in fours C². A1 Title, verso blank. A—C2 Text, beginning, On Monday 15th October 1571, &c.

Class IV. *B.M.*

73. A Treatise concerning the Defence of the Honovr of the Right High, Mightie and Noble Princesse, Marie Queene of Scotland, and Douager of France, with a Declaration, as wel of her Right, Title, and Interest, to the Succession of the Croune of England: as that the Regiment of women is conformable to the lawe of God and Nature. Made by Morgan Philippes, Bachelar of Diuinitie, An. 1570. [Printer's ornament.]

Leodii Apud Gualterum Morberium. 1571.

8vo (6¼ × 4). ❧ + ❧❧ + A—F in eights + G² + a—h in eights + i¹ + Aa—Dd in eights. ❧1 Title, verso blank. ❧2—❧❧8 To the Reader. A1 (probably a blank leaf). A2—G3 A Defence of the Honovr of the Right High, Right mightie and Noble Princesse, Marie Queene of Scotlande, and Douager of France. The First Booke. 50 numbered leaves with catchwords. a1³ A Treatise tovching the Right, Title and Interest of the mightie and noble Princesse Marie, Queene of Scotland, to the succession of the Croune of England. Made by Morgan Philippes, Bachelar of Diuinitie, assisted with the aduise of Antonie Broune Knight, one of the Iustices of the Common

Place. An. 1567. [Small Printer's ornament.] Leodii Apud Gualterum Morberium. 1571. a2^b blank. a2^a—i4^a Repetition of above second title, with addition of the words 'The Seconde Booke,' and Text. 67 numbered leaves. i4^b An imprimatur dated Louanii 6. Martii 1571. Aa1 (probably a blank leaf). Aa2—Dd7 A Treatise wherein is declared that the Regiment of Women is conformable to the lawe of God and nature. The Third Booke. 30 numbered leaves, with catchwords. Imprimatur is repeated at bottom of Dd7^b in which the words 'Hos tres libros' are used. Dd8^a Errata Libri secundi et lebri Tertii. Dd8^b Printer's ornament.

This edition of Bishop John Lesley's book (see No. 62) was issued from Liege, in 1571, as the production of Morgan Philippes, a pseudonym very apparent to any one who was acquainted with the history of the edition of 1569, which is not mentioned. The book professes to contain three original treatises, which have separate title-pages. Certain differences, however, exist between the two issues. The address to the reader has been rewritten and much extended. Passages have been suppressed which, in the first edition, mentioned Queen Elizabeth with respect, and placed Queen Mary's rights to the English throne as secondary to those of Queen Elizabeth, or any issue that might spring from her. The second edition artfully reverses the position, and treats Queen Mary as the only true heir to the throne of England. It consequently gave greater offence to the English Court than the prior edition, and was strenuously suppressed. Anderson (Collections, &c., Edinburgh, 1727, 4 vols. 4to, Vol. I. p. 55) has reprinted the first book of this edition in full, and in his preface has given many details of the vicissitudes through which the author and his book passed.

See also A Collection of State Papers, &c., left by William Cecill Lord Burghley, by W. Murdin (London, 1759, 2 vols. fol.), Vol. I. pp. 1-32, for documents bearing on the reception of the book in England.

Some copies, immediately on their arrival, were seized at Dover, to which place they had been brought by Charles Bailley, one of Queen Mary's servants. For an account of Bailley, see *The Scottish Antiquary.* Edinburgh, 1895. Vol. x.

Class IV. *B.M. Adv. S.*

74. A Treatise touching the Right, Title and Interest of the mightie and noble Princesse Marie, Queene of Scotland, to the succession of the Croune of England. Made by Morgan Philippes, Bachelor of Diuinitie, assisted with the aduise of Antonie Broune Knight, one of the Iustices of the Common Place. An. 1567.
Leodii. Apud Gualterum Morberium. 1571.

Small 8vo (6 × 4). a—h in eights i^4. 67 ll. numbered with catchwords.
This is the second book of Bishop Lesley's Treatise, No. 73. It is not unfrequently found in this state, and it seems to have been issued separately.

Class IV. *B.M. S.*

75. De Maria Scotorum Regina, totáque eius contra Regem coniuratione, fœdo cum Bothuelio adulterio, nefaria in maritum crudelitate & rabie, horrendo insuper & deterrimo eiusdem parricidio : plena, & tragica planè Historia.

8vo (5$\frac{3}{4}$ × 3$\frac{1}{2}$) A—Q in fours. A1^a Title, verso blank. A2^a—Q2^b Text, 122 numbered pages, with catchwords. Q3—4 without pagination, containing two Latin poems on Queen Mary, the latter signed P. R. Scotus.

The date of issue of this "little book," which, with its translations, has been the object of intense critical examination, is given by some bibliographers (Ames and Herbert, Lowndes, Dickson and Edmond), by other writers, and by most catalogues, as 1572. It seems, however, to be certain that while the first portion (Detectio) circulated to some extent in MS. after 1568, it was printed in 1571.

A letter of Queen Mary to De la Mothe Fenelon, the French Ambassador to England (Labanoff Recueil, Vol. IV. p. 3), dated from Sheffield, November 22nd, 1571, is devoted to an indignant complaint of the treatment she had received in having had sent to her, apparently by authority, a copy of the book, the composition of which she attributes to "ung athée Buccanan." George Buchanan was commonly accepted at the time of publication as the author of the whole tract, and it is reprinted in the collected edition of his works, edited by Ruddiman (Edinburgh, 1715, folio, 2 vols.); but more recent criticism and examination of authorities tend to the conclusion that the second part (Actio contra Mariam) is not of his composition.

William Herbert's copy (Ames and Herbert, p. 1629) contained two contemporary MS. notes to the following effect :—" Istas actiones scripsit Thomas Smythus à secretis Dominae nostrae Reginae Elizabethae, sicut fama est: Thomas Willsonus à supplicum libellis, quod mihi magis placet."
"Thomas Willsonus creditur hos literas e Gallico transtulisse eū autem Gallicam phrasim vix credo intelligere: Thomas vero Smith hoc optime potuit praestari eo quod legat. Parisiis diu est commoratus."

On these notes Malcolm Laing (*History of Scotland*, London, 1819, 8vo, Vol. I. p. 254) founds a lengthened argument to prove that Dr Thomas Wylson, the Master of the Requests, who afterwards succeeded Sir Thomas Smith, in 1590, as Secretary, is the author of the Actio, and the translator into Latin of the three letters of Queen Mary attached thereto. From documentary evidence additional to Queen Mary's letter, referred to above, the book seems to have been published prior to November 1st, 1571, and there seems to be no doubt that John Day was the printer.

In Ruddiman's reprint the title is given as Detectio sive de Mariae Scot. Reginae . . . Historia, and this title is adopted by Jebb, who reproduces it from the collected edition, Vol. I. p. 217.

Class IV.   *B.M. Adv. Signet. S.*

76. Ane Detectiovn of the duinges of Marie Quene of Scottes, touchand the Murder of hir husband, and hir conspiracie, adulterie, and pretended mariage with the Erle Bothwell. And ane defence of the trew Lordes mainteiners of the Kingis grace ctioun and authavritie. Translatit out of the Latine quhilke was written by G. B.

Svo ($5 \times 3\frac{3}{4}$). A—Y in fours. A1 Title, printed in roman letter, verso blank. A2—F4ᵃ. Whairas of things judicially determinit, &c., in black letter. F4ᵇ—O1ᵇ Ane oratioun with declaration of euidence against Marie the Scotische Quene, &c. O2ᵃ—O4ᵇ Memorandum that in the Castel of Edenburgh there was left by the Erle Bothwell, &c. P1—Q3 italic letter, Curia Iusticiariae s.p. n. Reginae, &c. Q4—Y2ᵇ The wrytynges & letters found in the gard casket, &c., in mixed black letter and italic. Y3 in roman letter, the lines : Now judge Englischmen if it be gud to change Quenes, &c., verso blank. Y4 blank.

Lowndes (Bibliog. Manual, p. 301) omits any mention of this the first edition of the translation of the Latin version (No. 75). It is now of the greatest rarity, and is easily distinguished by the absence on the title of the letter "a" in the word actioun. In a letter written by Dr Wylson to Cecil, November 8, 1571 (Murdin, Vol. I. p. 57), the writer says :—" I doe sende to your Honor enclosed, so muche as his translated into handsome Scottishe, desierynge you to sende unto me Paris closely sealed, and it shall not bee knowne frome whense it cometh." The request for " Paris " refers to the declaration of Hubert Paris, emitted since the Westminster conferences, and not given in the Latin version. It does not, however, appear in this translation, which was issued before the end of 1571, and is believed to be from the press of John Day.

It is unnecessary here to enter on the question whether Buchanan took part in the translation, or whether it is solely Dr Wylson's.

At the end of the book (Sign. Y3) a supplement occurs which is not translated from the Latin original. It comprises eighteen lines, commencing as follows :—

      "Now judge Englishmen if
       it be gud to change Quenes.
        O vnityng confounding," &c.

These scurrilous lines seem to have attracted attention in Scotland at the moment of publication, as they are noticed in a letter (Goodal, Vol. II. p. 371) from Alexander Hay, Clerk to the Regent Murray's Privy Council, to John Knox, dated December 12, 1571. The passage is as follows:—
"Sic things as are newlie set out in print, I trust be not needful to be written . . . all quilk are set out baith in Latin and Ingliss. In the end of quilk Ingliss buik thir sentences or conclusiounis are written, quhilks I thocht not guid heir to slip: Now judge Englishmen," &c.

Class IV.   *B.M. Adv. (imperfect).*

1572

77. The Lamentation of Lady Scotland Compylit be hir self, speiking in maner of ane Epistle, in the Moneth of Marche the zeir of God 1572.

¶ Imprentit at Sanctandrois Be Robert Lekpreuik. 1572.

8vo (5¾ × 3¾). B. L. A⁸ without pagination, but with catchwords on verso. A1 Title, blank on verso. A2ᵃ Dedication To The Richt Honourabill and Godly Leirnit Gentilman, the Laird of Dune, John Areskine, Minister of Gods word, and Superintendent of his Kirk in Angous Mernis & P. R. his humbill servant. S. A2ᵇ-8 Text of the Poem.

This is one of the poems of Robert Sempill. Reprinted in Scottish Poems of the Sixteenth Century, collected by John G. Dalyell. Edinburgh, 1801; and in The Sempill Ballates. T. G. Stevenson, Edinburgh, 1872.

Class IV.   *Adv.*

78. ane new ballat set out be ane Fugitue Scottisman that fled out of Paris at this lait Murther.

¶ Finis ☞ Quod Simpell ¶ Imprentit at Sanctandrois be Robert Lekpriuik Anno Do. 1572.

Broadside. Folio. B. L. Printed in double columns.

One of the poems of Robert Sempill. Reprinted by the Philobiblion Society, 1869; also in A Collection of Ballads by Joseph Lilly. London, 1869; and in The Sempill Ballates. T. G. Stevenson, Edinburgh, 1872.

The only known copy was formerly in the collection of Mr George Daniel, and is now in the Huth Library. The Poem commences—

   "Now Katherine de Medicis hes maid sic a gyis
    To tary in Paris the papistes ar tykit,
   At Bastinnes brydell howbeit sho denyis,
    Giue Mary slew Hary, it was not unlykit;
   Zit a man is nane respectand this number,
    I dar not say wemen hes wyte of this cummer."

Class IV.   *Huth Library.*

79. Historia Nova nella qvale si contengono tutti i successi della guerra Turchesca, la Congiura del Duca de Nortfolch contra la Regina d'Inghilterra; la guerra di Fiandra, Flisinga, Zelanda, & Holanda; l'uccisione d'Vgonotti, le morti de Prencipi, l'elettioni de noui, e finalmente tutto quello che nel mondo è occorso, da l'anno. M.DLXX. fino all 'hora presente. Composta dall Molto Magnifico, & Eccellentissimo Sig. Emilio Maria Manolesso, Dottor dell'Arti, delle leggi Ciuili, e Canoniche, e della Sacra Theologia. Dedicata al Serenissimo Prencipe di Venetia &c. & alli Illus. Legato Apostol. & Orator Catolico. [Printer's Mark].

1572]

Stampata in Padoua Per Lorenzo Pasquati Anno MDLXXII
    4to (8 × 5¾). a—Bb in fours. Title and dedication 2 ll. and 100 numbered ll.
    The account of Norfolk's conspiracy and of Queen Mary occurs at fols. 78 verso to 80 verso.
Class IV.   *S.*

80.   Ane Detectioun of the Doinges of Marie Quene of Scottes, tuiching the Murther of hir husband, and hir Conspiracie, Adulterie Mariage with the Erle of Bothwell. And ane Defence of the trew Lordis, Maintenaris of the Kingis Grace Actioun and Authoritie.
    ☞ Translatit out of the Latine quhilk was written be M. G. B.
    ☞ Imprentit at Sanctandrois be Robert Lekpreuik Anno Do. M.D.LXX.II.
    8vo (5⅝ × 3⅞). A—H in eights, and one leaf blank on verso without signature. No pagination. Catchwords on verso. The Title, with the exception of the first word, is in black letter. The Text is in black letter, with the exception of the Sonnets, Letters, &c., which are in roman type.
    This is the earliest of the English translations of the Detectio having on the title the place of printing and a date. The text, which is in substance the same as No. 76, has been altered to bring it into conformity with true Scottish idiom and mode of spelling. The reprint given in Anderson's Collections is drawn from this edition, which he believed erroneously to be anterior to the London version (No. 76). He rightly appreciates the extreme rarity of both editions, and states that he had seen only one copy, which was then in the possession of the Earl of Oxford. Possibly this is the copy now in the Advocates' Library, no other having been observed. This translation does not contain the scurrilous supplement mentioned in No. 76.
Class IV.   *Adv.*

81.   Ane Detectiovn of the duinges of Marie Quene of Scottes, touchand the murder of hir husband, and hir conspiracie, adulterie, and pretended mariage with the Erle Bothwell. And ane defence of the trew Lordis, mainteineris of the Kingis graces actioun and authoritie. Translatit out of the Latine quhilke was written by G. B.
    [London John Day 1572.]
    8vo (5⅝ × 3⅞). A—N in fours V². No pagination. Catchwords. A1 Title, printed in roman letter, verso blank. A2—V2 Text. The French sonnet in italic letter. Some copies have an extra leaf with the lines beginning Now judge Englishmen, &c., which, it would appear, were added to certain copies as occasion required. It is a reprint of No. 76.
Class IV.   *B.M.*   *Adv.*   *S.*

82.   Histoire de Marie Royne d'Escosse, tovchant la conjuration faicte contre le Roy, & l'adultere commis auec le Comte de Bothvvel, histoire vrayement tragique, traduicte de Latin en François.
    A Edimbovrg par Thomas Vvaltem. 1572.
    8vo (6¾ × 4⅜). A—Y in fours. 88 numbered ll. with occasional catchwords. A1 Title, verso blank. A2 Av Lectevr. A3—V4 Text. At the end, Acheué d'imprimer à Edimbourg ville capitalle d'Escosse, le 13. de Feurier, 1572. par moy Thomas Vvaltem.
    Much argument has been expended in endeavouring to determine the real place and time of issue, and the names of the translator and printer of this translation of the Latin Detectio (No. 75). The Edinburgh imprint is evidently fictitious (see Malcolm Laing's History of Scotland, Vol. I. p. 262, and Goodal, Vol. I. p. 38). Some writers have suggested that it was produced in London under Cecil's auspices, but, notwithstanding the passage quoted below from L'Innocence de Marie, &c., it appears to be certain that the place of printing was La Rochelle. However this may be, it

is evident that Cecil, within a few days of the publication of the book, must have furnished the supplement found at p. 83, which is not a translation from any part of the Detectio, as it appeared either in Latin or English.

The name usually assigned by bibliographers to the translator is P. Camuz, but it may be noted that a recent writer (Henderson: The Casket Letters, Edinburgh, 1889; 8vo; p. 48) has altered this into Cumez. The authority for the adoption of the name of Camuz may be found in L'Innocence, &c. (No. 85), in the following passage (Advertissement av Lecteur. Sign. a3ᵇ), describing the issue in France of this book, and referring to the imprisonment of Queen Mary and the Duke of Norfolk: "Veu qu'on les a priuez de leur liberté personelle, denigrez en leur honneur, & reputation qu'ils auoyent aquise enuers touts les Princes Chrestiës, & cecy, auec vne infinité de faux raports, parolles scandaleuses, & libelles diffamatoires, espars, & publiez par tout: et nommement vn, imprimé du 17 Feburier 1572, enuoyé secretement, & à cachette exposé par la France, contre celle Royne d'Escosse . . . . . Fut faite (dis-ic) vn libelle, aïãt ce titre Histoire de Marie royne d'Escosse, touchant la coniuration faite côtre le roy &c. Et iceluy premieremẽt composé (cõme il me semble) par George Bucchanan Escossoys & depuis traduit en lãgue Françoise par vn Huguenot, Poiteuin (aduocat de vocation) Camuz soy disant gentilhomme, & vn des plus remarquez seditieux de France et depuis augmente d'vn abregé d'vn liuret publie en Angleterre le 13 Octobre l'an 1571, auec la souscription de ces deux lettres R. & G. & portant pour tiltre en François, Le Recueil des conspirations faites par la Royne d'Escosse." Jebb reprinted the book, but without the supplement regarding the Duke of Norfolk. Is it possible, in the light of the latter part of the quotation from L'Innocence, that some copies were issued without the supplement? (see Brunet Manuel du Libraire, Vol. I. 1369). It is also reprinted in Memoirs de l'Estat de France. 8vo, Vol. III., 1579 (No. 103).

Class IV.   *B.M. (imperfect). Adv. S.*

83. A Treatise of Treasons against Q. Elizabeth, and the Croune of England, diuided into two partes: whereof, The first parte answereth certaine Treasons pretended, that neuer were intended: And the second, discouereth greater Treasons committed, that are by few perceiued: as more largely appeareth in the Page following. [Printer's Mark.]

Imprinted in the Moneth of Ianuarie, and in the Yeare of our Lord M.D.LXXII.

8vo (5½ × 3⅜). ¶. ℔. a+e+i+A—X in eights+V⁶. a1ᵃ Title, printed in roman, italic, and Gothic letters. a1ᵇ The Argument of this Treatise diuided into two partes. a2—i6 The Preface to the English Reader. i7ᵃ Allusio ad presentem Angliæ conditionem, ex Æneid Lib. 2. i7ᵇ—i8ᵃ blank. i8ᵇ Printer's Ornament. A—V6ᵃ Text. V6ᵇ Faultes escaped in the Printing. 174 numbered ll.

This book is of great rarity. It was printed either at Paris or Antwerp.

The author, in his preface, professes that he was a stranger who had lived in England for thirty years. The first part is a reply, paragraph by paragraph, to the tract (No. 69) Salutem in Christo. The second part is composed of a virulent attack on Cecil and Bacon, the former of whom is designated as Synon. They are accused of abusing Queen Elizabeth and her people, by not only desiring to destroy Queen Mary and her son, but Queen Elizabeth herself, so as to settle the Suffolk family on the throne.

The author of this powerful invective is supposed by Strype (Annals of the Reformation, Vol. II. p. 178) to be some French rancorous person having his instructions from some crafty rebellious papist of England. The many references to incidents in Scottish contemporary history would lead to the supposition that he was a Scotsman. He says in the Preface, in excusing himself for having written the treatise, that he would "aventure to tye this bel about the Catte's necke." He gives a curious list of persons destroyed by the machinations of Sinon and his associates, which includes Lord Huntly, Lord Darnley, the Archbishop of St Andrews (Hamilton), and David the Secretary. He further says (fol. 37): "Can it be doubted, from whome and from whence the Earle of Lineux was sent, and set uppe : when he caused Dumbarton to be betraied, and quartered the Archebishop of S. Androwes most barbarousely."

Class IV. *Lambeth. B.M.*

84. The copie of a letter written by one in London to his frend concernyng the credit of the late published detection of the doynges of the Ladie Marie of Scotland.

    8vo (5¼ × 3½). A—B in fours. The above title is printed in roman letter on the upper fourth of recto of sign. A, verso blank. A2—B4 Text, ℌ. ℒ. 8 ll. With catchwords, but no pagination. The type seems to be that of John Day.

    Reprinted in Anderson's Collections (Vol. II., p. 261), and in The Harleian Miscell. (London, 1809, Vol. III. p. 561). It seems probable that this letter is the production of Buchanan himself. It is extremely rare.

Class IV. *B.M. Adv.*

85. L'Innocence de la tresillvstre tres-chaste, et debonnaire Princesse, Madame Marie Royne d'Escosse. Ou sont amplement refutées les calomnies faulces, & impositions iniques, publieés par vn liure secrettement diuulgé en France, l'an 1572. tovchant tant la mort du Seigneur d'Arley son espouse, que autres crimes, dont elle est faulcement accusée. Plus, vn autre discours auquel sont descouuertes plusieurs trahisons tant manifestes, que iusques icy, cachées, perpetrées par les mesmes calomniateurs.
Imprimé l'an 1572.

    8vo (6¾ × 4½). a+b in eights+c⁴ +A—M in eights +N⁴+O²+P—Aa in eights, a1 Title, verso blank. a2—c4ᵃ Advertissement av Lecteur. C4ᵇ blank. A1—O1ᵇ Contre les peruerses calomnies des trahistres accusans la tresillustre, treschaste, & debonnaire Princesse Madame Marie Royne naturelle, legitime & souueraine d'Escosse. With a running title, L'Innocence de la Royne d'Escosse. With very irregularly numbered leaves, which should number 100, but leaf O1 is numbered 11, following N4, which is 110. O2ᵃ blank, with the exception of having a printer's ornament in the centre of the page. O2ᵇ blank. P1—Aa6ᵃ Discours contre les conspirations faites sur l'estat d'Angleterre : avec les responses à celuy qui defend la cause de la tres illustre Royne d'Escosse traduict d'Anglois en François, l'an 1572, with running title as in first part. 78 irregularly numbered leaves. There are a few catchwords at intervals.

    The copies of this work noted below present considerable differences ; this collation being taken from my copy No. 2. The book, which is of considerable rarity, has been treated by many bibliographers as an original work ; the authorship they attribute to François de Belleforest, a voluminous French author and translator. It is manifest, however, that if Belleforest had any part in its production, it was only as editor and translator.

    The Introduction is a reproduction of the second part of the Treatise of Treasons (No. 83). The first part (A1—O1ᵇ) is a reply to the French translation of George Buchanan's Detectio, Histoire de Marie, Royne d'Escosse (No. 82); but it could not have been produced by a Frenchman, at least not without instruction from some person having an intimate knowledge of the details of recent events in Scotland.

    The third part (P1—Aa6ᵃ) is the reply to the tract Salutem in Christo (No. 69), translated from the Treatise of Treasons (No. 83). Labanoff (Recueil, Vol. VII., Notice des ouvrages imprimés renfermant des lettres de Marie Stuart, p. 6), mentions an edition with the imprint Lyon, De Tournes, 1572. This is probably on the authority of Le Long (Bibliotheque Historique de la France. Paris, 1769. 4 vols. folio. Vol. II., p. 651), who names this place of printing, and says: "Francois de Belleforest est l'auteur de cette apologie," but does not quote any edition without place of printing.

Brunet (Manuel du Libraire) asserts the place of printing to be Paris, but however this may be, all the copies observed are from the same fount of type, and none bear a place of printing. Without signalising minor differences, which probably could be established in very numerous instances, the following have been observed in the copies examined :—

1. The British Museum copies, Nos. 1, 2, and 3, and the Signet copy want 2 ll. of Sign. P.
2. Copy No. 4 in British Museum, the Advocates', and my No. 1 copy have a leaf with altered matter in the *Advertissement*; and the copy in British Museum has a Title differing from the others in the setting, although having the same wording.
3. In sheet M the first and last leaves have been twice set, showing several differences. The one variety is found in copies 1, 2, and 3 in the British Museum, in the Advocates', and in my No. 1 copy; the other in the Signet and in my No. 2 copy.
4. My copy No. 2, besides minor changes, differs in matter and arrangement in many places from all the other copies, specially in changes and additions to sheet N, and in having a sheet O not found in any of them.

Some of the copies have two leaves of errata following two blank leaves, which complete Sign. Aa. My copy No. 2 has attached to it the leaves of errata, which apparently belong to one of the other varieties.

The space at disposal in this note does not permit more than the above instances of the curious variations which the several versions display. Differences are caused by the addition or removal of passages offensive to many of the actors in the drama, more especially to Murray.

The typographical and editorial ingenuity displayed in making the altered pages fit in with those which have been allowed to remain intact is specially remarkable. The book has been reprinted by Jebb, Vol. 1. pp. 423-606, apparently in the form in which it is found in my copy No. 2.

Attention was first called to the variations in the copies of this book in a paper read to the Edinburgh Bibliographical Society by Mr William Brown on 23rd March 1893.

Class IV.   *B.M. (four copies.)*   *Adv.*   *Signet.*   *S.*

86.   Copie d'vne Lettre de la Royne d'Escosse escripte de sa Prison de Cheifeild touchant ses aduersitez, & le bannissement de ses fidelz Seruiteurs.

A Paris chez Robert Coulombel, Rue S. Jaques, a l'enseigne d'Alde. 1572. Avec Privilege.

8vo, 3 ll. According to Brunet (Manuel, Vol. III. 1426), a reprint of ten copies, four on vellum, was made by P. A. Tossi, Bookseller at Milan, in 1836, not from an edition of Paris, which never existed, but from a MS. One vellum copy and one on paper are in the British Museum, and copies of each of the varieties are in my collection.

Lowndes (Bibliog. Manual) says that the letter is a forgery.

Tossi issued another edition of ten copies in small 4to in 1839.

Class IV.   *B.M.*   *S.*

1574

87.   The Three Partes of Commentaries, Containing the whole and perfect discourse of the Ciuill warres of Fraunce, vnder the raignes of Henry the second, Frances the second, and of Charles the ninth. with an Addition of the cruell Murther of the Admirall Chastilion & diuers other Nobles, committed the 24. daye of August. Anno. 1572. Translated out of Latine into English by Thomas Timme Minister. Seene and allowed. Deuteron. 32. Remember the dayes of olde &c.

Imprinted at London, by Frances Coldocke. Anno 1574.

4to (7¼ × 5½). N. L. Title within woodcut border. Each part has separate Title, signatures, and pagination. A fourth part was added with separate title in 1576, printed by Henric Binneman, but it has no reference to Queen Mary.

Queen Mary is mentioned in several places in Part I., especially (p. 62) regarding her assumption, at the instigation of the Guises, of the Queenship of England.

Class IV.   *B.M.*

88. Dialogi ab Evsebio Philadelpho Cosmopolita in Gallorum et cæterarum nationum gratiam compositi, quorum primus ab ipso auctore recognitus & auctus : alter verò in lucem nunc primum editus fuit.

Edimbvrgi Ex Typographia Iacobi Iamæi 1574.

8vo ($7\frac{1}{2} \times 4\frac{1}{4}$). 2 leaves unsigned + ¶² + *² + *,*,* + a—o in fours. Title, verso blank, and Typographus Lectoris. ¶1—¶,6 Preliminary. ¶7-8 blank. a—o Dialogus I. pp. 112. The second Dialogue has a separate Title : Dialogvs Secvndvs ab Eusebio Philadelpho Cosmopolita in Gallorum et vicinarum gentium gratiam conscriptus & nunc primum in lucem editus Edimburgi Ex Typographia Iacobi Iamaei 1574. A—R in fours, pp. 1-136. The references to Queen Mary are at pp. 21, 24, 29 and 30.

Brunet (Manuel, Vol. IV. p. 599) has a lengthy account of the various forms in which this book was published. Some bibliographers attribute the authorship to Theodore Beza, others to Nicholas Bernand. This and the following number are among the books issued about this period with the counterfeit imprint of Edinburgh, but they were probably printed at Geneva.

See Laing's History of Scotland, Vol. I. p. 268.

Class IV.   *Adv.*

89. Le Reveille-Matin des Francois, et de levrs voisins. Composé par Eusebe Philadelphe Cosmopolite, en forme de Dialogues.

A Edimbourg, de l'imprimerie de Iaques Iames. Auec permission. 1574.

8vo ($7\frac{1}{2} \times 4\frac{1}{4}$). a—b in eights + c⁴ + A—K + a—m in eights. a1 Title, verso blank. a2ᵃ L'Imprimeur aux Français &c. a2ᵇ—a3ᵃ Dedication to Queen Elizabeth. a3ᵇ—b3ᵃ Epistre &c. b3ᵇ—b7 Lettre au Duc de Guise. b8—c2 Dialogisme svr L'Effigie de la Paix. c3 Argument du Premier dialogue. c4 blank. A1—K8ᵃ Dialogve I. K8ᵇ blank. a1ᵃ Dialogve Second (similar title to first). a1ᵇ Argvment du second Dialogve. a2—m8 Dialogve II. The pagination of each Dialogue is separate. Special References to Queen Mary are at pp. 34, 35, 41 and 46-48 of Dialogue II.

This is a translation of No. 88.

Class IV.   *Adv. S.*

90. The Ordovre and Doctrine Of The Generall Fast, appointed by the Generall Assemblie of the Kirkes of Scotland. Halden at Edinburgh the 25. day of December 1565.

Ioel 2. Therefore also now the Lord sayeth, Turne yow vnto me, with all your hart, and with Fasting, and with weaping and with murning.

Imprented at Edenbvrgh Be Robert Lekpreuik Anno 1574.

8vo. 38 leaves printed in roman letter without pagination, but with catchwords on verso, two on recto. A—D in eights E⁴ F². F1-2 Certaine Chapters and Partes of the Scriptures used be the Ministers of Edinburgh & Halyrudhous, in the tyme of Godes visitation be the Pest ; in the tyme when the Court rang all impietie, as murther, huredome, in contempt of God's word, bot especially in the tyme when the Quene was strikken be Gods hand in Jedburgh : &c. &c.

These Chapters are repeated in most of the Editions of the Book of Common Order up to 1635, and in Knox's Works, Laing's Ed., Vol. VI. p. 427. See Dickson and Edmond's Annals, p. 263.

Class VIII.   *Trin. Coll. Camb. Lambeth Palace. Bodl.*

91. Ioannis Leslæi Scoti, Episcopi Rossen. Libri Dvo : quorum vno, Piæ afflicti animi consolationes, diuináque remedia : altero, Animi tranqvilli mvnimentvm & conseruatio, Continentur. Ad serenissimam Principem D. Mariam Scotorum Reginam. His adiecimvs eivsdem Principis Epistolam ad Rossensem Episcopum, & versus item Gallicos Latino carmine translatos, pias etiam aliquot preces. Opus iis omnibus, qui haec calamitosa tempora pio fortique animo transigere cupiunt, admodum vtile : ab eodem auctore, dum pro dicta Principe apud Anglos legatione fungeretur, in carcere conscriptum, & ad eandem missum, nunc verò in communem aliorum vsum in lucem editum. Cum placuerint Domino viae hominis, inimicos eius conuertet. ad pacem Prouerb. 16.

Parisiis, Ex officina Petri l'Huillier, via Jacobæa, sub signo Oliuæ. 1574. Cvm Privilegio Regis.

8vo (5¼ × 4). †+A–R in eights. A–Q3 leaves numbered 1–123. †1 Title, verso blank. †2–†6a Serenissimae Principi, Dominaeque svae benignissimae, Mariae Scotorum Reginae, Jo. Leslaeus Episcopus Rossen. Humilimus ipsius subditus, & apud Anglos orator, mentem tranquillam incolume corpus ac optima quaeque precatur. †6ᵇ–†7ᵃ Two Odes addressed to Bishop Lesley, signed respectively A. B. and T. S. †7ᵇ Typographvs Lectori. †8 blank. A1–E4ᵃ Consolationum Afflicti Animi Lib. 1. E4ᵇ Printer's ornament. E5–E6ᵃ Literarvm Seren. D. Mariae Scot. Reg. ad Episc. Rossen. Scotico idiomate scriptatum versio Latina. E Castro Shefeldiae, prid. id. August. 1572. E6ᵇ–F2ᵃ Meditation facte par la Royne d'Escosse, in French and Latin. F2ᵇ Animi Tranqvilli Mvnimentvm et Praeservatio, Liber alter. F3ᵃ Hymn in Sapphic verse to the Queen. F3ᵇ–F6ᵃ Seren. Prin. D. Mariae, Joan. Epis. Rossen. Epistola. F6ᵇ–O8 Munimentvm. P1–Q3 Precationes aliquot. Q4 Ad Devm . . . Mariae Scotorvm Reginae . . . Quotidianvs Hymnvs. Q5–R7ᵃ Indices. R7ᵇ Auctoris ad lectorem admonitio. R8 Errata, verso blank.

Class IV. I 2.   *B.M. Adv. S.*

92. Ioannis Leslæi Scoti Episcopi Rossensis pro libertate impetranda Oratio ad Reginam Angliæ.

Parisiis. 1574.

8vo. This book is noted in Lowndes' Manual as having been in the libraries of Heber and Bright, but no copy has been observed. Anderson (Collections, Vol. III. p. 251) quotes from it in his notes to Lesley's Negotiations.

Class IV.

1575

93. The Flovver of Fame Containing the bright Renowne & moste fortunate raigne of King Henry the VIII. Wherein is mentioned of matters, by the rest of our Cronographers ouerpassed. Compyled by Ulpian Fulwell (∴). ¶ Hereunto is annexed (by the Author) a short treatice of III noble and vertuous Queenes. And a discours of the worthie seruice that was done at Hadington in Scotlande, the seconde yere of the raigne of King Edward the sixt. Viuit post funera virtus. 1575.

Imprinted at London in Fleete streate at the Temple Gate by VVilliam Hoskins (∴)

4to (7¼ × 5¼). 𝔅. 𝔏. 2ll. unsigned + B–R in fours. 1 Title, within woodent border, printed in roman, italic, and black letter. Verso Royal arms with motto, Cor vnvm. via vna. 2 Dedication to Sir William Cecill Baron of Burghleygh signed by Ulpian Fulwell. B1 Table of contents. B2–B3ᵃ To the reader. B3ᵇ–B4ᵃ Ulpian Fulwell to his booke. B4ᵇ In Ulpiani Fulwelli operis laudem. Rich. Coppoci carmen. C—R3ª, Fol. 1-59, Text, ending with colophon similar to imprint. The History of the winning of Hadington, in Scotlande, An. 2. Reg. Edwardi 6 (∴) is at folios 49-55, and in prose.

This book, which is of great rarity, gives, in very quaint terms, a curious contemporary account of the defence of Haddington by the English army in 1548. It supplies a version of the incidents of the siege from the defenders' side, and is thus a companion volume to the narrative of De Beaugué (No. 9).

The author's opinion of the French commander may be contrasted with that of De Beaugué. He says, "This Mounsier Dassey [D'Essé] captaine generall of the French Armie was complayned on to the Kyng his maister, for his too much rashenesse, whereby hee lost manye of his best souldiers: so that he was sent for home in great displeasure and in his place was sent Monsieur de Termes who remoued the siege, and came not neare the towne by three myles."

The Flovver of Fame is reprinted in Park's Supplement to the Harleian Miscellany. London, 1808. Vol. IX., pp. 337-375, where a short biographical account of the author is given. (See Censura Literaria. London, 1807. Vol. v., pp. 164-168.)

Class I.   *B.M.* *Huth Library.*

94. The Firste parte of Churchyardes Chippes, contayning twelve seuerall Labours. Deuised and published, only by Thomas Churchyard Gentilman.

Imprinted at London in Fletestreate neare vnto Saint Dunstones Church by Thomas Marshe. 1575. Cum priuilegio.

8vo (7×5). ¶. ℔. *¹+A—N in eights+O⁸. *1ᵃ Title, printed partly in roman, italic, and black letter. *1ᵇ The contents of this booke; among which is The Siege of Leith, The Rode into Scotland by Sir William Druery, Knight, and the Siege of Edenborough Castle. *2—*3ᵃ Dedication to Maister Christofer Hatton, Esquier, Captaine Queenes Maiesties Gard. *3ᵇ—*4ᵃ To the despisers of other mens workes that shoes nothing of their owne (in verse). *4ᵇ blank. A—O6 Text, 110 numbered leaves with catchwords. Ll, 1-12, The Seige of Leeth more aptlie called the schole of warre, (The Lord Gray of Wilton generall thereof) in the seconde yeare of the raigne of our Soueraigne Lady Queene Elizabeth. Anno 1560. 38-46, The Roed made by Syr william Druery Knight, into Skotland, from the East Seas to the West, (with sundry Gentlemen of good calling) for the reformation of such causes as the Queens Maiestie and her Counsel thoght convenient. In the XIII year of the raign of our Soueraigne Lady Queene Elizabeth. [In Prose.] 93-99, The Siege of Edinbrough Castell in the XV. yeer of the raigne of our soueraigne Lady Queen Elizabeth, at which seruice Sir VVilliam Druery Knight was generall, hauyng at that time vnder him these Captaynes and Gentlemen following, &c.

Although this is called in the title the first part, no second was ever printed. Other editions were issued in 1565 and 1578. The pieces named above were reprinted in Churchyard's Chips concerning Scotland . . . with historical notices and a life of the author by George Chalmers, London, 1817. 8vo. Chalmers gives a complete list of Churchyard's works.

Class I.   *B.M.*

95. Catharinæ Mediceæ Reginae Matris, vitæ, actorum, & consiliorum, Quibus Universum regni Gallici statum turbare conata est, stupenda eáque vera enarratio. M.D.LXXV.

8vo (6½×4). A—G in eights H⁴. (B4 and G2 are signed respectively A4 and F2.) A1 Title, verso blank. A2 Pacis et tranquilitatis studioso lectori. S. pp. 3-4. A3—H3ª Text, pp. 5-116. H3ᵇ—H4 blank. The earlier edition of the Latin version of No. 96. Another of 103 pp. was issued in the same year with the title Legenda Sanctae Catharinae.

Queen Mary is referred to, p. 19.

Class II.   *S.*

96. Discovrs Merveillevx de la vie, actions, & deportemens de Catherine de Medicis Royne mere, Auquel sont recitez les moyens qu'elle a tenu pour vsurper le gouuernement du Royaume de France, & ruiner l'estat d'iceluy. M.D.LXXV.

    8vo (7 × 4½). A—K in eights L², pp. 1-164. A1 Title, verso blank. A2—L2 Text. s. l. et n. i. (see Latin version, No. 95).

    Queen Mary is referred to in several passages.

Class II.   *S.*

1576

97. La Legende de Charles Cardinal de Lorraine, & de ses freres, de la maison de Guise. Descrite en trois liures par François de l'Isle.

A Reims, de l'Imprimerie de Jacques Martin. 1576.

    8vo (6 × 3⅞). ¶+a—p in eights. ¶1 Title, verso blank. ¶2—6 Preface and errata. ¶7-8 blank. a1—p7 Text, 119 numbered leaves. p8 blank. Text ends with the words Fin de livre premier, but no more was issued. The author of this famous satyre on the Guises was Louis Regnier de la Planche, under the pseudonym of F. de l'Isle. The references to Queen Mary's early life in France convey most scandalous charges against her uncles, and insulting to herself.

    Another impression of this book was printed at Reims by Pierre Martin in 1579 (No. 112), and it is also reproduced in Memoires de Condé; Supplement, 1743. Paris. 4to.

Class II.   *S.*

1577

98. A Legendarie conteining an Ample Discovrse of the life and behauiour of Charles Cardinal of Lorraine, and of his brethren of the house of Guise. Written in French by Francis de L'isle. [Printer's Mark.] Imprinted 1577.

    8vo (6⅞ × 4). A—M in eights N². A1 Title, verso blank. A2—A5ᵃ Francis de Lisle vnto the reader. A5ᵇ blank. A6—N2ᵃ Text, with catchwords, but without pagination. N2ᵇ blank.

    This is a close translation of No. 97.

Class II.   *B.M.*

99. The firste volume of the Chronicles of England, Scotlande, and Ireland conteyning The description and Chronicles of England from the first inhabiting vnto the conquest.

    The description and Chronicles of Scotland from the first original of the Scottes nation, till the yeare of our Lorde 1571.

    The description & chronicles of Yrelande, likewise from the firste originall of that Nation, untill the yeare 1547.

    Faithfully gathered and set forth by Raphael Holinshed.

    At London Imprinted for John Harrison.

    The laste volume of the Chronicles of England, Scotlande and Ireland with their descriptions. Conteyning The Chronicles of Englande from William Conqueror untill this present tyme. Faithfully gathered and compiled by Raphael Holinshed.

    At London Imprinted for John Harrison.

    2 vols. Folio (11¼ × 7¾). ℔. T.

    The First Edition with numerous woodcuts, commonly called the Shakespeare edition. Each title in a Woodcut border with 1577 at top and God save the Queene at bottom.

    Vol. 1. Title, as above—one leaf with armorial bearings on verso. Dedication of the whole work to Sir W. Cecil Lord Burghleygh—two leaves. The Preface to the Reader—two leaves. Dedication to Sir W. Brooke Baron-Cobham—one leaf. An Historical Description of the Islande of Britagne, an Index of the Chapter and List of Authors—two leaves. Text of the Description—126 leaves (the last misprinted 124). Faultes escaped—one leaf (blank on verso). The Historie of Englande—pp. 1-290, last blank. The Historie of Scotlande (within the same woodcut border as the main title) At London Imprinted for John Hunne—one leaf, with armorial bearings and list of Authors out of whom this History of Scotlande has been gathered on verso. Dedication to Lord Robert Dudley Earl of Leycester—one leaf. The Description of Scotlande, written at first by Hector Boethus in Latin and translated by John Bellenden, contents of the chapters—one leaf (blank on verso). Dedication to Mr Thomas Seaford—one leaf (blank on verso). The Description of Scotland—pp. 1-22. The Historie of Scotland—pp. 1-518. A Table of the principal matters—13 leaves without pagination. The Historie of Irelande (within the same woodcut border as the main title). At London imprinted for John Hunne, with armorial bearings and list of Authors on verso. Dedication to Sir Henry Sydney—one leaf. The description of Ireland—28 leaves numbered. The Historie of Irelande—pp. 1-116, the latter containing the names of the Governors. A Table—3 leaves (blank on verso) Faultes and ouersightes escaped in the printing of the Hystorie of Scotlande—one leaf with the same for Ireland on verso.

Vol. II. Title as given above—one leaf with armorial bearings on verso. The Preface to the reader—one leaf (blank on verso). The Politique Conquest of William the First—pp. 291-1876, in continuation of the paging of The Historie of England in Vol. I. Between folios 1868 and 9 is a folding woodcut view of Edinburgh with a list printed on the verso of inner side of the woodcut of The names of such Gentlemen and Captaines as had charge at the siege and wynning of Edenburgh Castell Anno 1573. A Table serving unto both parts of the Chronicle of England—50 leaves, not numbered. Faultes and ouersightes escaped in the printing of the first part of the English Historie—two leaves. At sign. Eeee v is an extra leaf (blank on verso) containing the names of the Knights made at Leith after the brenning of Edenburgh.

This book is rarely found in perfect and fine condition. Neither of the two copies in the British Museum are perfect, but one of them contains an addition of several cancelled leaves at pp. 74 and 90-91 of the History of Ireland.

Class X. B.M. Adv. Signet. Huth. S.

1578

100. De Origine Moribvs, et Rebvs Gestis Scotorvm Libri Decem. E quibus septem, ueterum Scotorum res in primis memorabiles contractius, reliqui uerò tres, posteriorum Regum ad nostra tempora historiam, quae hucusque desiderabatur, fusius explicant. Accessit noua & accurata Regionum & Insularum Scotiæ, cum vera eiusdem tabula topographica, descriptio. Avthore Ioanne Leslaeo, Scoto, Episcopo Rossensi. (Printer's Mark with letters s. p. q. r. on centre of shield.)

Romæ, in Aedibus populi Romani. MDLXXVIII. Cum priuilegio, & Facultate Superiorum.

4to (8¾ × 6½). a—e in fours+A—R in eights+S⁴+T—Oo in eights+Pp—Rr in fours+Ss⁶. a1 Title, verso blank. a2—b2ᵇ Dedication to Pope Gregory XIII. Dated from Rome Kalend. Janua. 1578. b3—b4 Letter to Cardinal Sermoneta, Protector of the Scottish Nation and a Latin Poem by Ninean Vinzet Abbot of the Scottish Monastery at Ratisbon. c—e2 Ad Nobilitatem Popvlvmqve Scoticvm. and Epigrams by Alexander Seton and Aurelius Vrsius. e3 Order of the Scottish Kings. e4 Archbishoprics and Provinces of Scotland. On an unsigned sheet the Map of Scotland with Title Scotiae Regni Antiqvissimi Accvrata Descriptio. A1—Pp2 Text (pp. 1-588) with ten copper-plate engravings of the Scottish Kings and their genealogical trees. The last is of Queen Mary (with the motto : Optimam partem elegit.) and of King James VI. in his 12th year (*see Facsimile No. XI.*) Pp3—Ss6 Index, Errata and Register, without pagination.

The Map of Scotland is of considerable rarity, being wanting in many copies.

The second portion of the History from 1436 to 1572 has a separate Title-page, sign. T (pp. 281-282), with a copper-plate of the Royal Arms of Scotland on verso, and an Epigram to Queen Mary by Alexander Seton. Pp. 283-287 Dedicatory Letter to Queen Mary dated Rome IX Kalend Januarii 1578. It refers to the Queen as being detained in prison and to the fact that Lesley had formerly, in 1570, presented to the Queen this History of the later period of Scotland, never before written in the Scottish Tongue.

The original MS. of this Scottish version, which must at some period have been in the Queen's possession, has not been traced, but several more or less imperfect copies still exist, from which the Bannatyne Club printed a hundred copies, Edinburgh, 1830, 4to. The title as there produced is as follows:—"The Historie of Scotland fra the death of King James the first in the year of God M.CCCC.XXX.VI. to the year M.D.LXI. and sae of the four late Kingis called James Steuartis, and of Quene Marie now Quene of Scotland: Newly collected be Johne Leslye Bischop of Rosse, during the time of his remaning as Ambassadour for the Quene his Soverane in Ingland. M.D.LXX."

The Scottish Text Society has further printed, in 8vo, The Historie of Scotland, Wrytten first in Latin by the Most Reverend and worthy John Leslie, Bishop of Ross; and translated in Scottish by Father James Dalrymple, Religious of the Scottish Cloister of Regensberg, the year of God 1596. Edited from the Fort Augustus MS. by the Rev. Father E. G. Cody, O.S.B.

Class V. X.   *Adv. Signet. S.*

101.   Ad Nobilitatem Popvlvmq. Scoticvm, qvo Maiorum svorvm cvm in caeteris virtvtibvs, tvm in avita religione maxime vestgiis insistant; Ioannis Leslæi Episcopi Rossensis Paraenesis; Scotorvm Historiæ Nvper ab eodem auctore editæ, praefixa. Cvi omnivm Regvm Scotiae Genealogiae in Stemmata destinctæ, ac eorum, qui inter illos illustriores habentur, imagines, cum carta Cosmographica accesserunt (The Royal Arms of Scotland with Motto below Optimam partem elegit.)

Romæ, in Aedibus Populi Romani. M.D.LXXVIII.

4to (8¾ × 6¼). The Paraenesis (which does not occur in the copy from which this is described) is no doubt the same as that which precedes the Roman Edition of Bishop Lesley's History (No. 100). The rare map and portraits are duplicates of those in that work, but are arranged in different order, those of Henry VII. and Queen Mary taking precedence.

This book, which appears to be of great rarity, is printed on thick paper, and the plates are of greater brilliancy than those attached to the History, as a forerunner to which it was probably issued. The Royal Arms of Queen Mary on title-page of this Bibliography and Facsimiles Nos. X. and XI. are reproduced from these plates.

Class X.   *S.*

102.   Promtvarii Iconvm Insigniorvm à secvlo hominvm subiectis eorum vitis, per compendiû ex probatissimis autoribus desumptis, Editio secunda, illustrium virorum, qui à prima successerunt, imaginibus aucta atque locupletata. Prima Pars. [G. Rouille's Printer's mark, an eagle attacked by serpents, with motto, In virtute, et fortvna.]

Lvgdvni, Apud Gulielmum Rouillium. 1578.

8vo (9 × 8½). Aa⁸ + Bb⁴ + Cc—Mm in eights. Aa1 Title within woodcut border, verso blank. Aa2 Ad Christ. Franciæ Regem Henricvm II. Gul. Rouillij Epistola. Aa3—Aa6ᵃ Epistolae and List of authors cited. Aa6ᵇ blank, with printer's ornament in centre. Aa7—Mm6 Text, with woodcut portraits at top of each page, pp. 1-172. Mm6-7 Index.

The second part has separate title. Promtvarii Iconvm pars secvnda Incipiens à Christo nato & perpetuam ducens seriem ad vsque Chris. Franciæ ac Poloniæ Regem HENRICVM hoc nomine

tertium, hodie feliciter regnantem. Hac secunda editione valde aucta. Lex per Mosen data est : gratia & veritas per Iesum Christum facta est. Ioan. cap. 1. [A printer's mark of Moses with the tables of the law, and the motto, Nox praecessit : Dies svccessit.] Lvgdvni Apvd Gvlielmvm Rovillivm. M.D.LXXXI. Aaa—Vvv in eights. Aaa Title, Nativitas D. Nostri Salvatoris on verso. Aaa2—Vvv4ª Text, with woodcut portraits at top of each page, pp. 3-361. Vvv4ᵇ—Vvv8ª Index. Vvv8ᵇ blank. Many of the woodcuts are of merit. At p. 282 the portraits of Francis II. and Queen Mary are to be found with short biographies. That of the Queen terminates with the following words :—" Cū hec esset Francine Regina, habita est ab omnibus omnium formosissima & virtute prestantissima verum fortune iniuriis, post regis obitum, in patriam reuersa, fuit obnoxia, & hodie ob suspicionem alicuius facinoris, in carcere detinetur."

The first edition of this book was issued by G. Rovillius, Lugduni, 1553, 8vo (*Adv. S.*), but it does not contain any notice of the Dauphin or Queen Mary. At p. 243 a portrait and short notice of Magdalene, the unfortunate consort of James V., is to be found.

Class VII. S.

103. Memoires de l'Estat de France, sous Charles Neufiesme. Contenans les choses plus notables, faites & publiees tant par les Catholiques que par ceux de la Religion, depuis le troisiesme Edit de Pacification fait au mois d'Aoust 1570, jusques au Regne de Henry troisiesme et reduits en trois volumes. chascun desquelles a vn indice des principales matieres y contenues. Seconde Edition reueuë, corrigee, et augmentee de plusieurs particularitez et traitez notables.

A Meidelbourg par Henrich Wolf 1578.

8vo (6½ × 4¼). 3 vols.
Vol. I. Title and Preface 8ll. Text 1-475 numbered ll. Index 4 ll.
Vol. II. Title and Preface 2 ll. Index 2 ll. Text pp. 1-790.
Vol. III. Title 1 l. Text 1-357 numbered ll. Index 4 ll.

This curious book, published by the Protestant party of France, was originally issued in a less complete state in 1576 and 1577. Another edition, similar to the present, was also issued in 1578 with some copies dated 1579, one of which is in the British Museum. The second and third Volumes do not contain any reference to Queen Mary.

The first Volume includes many curious passages having reference to the Queen, and it reprints entire the French translation of the Detectio (No. 82). The following introduction to the reprint seems to establish the extreme rarity of the original book. L. 81 : " Mais puis que nous sommes entrez de France en Angleterre & Escosse, auant que d'en sortir nous prierons les lecteurs de nous supporter, si nous leurs presentons l'ample recit de la vie de la Royne d'Escosse. Car outre ce que telle histoire à esté veuë de peu de gēs . . . . . Que si quelqu'vn replique, qu'au lieu de memoirs de France, ie passe en Escosse & traite de choses passees de long temps : ie repondray que ci ceux de Guise . . . . . n'eussent voulu seruir de Marie Stuard pour faire beaucoup de remuemens, ie l'eusse laissee pour telle qu'elle est."

The only omission in the reprint is the list of the names of the Peers who tried the Duke of Norfolk, but to the text of the original the compiler adds the following words: " Quant à la Royne d'Escosse, les estats de son pays luy firent son proces, & asseure-on qu'elle a esté par eux condamne à estre bruslee viue. Sa detention en Angleterre & la patience de Dieu la garantie de ce supplice. Le temps en fera voir la fin."

This passage is followed by a reprint of a considerable portion of the 2nd Dialogue of the Reveille Matin., Edin., 1574 (No. 89) pp. 12-49. It is headed " Discovrs svr la detention de la Royne d'Escosse, & si elle est iusticiable de la Royne d'Angleterre."

The portion of the volume which contains these reprints (ll. 81-144) has a running title, "Histoire Tragique de la Royne d'Escosse."

Class IV. B.M. S.

[1579

1579

104. The Discoverie of a Gaping Gvlf vvhereinto England is like to be swallowed by another French mariage, if the Lord forbid not the banes, by letting her Maiestie see the sin and punishment thereof.
 Saue Lord, let the King here vs in the day that vve call. Psal. 20. verse 9.
 Mense Augusti Anno. 1579.

    8vo (5⅝ × 3⅞). A—E in eights F⁴. 44 ll. with catchwords on both sides, but without pagination. A1 Title, printed in minute roman type; verso blank. A2—F4 Text, with rubrics on margins.
     This tract was inspired by the negotiations for the marriage of Queen Elizabeth to the French King's brother.
     At E5ᵇ—E6ᵇ there is a very violent passage directed against Mary Queen of Scots, in which John Lesley, Bishop of Ross, is named, " And thys is also a deuise fit ynough for such a solicitor, as is that false Scot prelate Rosse, mortall enemy hether, who is presently in Fraunce and like ynough, hyr agēt to procure this deuise." The passage ends thus, " She already cost vs ynough of our Englishe blood, and she cares not though she make hauock of nobilitye & people : she seeks her owne turne by hooke or crooke. Aboue all the dangers to her Maiestie I wold she had one that might euery day cry vvith a loud voyce TAKE HEEDE OH ELIZABETH OF ENGLAND AND BEWARE OF SCOTTISH MARY. The Lord her God defend her from all hyr popish enemies."
     The death of Francis II. is mentioned as having arisen from a "disease in the ear which rotted hym while he was yet alive."
     The right hand of John Stubbes, the author, and Page, the publisher, were both cut off with a butcher's knife and a mallet in the market-place at Westminster. Stapleton the printer, was pardoned. In Park's edition of Harington's Nugae Antiquae will be found much curious matter regarding this work—viz., " An Order of Council to the Lord Mayor of London concerning Stubbes book and A Petition to Q. Elizabeth by Stubbes and his wordes upon the Scaffolde when he lost his haunde on Tewsday 3 Novr. 1579 and his Supplication to the Privie Counsell likewise the wordes of Robert Page." The original MS. of this book is in the Douce Collection in the Bodleian Library. See Lowndes' Bibliog. Manual, p. 2539.

Class IV.   *B.M.*

105. A generall rehearsall of Warres, called Churchyardes Choise : wherin is fiue hundred severall services of land and sea . . . & joyned to the same some Tragedies & Epitaphs. Written by Thomas Churchyard Gent. 1579.
 Imprinted at London by Edward White, dwellyng at the little North-doore of S. Paules Churche, at the signe of the Gunne.

    4to (7 × 5). ¶. ¶. *+**+A—Ee in fours. *1 Title, verso blank. *2—**4 Dedication and Preface. A—Ee Text.
     The Running Title is Churchyards Choise. A second copy of this work in the British Museum has a title-page differing slightly from the above, and without date.

Class I.   *B.M.*

106. Discovrs des plvs memorables faicts des Roys & grāds Seigneurs d'Angleterre depuis cinq cens ans : Auec les Genealogies des Roynes d'Angleterre, & d'Ecosse. Plus vn traicté de la Guide des chemins, les assiettes & descriptions des principales villes, Chasteaux & rivieres d'Angleterre. Par Iean Bernard Secretaire de la Chambre du Roy.

A Paris chez Geruais Mallot, ruë S. Iacques, à l'enseigne de l'Aigle d'or. Auec Priuilege du Roy.
    8vo (6½ × 4). A—K in eights + L⁴ + M². A1—A8 Title, &c. B1—M2 Text, 64 ll. numbered.
    The signatures continue through La Guide, which is without pagination, but has a separate Title.
Class VII.   *S.*

107.   Histoire Abbregee de tovs les Roys de France, Angleterre et Escosse, mise en ordre par forme d'Harmonie : contenant aussi vn brief discours de l'ancienne alliance, & mutuel secours entre la France & l'Escosse. Plus, l'Epitome de l'histoire Romaine des Papes & Empereurs y est adiousté, & celle d'iceux roys augmentee selon la mesme methode. Dedié au treschrestien Roy de France, & de Polongne, Henry III. Le tout recueilli & mis en lumiere, avec la recerche tant des singularitez plus remarquables concernant l'estat d'Escosse : que de la succession des femmes aux biens, et gouuernement des Empires & Royaumes. Par David Chambre Ecossois, conseiller en la cour de Parlement à Edinbourg ville capitale d'Escosse.
    A Paris chez Jean Feurier, pres le college de Reims. 1579. Auec priuilege du Roy.
    8vo (6½ × 4½). ā + ē + a—z + A—G in eights and one l. Privilege and errata. ā1 Title, verso blank. ā2—ā4ᵃ Dedication to Henry III. of France. ā4ᵇ—ā5ᵇ Dedication to Charles IX. of France. ā6—ā7 Preface. ā8—ē8 La Descente des Romains, &c. a—G4ᵃ Text. G4ᵇ—G8ᵇ Table. 235 numbered and 6 unnumbered ll. The Privilege is granted to Jenn Feurier, Michel Godouleau, and Robert Coulombel, and the latter printer also issued an edition of the work. The Author of this and the books described in the two succeeding Nos. was David Chambers of Ormond, one of the Senators of the College of Justice. Although issued together under the above title, they are frequently found separate, and are so treated here. The Life of Queen Mary is to be found on verso l. 212 to recto l. 217.
Class IV. VII.   *Adv. Signet. S.*

108.   La Recerche des Singvlaritez plvs remarqvables, concernant l'estat d'Escosse. Vové a tresauguste & tresclemente Princesse Marie Royne d'Escosse, & doüairiere de France. Par Dauid Chambre Escossois, conseiller en la cour de Parlement à Edinbourg, ville capitale d'Escosse. [Feurier's Printer's mark.]
    A Paris, chez Jean Feurier, pres le College de Reims. 1579. Auec priuilege du Roy.
    8vo. (6½ × 4½). Title, Dedication, and Preface, four ll. A—D in eights, Text 32 ll. numbered.
Class IV. V.   *Adv. Signet. S.*

109.   Discovrs de la Legitime Svccession des Femmes aux Possessions de leurs parens : & de gouuernement des princesses aux Empires & Royaumes. A treshaute & tressage princesse Catherine de Medici, Royne-mere du Roy treschrestien. Par David Chambre Escossois &c. [Feurier's Printer's mark.]
    A Paris, Chez Jean Feurier, pres le College de Reims. 1579.
    8vo (6½ × 4½). a1—4 + A—D in eights E³. a1 Title. a2—4 Dedication to Catherine de Medici and Preface. A1—E2 Text. 33 ll. numbered and one leaf of Table.
Class IV.   *Adv. Signet. S.*

110.   De Ivre Regni apvd Scotos, Dialogvs, Avthore Georgio Bvchanano Scoto. [John Ross' Printer's mark, a female figure with *Verbum Dei* in her right hand, and a candle in her left, surrounded by the motto, *Veritas vincit tandem*, and flanked by the letters I.R.]

Edinbvrgi apud Iohannem Rosseum, pro Henrico Charteris. Anno. Do. 1579. Cvm Privilegio Regali.
  4to (7 × 5). A—O in fours, printed in roman letter. A1 Title, enclosed within a woodcut border, verso blank. A2 Dedication to James VI., dated Sterlini 10 Jan. 1579. A3—O2ᵇ Text, pp. 1-104. O3ᵃ Errata, one leaf unpaged, verso blank. O4 blank.
  With the exception of the Title-page this edition is identical with those of 1579 and 1580, issued without printer's name.
Class IV.   *S.*

111. De Ivre Regni apud Scotos, Dialogus, Avthore Georgio Bvchanano Scoto. Anno. Do. 1579.
  4to (7 × 5). A—O in fours. Printed in roman letter. S. l. et n. i.
  With the exception of the Title-page, this edition is in every way the same as No. 110.
Class IV.   *Adv. S.*

112. La Legende de Charles, Cardinal de Lorraine, & de ses freres de la maison de Guise. Descrite en trois liures par François de l'Isle.
 A Reims de l'Imprimerie de Pierre Martin. MDLXXIX.
  8vo (6 × 3¾). ¶⁰ + A—I in eights + 2 ll. unsigned. ¶1 Title, verso blank. ¶2—6ᵃ Preface. ¶6ᵇ blank. A—[recto of last leaf] Text, ending with the words Fin de premier livre (see No. 97).
Class II.   *B.M.*

1580

113. De Jvre Regni apud Scotos, Avthore Georgio Bvchanano Scoto. Anno. Do. 1580.
  4to (7 × 5). A—O in fours. Printed in roman letter. S. l. et n. i.
  The woodcut border surrounding the Title is similar to that of No. 110, but it appears to be printed from a new block.
Class IV.   *Adv. S.*

114. De Ivre Regni apvd Scotos Dialogos, Auctore Georgio Bvchanano Scoto. Ad Jacobvm VI. Scotorvm Regem. Editio Secunda. M.D.LXXX.
 Ad exemplar Ioannis Rossei Edimbvrgi Cvm privilegio Scotorvm Regis.
  8vo (6 × 3¾), A—F in eights. A1 Title, verso blank. A2—A3 Dedication, pp. 1-4. A4—F7ᵃ Text, pp. 5-93. F7ᵇ—F8ᵃ containing Rex Stoicus, without pagination. F8ᵇ blank.
  Editio Tertia similar to this was issued in 1581.
Class IV.   *B.M. Adv. S.*

115. De Titvlo et Jure Serenissimæ Principis Mariæ Scotorum Reginæ, quo Regni Angliæ, successionem sibi justè vendicat, Libellus : Simul & Regum Anglie à Gulielmo Duce Normandie, qui Conquestor dictus est, genealogiam et successionis seriem in tabula descriptam : Competitorum quoque à Lancastrensi & Eboracensi familiis descendentium historiam summatim complectens. Opera Io. Leslæi Episcopi Rossensis Scoti, dum pro eadem Serenissima Principe iampridem in Anglia Oratorem ageret, patrio primum, nunc verò Latino sermone in lucem editus. Accessit ad Anglos & Scotos, vt qui temporis bellorumque inuria iam diu destracti fuerunt, tandem aliquando animis consentiant, & perpetua amicitia in vnum coalescant, Paraenesis.

Post varios caedes, vnita Britannia tandem
Florebit, pace & relligione pia.
Rhemis, Excudebat Joannis Fognaeus, sub Leone. 1580. Cvm Priuilegio.

> 4to (8½ × 6). a + e + A—B in fours C² D—P in fours Q², a—e Title and Dedicatory epistles (a4 and e4 blank). A—Q1, 59 numbered leaves, De Titvlo, &c., Q2 blank. The Paraenesis follows with separate signatures a⁴ b⁴ c² (in some copies two leaves of a are signed R), and the genealogical table, frequently wanting, is on a separate sheet. The title is enclosed in a woodcut border used in many of Lesley's works. *See Facsimile No. XII.* for a smaller form of the same cut.
> Some copies end with the Paraenesis, but the De Illvs. Foemenarum . . . Libellus (No. 116) is usually found attached. This book and No. 116 are the Latin translations of the second and third books of Lesley's English treatises, dropping the pseudonym of Morgan Phillipes.

Class IV.   *B.M. Adv. S.*

116. De Illvstrivm Foeminarvm in Repvb. Administranda, ac ferendis legibus authoritate, Libellus. Opera Io. Leslæi Episcopi Rosiensis Scoti, dum pro Serenissima Principe Maria Scotorum Regina iam pridem in Anglia Legatum ageret, patrio primum, nunc verò Latino sermone in lucem editus.
Rhemis excudebat Ioannes Fognæus, sub Leone. 1580 Cvm Priuilegio.

> 4to (8½ × 6). A—F in fours G², 26 ll. numbered with catchwords, and leaf of errata. The Title has the woodcut border used in most of Lesley's works.

Class IV.   *B.M. Adv. S.*

1581

117. Adversvs Georgii Bvchanani Dialogvm, de Jvre Regni apvd Scotos, pro regibus apologia. Per Adamum Blacuodæum Senatorem apud Pictauos.
Pictavis Apud Franciscum Pagæum Typographum Regium. Cum Priuilegio Regis ad Decennium. 1581.

> 4to (7½ × 5¼). *⁴ + ⁂² + A—Tt in fours. *1—⁂2 Title and Dedication to Queen Mary and her son, Poems, &c. 6 ll. unpaged. A—Tt3 Text, pp. 1-341 with irregular catchwords, having none on the signed leaves. Tt4 Errata, unpaged.
> The verso of p. 341 contains an interesting address to the reader.

Class IV.   *Adv. S.*

118. Ane Catholik and facile Traictise, Drauin out of the halie scriptures, treulie exponit be the anciēt doctores, to confirme the real and corporell praesence of chrystis pretious bodie and blude in the sacrament of the alter. Dedicat. To his souuerane Marie the quenes maiestie of scotland. Be Johne Hamilton student in theologie, and regent in philosophie to the maist excellent and catholik prince Charles of Bovrbon in the royal college of Nauarre.
Imprentit at Paris the first of April. 1581.

> 16mo (4½ × 3). A—V in eights. A1 Title, quotations from Scripture in Latin and Scottish on verso. A2—B2 Epistle to Queen Mary numbered 2-10. B3—P4ᵇ Text, ll. 11-116, no catchwords. P5—P8 To the richt noble vertuous and michtie Prince James the Saxt King of Scotland, without pagination or catchwords. Q1—V8 Certain orthodox and Catholik conclusions, &c., without numeration or catchwords.

Class V.   *Signet. S.*

119. De vita et moribvs atqve rebvs gestis Hæreticorvm nostri temporis &c. Traductis ex sermone Gallico in Latinum, quibus multa addita sunt quæ in priori editione quorumdam, negligentia omissa fuere. Authore Iacobi Laingæo Scoto Doctore Sorbonico. [Printing press: De Roigny's Printer's mark.]
Parisiis. Apud Michaëlem de Roigny via Jacobea sub signo quatuor Elementorum. 1581. Cvm privilegio.

8vo (6½ × 4). a⁸ + e⁴ + i⁸ + A—O in eights + 1⁶. a1 Title, privilege on verso. a2—e4ᵃ Dedication to Queen Mary and King James VI., printed in italic letter. e4ᵇ blank. i1—i7 index. i8 blank. 20 ll. without pagination. A1—P4 Text, 115 numbered leaves. P5—P6 Errata without pagination.

Class V. *Adv. S.*

120. The Dispvtation concerning the controversit headdis of Religion, haldin in the Realme of Scotland, the zeir of God ane thousand, fyue hundreth fourscoir zeiris. Betuix. The pretendit Ministeris of the deformed Kirk in Scotland. And, Nicol Burne Professor of philosophie in S. Leonardis college, in the Citie of Sanctandrois, brocht vp from his tender eage in the peruersit sect of the Caluinistis, and nou be ane special grace of God, ane membre of the halie and Catholik Kirk, Dedicat To his Souerane the Kingis M. of Scotland, King James the Saxt.
Nisi conuersi fueritis, gladium suum vibrabit: arcum suum tetendit, & parauit illum. 1. Vnles ze be conuerted, God vil drau his suord: he hes bendit his bovv, and preparit it. Psalm. 7.
Imprentit at Parise the first day of October. 1581.

8vo (6½ × 4). a+A—Z in eights. a1 Title, quotations in Latin and Scottish from Gospels of SS. Matthew and Mark on verso. a2—a5 To the Maist Nobil, Potent, and Gratiovs king of Scotland king Iames the saxt. a6—a8ᵃ To the Christiane reidar. a8ᵇ Quotations in Scottish from S. Paul, &c. A1—Z4 Text, 190 numbered ll. Z5-6 The Materis of Controversie qvhilk ar intreated in this conference ar thir. Z7ᵃ Quotations from Scripture in Latin and Scottish. Z7ᵇ Colophon: Imprentit at Pareis, the first day of October, the zeir of God, 1581. Z8ᵃ Arabesque ornament. Z8ᵇ blank.
Queen Mary is referred to in the Epistle to King James.

Class IV. *B.M. Adv. Signet. S.*

1582

121. Rervm Scoticarvm Historia Avctore Georgio Buchanano Scoto. [Arbuthnet's Printer's mark.]
Edimbvrgi apud Alexandrum Arbuthnetum Typographum Regium Anno M.D.LXXXII. Cvm privilegio Regali.

Folio (10 × 7¼). (*ₐ*)⁴ + A—Zz in sixes. (A, N, O, P and R in fours, Q in three.) (*ₐ*)1 Title, within a woodcut border, verso blank. (*ₐ*) 2-4 Dedication to King James VI., Latin poems by Andrew Melvin, Robert Rolock and John Lindsay terminating with the printer's small mark. A1—Zz Text. The last leaf contains Errata followed by the printer's small mark. Verso blank.

Class X. *B.M. Adv. Signet. S.*

1583

122. Rervm Scoticarvm Historia, Auctore Georgio Buchanano Scoto. Ad Iacobvm vi Scotorvm Regem. Accessit De Ivre Regni apud Scotos Dialogvs, eodem Georgio Bvchanano auctore.
ⅭⅠↃ.ⅠↃ.ⅩⅩⅭⅠⅠⅠ. Ad exemplar Alexandri Arbuthneti editum Edimbvrgi.

Folio (12½ × 8¼). Title, blank on verso, and Dedication with list of Kings, 2 ll. unsigned. A—Nn in sixes + Oo⁴ Text, 218 numbered leaves, last blank on verso. a⁶ + b⁶ + c⁴ + d⁴ De Iure Regni with a sub-title, Dedication on verso. On recto of d4 Latin verses of Andrew Melvin. Index and Errata 6 ll., last blank on verso. This Edition was printed in Geneva.

Class X. *B.M. S.*

1584

123. A Treatise Tovvching the right, title, and interest of the most excellent Princesse Marie, Queene of Scotland, And of the most noble king James, her Graces sonne, to the succession of the Croune of England. Wherein is conteined asvvell a Genealogie of the Competitors pretending title to the same Croune: as a resolution of their obiections.

Compiled and published before in latin, and after in Englishe, by the right reuerend father in God, John Lesley, Byshop of Rosse. With an exhortation to the English and Scottish nations for vniting of them selues in a true league of Amitie.

An. 1584.

All Britaine Yle (dissentions ouerpast)
In peace & faith will growe to one at last.

8vo (7¾ × 4¼). A⁴ + B—I in eights + K⁴ with catchwords. 71 numbered ll. A1ᵃ Title. A1ᵇ Portraits and verses (as under). A2—A4ᵃ To the most sacred and most mightie Emperour: and to the most high and pvissant Kynges and Soueraigne Princes of Christendome, John Lesley, Byshop of Rosse wysheth peace and perpetuall felicitie, &c. A4ᵇ blank. B1—B5ᵃ To the most excellent and most graciovse Qvene Marie, and to the most noble King James, her sonne, his vndoubted Souereignes, John Lesley Byshop of Rosse wisheth all true felicitie, &c. B5ᵇ—8ᵇ A preface conteyning the argument of this Treatise & the cavses mouying the Author to wryte the same. On C1ᵃ second Title (within a similar border to the first) in same form as far as the words, 'Croune of England,' then follow: And first, touching the Genealogie, or pedegrue of such competitors, as pretend title to the same croune. The Genealogical Table follows sign. C8. On I3 An Exhortation to the English and Scottishe Nations that after so long warres, they wolde now at last agree, and joyne together in one true league and fast frendshippe and amitie, &c.

Without place (Rheims) or name of printer. The title is enclosed in the woodcut border found on the title of many of Lesley's works. On verso of title are woodcut portraits of Queen Mary and her son King James, with the following verses respectively above and below the portraits:

Encrease of blesse expected long Through princelie grace and pietie
In Britain was begonne : Great is the mother's fame,
When suche a mother dyd bring foorth The King her sonne doth yeild much hope
VVith so good happe a sonne. To imitate the same.

This is the English version of the De Titulo et Jure Sereniss. Mariae (No. 115), which has been considerably altered by the author from the form in which it first appeared in English in 1569 (No. 62). It contains the Exhortation to Unity, but does not include the third book on the Regiment of women.

Class IV. V. *B.M. Adv. Signet. S.*

124. A discouerie of the treasons practised and attempted against the Queenes Maiestie and the Realme, by Francis Throckemorton, who was for the same arraigned and condemned in Guyld Hall, in the Citie of London, the one and twentie day of May last past. 1584.

4to (7¼ × 5¼). 2 ll. unsigned + A—C in fours. 1 Title, verso blank. 2 To the reader, &c. A—C A true and perfect declaration, &c. Without pagination, but with catchwords.

Class IV. *B.M. S.*

125. De Iustitia Britannica, siue Anglica, quæ contra Christi Martyres continenter exercetur.

Ingolstadii, ex Officina Typographica Davidis Sartorii. Anno cIɔ.Iɔ.xxciv.

8vo (6¼ × 4). A—G in eights. A1 Title, verso blank. A2ª—A6ª Præfatio Typographi ad Lectorem. A6ᵇ—A8ᵇ Exemplvm Literarvm P. Richardi Barretti ad P. Rectorem Collegii Anglorum de Vrbi, Rhemis VI Aprilis M.D.LXXXIIII. B1—G6ᵇ Series et Catalogvs Eorvm, quæ in Anglia svperioribvs annis contra Christi Ecclesiam acciderunt, ex doctissimi Theologi Nicolai Sanderi libris de Monarchia Ecclesiæ, pp. 92, with running title, De Justitia Britannica. G7ª Qui svbseqventivm annorvm persecvtiones & martyria cognoscere voluerit, librum earundē persecutionum cum vita & martyrio Edmundi Campiani & aliorum, qui libir vbiq; habetur, & in omnes pene linguas conuersus est, perlegere poterit. Cum facultate superiorum. G7ᵇ —G8 blank.

This book, although bearing the title De Justitia Britannica, is not to be confounded with that entitled Justitia Britannica, Londini, Excudebat Thomas Vautroullius 1584, 8vo, which latter is the Latin translation of the work usually attributed to Sir William Cecil, Lord Burghley, entitled The Execution of Justice in England for maintenance of publique and Christian peace, against certaine stirrers of sedition & adherents to the traytors and enemies of the Realme, without any Persecution of them for questions of Religion, as is falsely reported and published by the fautors and fosterers of their treasons. Imprinted at London mense Jan. 1583.

The latter book, although specially treating of the Roman Catholic plots and extenuating the use of torture, with the view of defeating them, contains no direct notices of Mary Queen of Scots. The work under consideration, however, embraces a list of the principal persons who had suffered for the Roman Catholic faith in England. Foremost among the women is placed the name of Mary Queen of Scots (p. 56), with a notice of some length of her devotion to the Roman Catholic faith, and an outline of her sufferings while detained in England.

The Justitia Britannica of Lord Burghley is referred to ironically in the preface, and the title has been chosen no doubt in the same sense.

Class IV. *S.*

126. Ad Persecvtores Anglos pro Catholicis domi forisque persecvtionem svfferentibus; contra falsum seditiosum, & contumeliosum Libellum, inscriptum Iustitia Britannica. Vera, sincera, & modesta Responsio: qua ostenditur, quàm injustè Protestantes Angli Catholicis perduellionem obijciant; quàm falsò negent se quenquam religionis causa persequi; & quàm callidè laborent hominibus externis imponere, ne earum quæ inferuntur afflictionum causam, modum & magnitudinem verè intelligant; cum aliis permultis ad hoc argumentum pertinentibus. Scripta primùm idiomate Anglicano, & deinde translata in Latinum.

Ps. 62. Ut obstruatur os loquentium iniqua.
Ps. 49. Os tuum abundauit malitia, & lingua tua concinabat dolos.

8vo (7 × 4¾). *+A—S in eights T⁴. *1 Title, verso blank. *2—*7 Præfatio ad Lectorem.

*8 Argumenta singvlorvm Capitvm. A1—S7ᵃ Text, pp. 1-285. S7ᵇ—T3ᵇ Tabvla particvlaris rervm in hoc libro insigniorvm. T4ᵃ Errata. T4ᵇ blank.
Printed probably at Ingolstadt or Douay about 1584.
The authorship of this book, which is a translation of A defence of the English Catholics against a slanderous Libel intituled the Execution of Justice in England, &c., is usually attributed to Cardinal Allen. Queen Mary, among other notices, is specially referred to in the Preface, and at pp. 107 and 175.
It is possible that the issue of this book may have been a little later than the end of the year 1584, as events occurring in Edinburgh on the 14th May 1584 are described.

Class IV. *S.*

1585

127. De vita et moribvs Theodori Bezae, omnivm Haereticorum nostri temporis facilé principis, & aliorum hæreticorum breuis recitatio. Cui adiectus est libellus, de morte Patris Edmundi Campionis & aliorum quorumdam Catholicorum, qui in Anglia pro fide Catholica interfecti fuerunt primo die Decembris. Anno domini. 1581. Authore Iacobo Laingæo Doctore Sorbonico.
Parisii, Apud Michaelem de Roigny via Jacobea, sub signo quatuor Elementorum, 1585. Cvm priuilegio.

8vo (6¼ × 4). aˢ + eᵉ + A—I in eights. a1 Title, verso blank. a2—a7ᵃ Dedication to Queen Mary and King James VI. printed in italic letter. a7ᵇ —e1ᵃ Haec disputatio habita est A.D. 1566, &c. e1ᵇ—e4ⁿ Preface, in roman letter. e4ᵇ blank with arabesque ornament. A—I Vita, &c., pp. 1-144 without catchwords.
This work of Laing is generally found bound with the De vita et moribus Haereticorum of same author. Paris, 1581. (No. 119.)

Class V. *Adv. S.*

128. Michaelis Hospitalii Galliarvm Cancellarii Epistolarvm sev Sermonvm Libri Sex.
Lutetiae Apud Mamertum Patissonium Typographum Regium, in officina Roberti Stephani. M.D.LXXXV. Cvm Privilegio.

Folio (13¼ × 8¼). Title, verso blank, and one leaf of Dedication to Henry III. printed in roman letter without sign. or pagination. a—I in sixes Text, pp. 1-381, and Index.
The Epithalamium on the Marriage of Francis II. and Queen Mary occurs at p. 240, and a poem on the accession to the throne of Francis II. at p. 253, in which the Queen is referred to.

Class II. VI. *S.*

129. A trve and plaine declaration of the horrible Treasons, practised by William Parry the Traitor, against the Queenes Maiestie. The maner of his Arraignement, Conuiction and Execution, together with the copies of sundry letters of his and others, tending to divers purposes for the proofes of his treason. Also an addition not impertinent thereunto, conteyning a short collection of his birth, education and course of life. Moreouer, a few obseruations &c.
At London by C.B. Cum Priuilegio.

4to (7 × 5¼). 𝔄. 𝔈. A—II in fours. Pages 1-53. Sign. H has separate pagination with catchwords. Colophon : Imprinted at London by C. B. (Christopher Barker).
Queen Mary is referred to at p. 15.

Class IV. *B.M. S.*

1586

130.   [The History of the Reformatioun of Religion within the Realme of Scotland: conteanying the maner and by what persons the light of Christis Evangell hath bene manifested unto this Realme, after that horrible and universal defectioun from the trewth, which has cume by the meanes of that Romane Antichrist.]

   8vo (6 × 4¼). B—Mm in eights.

   Thos. Vautrollier's unfinished and suppressed edition of John Knox's History, 1586-1587. All the copies were seized in London by the order of Archbishop Whitgift and Queen Elizabeth's Council. It commences on p. 17, sign. B. and ends on p. 560, sign. Mm8. It seems to have been suppressed prior to the printing of sheet A and the concluding sheets, as no copies have been found with more pages than those indicated. A small number of copies can be traced.

  Class X.   *B.M. Adv. (imperfect). Signet. S.*

131.   The Copie of a Letter to the Right Honourable the Earle of Leycester, Lieutenant generall of all her Maiesties forces in the vnited Prouinces of the lowe Countreys, written before but deliuered at his return from thence: With a report of certeine petitions and declarations made to the Queenes Maiestie at two seuerall times, from all the Lordes and Commons lately assembled in Parliament. And her Maiesties answeres thereunto by herselfe deliuered, though not expressed by the reporter with such grace and life, as the same were vttered by her Maiestie.

  Imprinted at London by Christopher Barker, Printer to the Queenes most excellent Maiestie. 1586.

   4to (6⅞ × 5⅛). A—D in fours E². A1ᵃ blank. A1ᵇ Royal Arms. A2ᵃ Title, verso blank. A3ᵃ—E3ᵇ Text, pp. 1-32. E3ᵇ Colophon. With pagination and catchwords. The Letter is signed R. C. [Richard Crompton].

  Class IV.   *Signet. S.*

132.   A Short Discourse: expressing the substaunce of all the late pretended Treasons against the Queenes Maiestie, and Estates of this Realme, by sondry Traytors: who were executed for the same on the 20. and 21. daies of September last past. 1586. Whereunto is adioyned a Godly Prayer for the safetie of her Highnesses person, her honorable Counsaile, and all other her obedient Subiects. Seene and Alowed. [Printer's ornament.]

  ¶ Imprinted at London by George Robinson for Thomas Nelson, and are to be solde at his Shop vpon London Bridge.

   4to (7 × 5⅜). A. E. A in fours. A1ᵃ Title. A1ᵇ Dedicatory Epistle by T. Nelson to Sir Owen Hopton, Lieutenant of the Tower. A2ᵃ A Godly Prayer giuen to Her Maiestie. A2ᵇ Acrostic written vpon the Alphabet of the Queenes name. A3ᵃ—4ᵃ The substance of all the late entended Treasons. A4ᵇ The names of those Traytors that were executed.

  This work, except the Dedication, is in verse. The eighth stanza thus refers to Queen Mary:—

    "And then for to invade the Realme by trowpes of foraine Power,
      To ouerthrowe the gouernment, and kill her in her Bower:
    Or forceably to dispossesse, The Queene of Englands Grace,
    And to proclaime the Scottish Queene, and set her in her place."

  Class IV.   *Lambeth Library. B.M.*

1587] 47

133. An Apologie of the Professors of the Gospel in Fravnce against the railing declamation of Peter Frarine a Louanian turned into English by John Fowler. Written by William Fulke.

8vo (6 × 4¼).

This tract, which has a separate title as above, is the third of three Treatises issued by William Charke. Printed by T. Thomas, Cambridge, 1586. Each part has a separate title and pagination. A new register commences at Part II. and is carried on to the end of the book. A copy is in the British Museum, press mark, 712. b. 4.

At p. 37 is the following passage : —" The Scottish Queenes behaviour hath so much dishonoured her Person that Frarine is to be pardoned if he spake anything in her praise, before the uttermost of her reproach was made manifest to the world."

At p. 38, referring to the conspiracy of Amboise and proceeding to refute the calumny, the following notice of Queen Mary occurs :—" By what scriptures (saith Frarine) did you conspire at Geneua like villaines & traitorous to murther King Frauncis, and the Scottish Queene his wife, his mother, brethren and all the nobles and Catholike officers of Fraunce."

Class IV.   *B.M.*

134. By the Queene. A true Copie of the Proclamation lately published by the Queenes Maiestie, vnder the Great Seale of England, for the declaring of the Sentence lately giuen against the Queene of Scottes, in fourme as followeth. [At the end] At our Manor of Richmont the iiii. day of December, the XXIX. yeere of our Reigne, and in the yeere of our Lord God, 1586. God save the Queene.

Imprinted at London by Christopher Barker, Printer to the Queenes most excellent Maiestie.

Broadside. Folio (34½ × 8½). B. L.

Class VIII.   *Adv. Edin. Univ.*

135. By de Coninginne De waerachtighe Copie van de proclamatie latelück ghepubliceert by de Coninginne / en hare Mayesteyt / onder de grote zeghel van Enghelant / omme de declaratie van de Sententie ghegheuen ieghens de Coninghinne van Schotlant in forme hier na volghende.

Gheprent na die Copie de tot Londen ghedruct is by Christoffel barker drucker der Coninginnes hooghe Mayesteyt.

4to (7¼ × 5¾). B. L. Four leaves without pagination, verso of title blank.

A Dutch Translation of Queen Elizabeth's Proclamation, which is dated 1586.

Class VIII.   *S.*

1587

136. Waerachtich verhael / hoe ende in wat manieren de Coninginne van Schotlandt haer heeft ghewillichlijck begeuen ter doot / achter volghende de sententie byde Conninghinne van Engelant ende haren Raet / den 16, Febrvarii 1587, gegeuen steruende int Catholicq Roomsche Gheloouc. [A rude woodcut of the Execution of Queen Mary.]

Gheprint Thantwerpen by Mattheus de Rische / op ons lief Vrouwen kerckhof / onder den Thoren / inden Gulden Sampson. Anno 1587. Met consent.

4to (7¼ × 5¼). 4 leaves without pagination.

Class IV.   *B.M.*

137.   Dv Droict et Tiltre de la Serenissime Princesse Marie Royne d'Escosse, & de tresillustre prince Jaques VI. Roy d'Escosse son fils, à la succession du Royaume d'Angleterre.   Auec la genealogie des Roys d'Angleterre ayans regné depuis cinq cens ans.   Premierement composé en Latin & Anglois, par R. P. en Dieu M. Jean de Lesselie Euesque de Rosse, Escossois, lors qu'il estoit Ambassadeur en Angleterre pour sa Majesté, & nouuellement mis en François par le mesme Autheur.
A Roven de l'Imprimerie de George l'Oyselet.

> 8vo (6½ × 4⅞). A—C in fours + D—K in eights without pagination; and a Genealogical Table. The title is enclosed in a woodcut border same as that of No. 115. The Dedication is addressed to Henry III. of France and dated Rouen, 1587.

Class IV. S.

138.   Declaration del Titvlo y derecho que la Serenissima Princesa Doña Maria Reyna de Escoçia, tiene a la Succession del Ingalaterra. Con la Genealogia y orden de la succession de los Reyes de Ingalaterra desde Guillermo Duque de Normandia por sobre nombre el Conquistador. Y sumeriamente la Historia de los compeditores descendientes de las casas de Lancastre y Eboraco dicha yore. Compuesto por el Reverdessimo Señor Don Johan Lesleo Obispo de Rossa Escoçes, Siendo Embaxador por la dicha Reyna de Escoçia, en Inglaterra traduzido de yngles en latin y de latin Español por el mismo author.

> Post varias caedes vnita Britannia, tãdẽ
> Florebit, pace & religione pia.

> 8vo (5⅞ × 4). 4 ll. Title and Dedication, with Genealogical Table. A—F in fours, last leaf blank. The Dedication is addressed to Philip II. of Spain and is dated from Roan (Rouen) 4 de Abril 1587.
> See *Facsimile No. XII.* of this title, the woodcut border of which is of the same design as that used in the original, and in each of the translations of Bishop Lesley's book, Nos. 115, 123, and 137. The Spanish translation is rarer than any of the others.

Class IV. S.

139.   A Dvtifvl Invective against the moste haynous Treasons of Ballard and Babington : with other their adherents, latelie executed. Together with the horrible attempts and actions of the Q. of Scottes : and the sentence pronounced against her at Fodderingay. Newlie compiled and set foorth in English verse.   For a Newyeares gifte to all loyall English subiects. by W. Kempe. [Printer's ornament.]
¶ Imprinted at London by Richard Iones, dwelling at the signe of the Rose and crowne neere Holborne bridge 1587.

> 4to (7 × 6). ¶ in four. ¶1ª Title. ¶1ᵇ Dedication to George Barne Lord Maior of the Cittie of London by W. Kempe. ¶2ª—¶4ᵇ A Joyful New-yeares Gift.
> The part of the poem regarding Queen Mary begins at bottom of p. 3. The verses are very bald.

Class IV. IX. B.M.

140.   A short declaration of the ende of Traytors, and false Conspirators against the state, & of the duetie of Subiectes to theyr soueraigne Gouernour : and wythall, howe necessarie, Lawes and execution of Justice are for the preservation of the Prince and Common wealth. Wherein are also breefely touched, sundry offences of the S. Queene,

Edin. Bibl. Soc.—*Queen Mary Literature. Facsimile No. XII.* See No. 138, page 48.

cōmitted against the crowne of this Land, and the manner of the honorable proceding for her conuiction thereof, and also the reasons & causes alledged & allowed in Parliament, why it was thought dangerous to the state, if she should haue liued.

Published by Richard Crompton, an apprentice of the common Lawes. Seene and allowed. Ecclesia. 10. Wish no euill to the King in thy thought, nor speake anie hurte of him in thy priuie Chamber: for a byrde of the ayre shall betray thy voyce, and with her fethers shee shall bewray thy wordes.

At London. Printed by J. Charlewood, for Thomas Gubbin, and Thomas Newman. 1587.

<blockquote>4to (7 × 5). B. L. A—F in fours. Catchwords, but no pagination. A1 Title within woodcut border, verso blank. A2—A3ª To the most reuerende Father in God John . . . Archbyshoppe of Canterbury . . . Richard Crompton wysheth euerlasting felicitie. A3ᵇ blank. A4—F4 Text.</blockquote>

Class IV.   *B.M. S.*

141. The Censure of a loyall Subiect: Upon certaine noted Speach and behauiours of those fourteen notable Traitors, at the place of their executions, the xx. and xxi. of September last past. Wherein is handled matter of necessarye instruction for all dutifull Subiectes: especially, the multitude of ignorant people. Feare God: be true to thy Prince: and obey the Lawes.

At London Printed by Richard Iones, dwelling at the Signe of the Rose and Crowne, neere Holborne-bridge, 1587.

<blockquote>4to (7 × 5). B. L. A—F in fours G². A1ª Title A1ᵇ An address to the reader by T. C. (Thomas Churchyard), editor of the book for his friend G. W. (George Whetstone), who signs the dedication (A2) to Lord Burghleigh. A—G2 Text. With catchwords and many marginal rubrics, but without pagination.

An edition of this book in the Advocates' Library, without date, has in the title the following inserted after the words "last past":—As also, of the Scottish Queen, now (thankes be to God) cut off by Iustice, as the principal Roote of al their treasons. On Wednesday the 8. of Februarie 1586. The special reference to Queen Mary occurs on the last two leaves, which are headed:—The Scottish Queene the root of all these treasons. The Traitors are Babington and his friends.</blockquote>

Class IV.   *B.M. S.*

142. Een warachtich verhael van seeckere requesten ende declaratien ghedaen aen de Con. Mᵗᵉʸᵗ tot twee diuersche stonden . . . belangende het vonnisse vande Coninginnie van Schotlant &c.

Tot Leyden, by Thomas Basson woonende aen de Breede-straat. Anno 1587.

<blockquote>4to (7¼ × 5⅞). A—C in fours. A1 Title, Privilege on verso. A2—C Text.

A translation of the Proclamation and Addresses by Parliament to Queen Elizabeth after the Babington conspiracy; Puckering's address to the Queen, 12th Nov. 1586, and her Majesty's reply.</blockquote>

Class VIII.   *B.M.*

143. Copye wan eenen brief | aen den E. den Grave van Leycester &c.

Gedruct by Richard Schilders, Drucker der Staten van Zeelandt. 1587.

<blockquote>4to (7½ × 5¼). A—F in fours, without pagination. Colophon: Middelburgh, by Richard Schilders, Drucker der Staten van Zeelandt 1587.</blockquote>

The letter is signed R.C. [Richard Crompton], and the volume contains a translation, from No. 131, of the Proclamation of the Sentence on Queen Mary, dated 4th Decr. 1586, and a translation of the Queen's correspondence with Anthony Babington.

Class VIII. *B.M.*

144. Martyre de la Royne d'Escosse Dovariere de France. Contenant le vray discours des traisons à elle faictes à la suscitation d'Elizabet Angloise, par lequel les mensonges calomnies & faulses accusations dressees contre ceste tresuertueuse, trescatholique & tresillustre princesse sont esclarcies & son innocence aueree. Pretiosa in conspectu Domini mors sanctorum eius.

A Edimbourg chez Jean Nafeild 1587.

8vo (6⅜ × 4¼). a+A—Hh in eights. a1ª Title, verso blank. a2ª—a4ᵇ Av Lectevr. a4—a8 Preliminary matter. A—Hh6, pp. 492, Text. Hh7 Epitaphium Elizabethae Titherae Angliae. Hh8 blank. Printed in a bold type of larger letter than the editions of 1588 and 1589. No Oraisons Funebres or Odes, as in the later Editions, occur in this the first impression of Adam Blackwood's famous book. The imprint of Edinburgh is, of course, fictitious. It was probably printed in Paris. Whether this edition of the Martyre or the Discours de la Mort, &c. (No. 160), was the first printed account of Queen Mary's execution is difficult to determine, but the evidence seems to point to the latter being entitled to preference of place.

Class VII. *Huth Lib.* *Adv.*

145. A Defence of the Honorable sentence and execution of the Queene of Scots: Exempled with analogies, and diuerse presidents of Emperors, Kings, and Popes: With the opinions of learned men in the point, and diuerse reasons gathered foorth out of both Lawes Ciuill and Canon. Together with the answere to certaine objections made by the fauourites of the late Scottish Queene. Vlpians Maxim. Juris executio nullam habet iniuriam. The execution of Lawe, is iniurious to no man.

At London, Printed by Iohn Windet.

4to (7⅜ × 5). ¶⁸ + A⁴ + B¹ + C—K in fours + L¹ + leaf unsigned + D—F in fours. With catchwords, but without pagination. ¶1 Title, verso blank. ¶2 Contents. A—L1ª Text, as noted in table of contents. L1ᵇ blank. l. unsigned, Errata to the first chapter, with catchword Anthony, verso blank. D—F3 Anthony Babington's letter to the Queene of Scots. The Queene of Scots' letter to Anthony Babington, &c. F⁴ blank. The author is usually stated to be Maurice Kyffin.

Of two copies in my possession, No. 1 has the collation given above; No. 2 stops at sign. L1, and is without the unsigned leaf of errata and Anthony Babington's letter (signs. D—F3).

It appears that No. 2 is the original form in which the book was issued, as No. 1 has a substituted leaf F1, which is introduced to enable the author to fortify, by modern examples, the opinion that Ambassadors may be put to death if they offend the laws of the country to which they are accredited.

Class IV. *B.M.* *Adv.* *S.*

146. Lettera di Sartorio Loscho su la morte della Reina di Scotia. Al molto Illustre Signor Conte Marc 'Antonio Martinengo.

In Bergamo per Comino Ventura, 1587.

This book is known to me by a facsimile reprint. A few copies were issued in Milan about 1860, one of which, printed on vellum, is in my possession.

Class IV. *S.*

147. Vera, e compita Relazione del svccesso della morte della Christianissima Regina di Scotia, con la dichiarazione del esequie fatte In Parigi dal Christianissimo Re suo Cognato e nome de' personaggi interuenutiui. [Curious woodcut of a kneeling Queen looking up to bright rays of light springing from the skye, trees on right and left in the middle distance, with a church in the background; the whole within a black border, relieved by small, white ornaments.]
Ad Instanzia di Francesco Dini da Colle.

 4to (8¼ × 5¾). A in four, with catchwords. No pagination. A1 Title, verso blank. A2ª—A4ᵇ Text, the concluding sentences of which are printed in an inverted conical arrangement, ending with the letters "me," the terminal of the word "lagrime," with the words "Il fine" below. There is no imprint or date either on title or in a colophon. The text is printed in italic letter.

 Mr Grenville has the following note in his catalogue in reference to the copy, now in the British Museum, from which this collation is taken, "This Italian account of the execution of Queen Mary is peculiarly interesting from its being followed by some names of the persons and ceremonies attending the funeral honours paid to her memory at Paris." He was probably unaware of the existence of the edition No. 148. The text of both issues is identical, but it is probable that No. 148 is the earlier. It will be observed that the latter does not bear the name of the author on the title, but has it attached to a dedication; while this edition without a dedication is issued "Ad instanzia de F. Dini da Colle."

 The publication of this book and those described under the five following numbers, all within a few months, testifies to the intense interest felt in Italy regarding the fate of the unfortunate Scottish Queen.

Class VII.   *B.M.*

148. Vera e compita relatione del svccesso della morte della Christianissima Regina di Scotia. Con la dichiaratione delle essequie fatte in Parigi, dal Christianissimo Re suo Cognato, E il nome de' personaggi interuenuti. [Curious woodcut of the Last Supper, Christ in the centre, six Apostles on one side of the table and five on the other.]
Stampata in Genoua, e ristampata in Vico. Con licenza de' Superiori.

 4to (8 × 5¼). A in four, catchwords, but no pagination. A1ª Title. A1ᵇ Dedication, alle venerande Madre e Venerande Suore di Casa Scala Religiose dignissime di San Clemente, signed by Francesco Dini da Colle. A2—A4 Text. The concluding sentences are arranged in an inverted cone, the last word, "lagrime," being printed entire in one line, unlike No. 147. The title and text are printed in roman letter.

Class VII.   *S.*

149. Vera, e Compita Relatione del successo della Morte della Christianissima Regina di Scotia. Con la dichiaratione delle Essequie fatte in Parigi, dal Christianissimo Rè suo Cognato, & il nome de Personagi interuenuti. [A very curious woodcut of the coronation of a King, Warriors, &c.] Con licenza de Superiori.
In Milano, Per Giacomo Picaglia, 1587.

 4to (8 × 5¼). A in four. With catchwords, but without pagination. The Dedication is similar to that attached to No. 148.

Class VII.   *S.*

150. Vera Relatione del svcesso della Sereniss. Regina di Scotia, condonnata à morte dalla Regina d'Inghilterra sua sorella. [A floreated cut with head in centre.]
In Milano et ristampata in Cremona Appresso Christofero Draconi 1587 Con licenza de' Superiori.

 8vo (5½ × 3⅞). A in four. A1 Title, verso blank. A2—A4ᵃ Text. Di Parigi alle 16 Marzo 1587 La Vera relatione della morte della Regina de Scotia. Catchwords, but no pagination. This is a reprint of the preceding work with an altered title.

Class VII.   *B.M.*

151. Il Compassionevole et Memorabil Caso. della morte della Regina di Scotia, moglie di Francesco II, Re de Francia. Con licenza de' Superiori [A Latin cross composed of printer's arabesque ornaments.]
In Parma, appresso Filandro Calestani. M.D.LXXXVII.

 4to (8 × 5). A in four. A1 Title, verso blank. A2—A4a Text. A4b blank. Title in roman and text in italic letter, with catchwords, but without pagination. The opening sentences of this tract give a curious perversion of Queen Mary's history. They run as follows :—Occorendo, molti anni sono, à questa Regina passare di Scotia in Francia, doue era stata prima maritata al Rè Francesco secondo, fu dalla malignita de venti spinta ne' porti d'Inghilterra, doue se bene con passaporto publico, segnato da quella Regina era stata assicurata di poter liberamente passare, & trattenarsi, fu nientedimeno da lei fatta prigione, per le pretensioni, & parti grande, che haueua detta Regina di Scotia nel Regno d'Inghilterra, nella qual prigionia ha vissuto disnoue anni continui. The conclusion of the tract is as follows : Di Parigi il di 14. di Marzo. La Regina era di eta di 45. anni.

Class VII.   *B.M. S.*

152. Il Compassionevole et Memorabil Caso, della Morte della Regina di Scotia, Moglie di Francesco II, Re di Francia. Con Licenza de' Superiori. [A printer's mark within an arabesque border, of a semi-nude female figure holding a bunch of flowers.]
In Vicenza, Appresso Agostino della Noce. MDLXXXVII.

 4to (8 × 5⅞). A in four. A1 Title, verso blank. A2—A4a. Text printed in italic letter. A4b blank.
 This is another edition of No. 151, corresponding entirely as to title and text, but of rather superior execution.

Class VII.   *S.*

153. De Iezabelis Angliæ Parricidio varii generis Poemata Latina et Gallica.

 4to (8¾ × 6¼). A—I in fours K², the last leaf being blank.
 This book has no Title, preliminary matter, Imprint, or Colophon. It is printed in italic type, with the titles of the poems in roman letter, and consists of Poems concerning the Execution of Queen Mary, in which Queen Elizabeth is handled with great severity. Several of the poems are signed G. C. S.; R. C. P.; A. A. R.; J. A. P. R.; N. R. P.; P. M. Q. P. M.; and at the end D. C. A. C. R.
 Brunet (Manuel du Lib., Vol. III. 530) describes this book probably from a copy in the Libri Sale. He believes it to have been printed in Paris, 1587 or 1588, but a contemporary MS. note in British Museum copy says Brusselles, 1587. In this form these poems are extremely rare, but they were reprinted in 1588 at the conclusion of Martyre de la Royne d'Escosse Anvers. Gaspar Fleyben 1588 (No. 174), without any notice of their having been drawn from a prior book.

Class IX.   *B.M. S.*

Persecutiones aduersus Catholicos à Protestantibus Caluinistis excitæ in Anglia.

Post varias clades miserorum, & cædis aceruos
Insontum, comes exornat spectacula mater
Supplicio, & regum soror & fidißima coniux.
Illa Caledonijs diademate claruit oris,
Sed micat in cælo fulgentior, inde corona
Sanguinis, infandaq́; manet vindicta securis.

L 3 NOMI

154. Marie der Konigin auss Schotlandt eigentliche Bildtnuss.
> Broadside (10½ × 7⅜). Gothic Letter. Below the German Text are some Latin verses printed in roman letter: (Epitaphium) Illa ego, quae fata sum regali stirpe parentum, &c. and which are similar to those in Broadside (No. 156), printed by Joan. Charlewood, London, in 1587.
> The Broadside gives an outline of Queen Mary's history from her birth till her execution. The British Museum copy has attached to it a coloured Portrait of the Queen, after De Leu (Jan Bussen exc.) surrounded by vignettes of her execution, the Arms of Scotland quartered with those of France, and Latin verses describing her imprisonment of twenty years and execution.

Class VI.   *B.M.*

155. Theatrvm Crudelitatum Hæreticorum Nostri Temporis.
Antverpiae apud Adrianum Huberti, Anno M.D.LXXXVII. Cum Priuilegio.
> 4to (8½ × 6½). A—M in fours. Engraved Title, Text, with copperplates, pp. 1-95, verso of last leaf blank. The portion regarding Queen Mary, with engraving of her execution is at p. 85, headed: Persecutiones aduersus Catholicos à Protestantibus Calvinistis excitae in Anglia, with six lines of Latin Hexameters (*see Facsimile No. XIII.*) On verso of preceding leaf there is a short life of Queen Mary. [By N. Verstegan.]
> The copy of this book in the Grenville Library, British Museum, has the following MS. note attached:—"This first edition is very rare and desirable from the superiority of the impressions. The Latin verses under the plates are by I. Bochius of Brussels. It is said that Verstegan, being at Paris after the publication of his Book, the English Embassador complained of him to Henri III for accusing Q. Elizabeth of the cruelties imputed to her in this work. Verstegan died about 1634."

Class IV.   *B.M. S.*

156. Mariæ Scotorvm Reginæ Epitaphium.
Londini Excudebat Joannes Charlewood pro Roberto VVallie.
> Broadside (10 × 8). Signed I. II. D. The Epitaph is surrounded by a woodcut border.
> Another broadside exists with same signature in honour of Sir Francis Drake by the same printers, which is dated 1587. On the latter broadside the initials are filled up in a contemporary hand as Joh. Hercusanus Danus.

Class VI.   *B.M.*

157. Execvtion oder Todt Marien Stuart Königinnen aus Schotlandt | gewesenen Königinnen zu Franckreich | welche Adi 18 Februarii Anno 1587 Stilo nouo, in Engelandt entheuptet worden ist | in Schlos Fodrigham | in Nortthamtoschir.
Erstlich gedruckt zu Königsperg | Anno 1587.
> 4to (7¼ × 5⅞). A—B in fours. The Title in Gothic letter except the first word. On verso of title in roman letter Mariæ Scotorvm Reginæ Epitaphivm. 16 lines same as those on broadside printed by Joh. Charlewood, London (No. 156). B4ᵇ blank.

Class IV.   *B.M.*

158. Kurtzer unnd gründtlicher bericht | wie die Edel unnd from Königin auss Schotlandt | Maria Stuarda, ir Mutter halb | auch von Königklichen Geblut in Franckreich dem Hausz Guisa geborn | den 18 Februarii Anno 87 in Engellandt gericht worden | und was sie fur ein Gottseliges end genommen.
Gedruckt zu München | bey Adam Berg Anno MDLXXXVII, Mit. Rom Kay. Mayestat Freiheit nit nachzudrucken.
> 4to (7½ × 5½). A in four, verso of last leaf blank. With catchwords, but no pagination.

Class IV.   *B.M.*

159. Mariae Stvartae Scotorvm Reginæ Principis Catholicae, Nvper ab Elizabetha Regina et ordinibvs Angliae, post nouendecim annorum capitiuitatem in arce Fodringhaye interfectæ Svpplcivm & Mors pro fide Catholica constantissima.

In Anglia Vernacvla Lingua primum conscripta: ideoque multis aspersa ex hostiû eius Reginæ sententia, quæ nec ipsa vnquam confessa est, nec hactenus debitè probata sunt. Nunc in gratiam Catholicorum fideliter, nullis planè omissis translata & edita: vt sanctissimae Principis martyrii feruor animique inuicta constantia, ipsorum aduersariorum testimonio comprobata, toti mundo elucescat. Additis svccinctis qvibvsdam animaduersionibus & notis: breuiq totius Reginæ eiusdem vitæ Chronologia, ex optimis quibusque auctorebus collecta.

Coloniae apud Godefridum Kempensem   Anno M.D.LXXXVII.

    8vo (5⅞ × 3½). A—D in eights. Catchwords, but no pagination. A1 Title, verso blank. A2—B2 Narratio svpplicii et mortis Mariae Stuart Reginae Scotiae, Dotalis Franciae, decollatæ in Anglia decimo octauo Februarij 1587. stylo nouo in Castello Fodringhaye. B3—B6a Animadversiones breves ad praecedens scriptum, datum Londini 27. Martii Anno Salutis 1587. continens gloriosum Martyrium Mariæ Scotiæ Reginæ, cuius nomen in benedictionibus est. B6ᵇ—B8 six Latin poems in honour of Queen Mary. C—D8ᵃ Brevis Chronologia vitae et gloriosi per Martyrivm exitius Mariæ Stuartæ, Scot. Reg. propter Catholicae fidei confessionem sub Elizabetha Angliæ Requia capite plexa. D8ᵇ blank.

    This is the first publication regarding Queen Mary's death issued by the Roman Catholic party. It was no doubt prepared in England, as stated in the title, but it does not appear to be a translation of any known work in the English language. It is of some rarity in this form, but it was afterwards incorporated in Summarium Rationum, &c. (No. 171).

Class VII.   *S.*

160. Discours de la Mort de Tres-haute & tres-illustre Princesse Madame Marie Stouard, Royne d'Ecosse Faict le le vingt troisiesme iour de Fevrier 1587.

    8vo (5⅞ × 3⅞). A in four. There is no title. The text, as above, is printed in italic letter down to the word Ecosse; the remainder is very minute roman letter. ll. 2 and 3 are signed A2 and A3, and pagination runs 2-4, from A1ᵇ—A4ᵇ.

    Following the above the text, printed in ordinary roman letter, continues as follows:—Le Samedy vingt-troiziesme iour de Feburier 1587 Monsieur Belé beau frere de Walsin Han, fut depesche sur le soir auec commission signé de la main de la Royne d'Angleterre, pour faire trancher la teste a la Royne d'Ecosse, & commandement au Conte de Chersbery, de Heut, & de Rotoland auec beaucoud [*the p is thus reversed*] d'autre Gentils-hommes voisins de Soeteringhan de assister à la dicte execution. . . . At p. 8 the narrative continues: Le Jeudi ensuiuant dixneufiesme lesquelles nouuelles ne furent long temps celees. Car des les trois heures apres Midy toutes les cloches de la ville de Londres commancerent à sonner, & se firent feux de Joye par toutes les Ruës, auec festins & banquets, en signe de grande reiouissance. Le bruit est que la dicte dame mourant a tonsiours persisté à dire qu'elle estoit innocente & qu'elle nauoit iamais pêse a faire tuer la Royne d'Angleterre & qu'elle pria Dieu pour elle & qu'elle chargea le dict Melun de dire au Roy son fils qu'elle prioit d'honorer la Royne d'Angleterre comme sa mere & de ne departir Iamais de son amitie. Fin.

    This little book must not be confounded with the work La Mort de la Royne d'Escosse (Nos. 172, 173, 179).

    No copies, except the three noted below, have been traced in this country. The British Museum copy, formerly in Mr Grenville's possession, and mine are exactly alike. That in the Signet Library is of the same setting, but the letter p in beaucoup is correctly printed, and the date of

EXECVTION
Oder
Todt Marien Stuarts

Königinnen aus Schotlandt gewesenen
Königinnen zu Franckreich / welche Adi 18. Februarij
Anno 1587. *Stilo Novo* / in Engelandt enthauptet worden ist / im Schloß Fodrigham / in Northamtoschir.

Zu Magdeburgk / bey Johan Francken
Anno 1588.

Edin. Bibl. Soc.—Queen Mary Literature. Facsimile No. XIV. See No. 162, page 55.

execution given above as "vingt troisiesme" is altered to "dixhuictiesme," the superfluous "le" being suppressed. It is bound with two other tracts regarding Queen Mary (Nos. 168 and 169), being marked as having been formerly in the library of Sir M. Masterman Sykes. It is evidently the copy mentioned by Lowndes (Manual, Vol. III., p. 1501), to which he attaches the place and date of printing as Anvers, 1589; but there is no trace of this on the book itself, which was clearly issued in Paris. Brunet (Manuel, Vol. I.), however, states that a reprint was made at Antwerp in 1589. It has again recently been reprinted, with interesting notes, in Varietés Historiques et Litteraires, &c., par E. Fournier. Paris, 1855-63. 8vo. 10 vols. Vol. V., pp. 279-289. The Text of the Discours is a reproduction of the greater portion of a despatch of Mons. de l'Aubespine de Chateauneuf, the French Ambassador to Queen Elizabeth, addressed by him to Henri III. a few days after the execution of Queen Mary.

This document, which is dated 27th February 1587, in the autograph of the Ambassador, is preserved in the Bibliothèque Nationale at Paris (Fonds de Béthune, No. 8880, fol. 7), and has been printed by Teulet, Papiers d'Etat relatifs à l'Histoire d'Ecosse. 3 vols. 4to. Bannatyne Club, Vol. II., pp. 890-899. Neither Teulet, Mignet, nor other recent authors who have quoted the despatch, seem to have known that it had been issued in a printed form so soon after the event.

The issue of an official document, in the form of the simple leaves of this little tract, bears testimony to the state of feeling of the people in Paris towards their unfortunate Queen, and it is evident that its publication must have taken place with the sanction, if not the encouragement, of the Queen mother and her son.

Class IV. VII.   *B.M. Signet. S.*

161. [A Tract, s. l. et a. Printed in Capitals.]

4to (7¾ × 5¾). A in fours as follows. A1ª P. M. P. Q. M. Adverte Hospes Qvod Nvnqvam accedit hoc. Heus? Address to Queen Mary follows: Maria Stuarta impiatorum violentia oppressa quiesco, &c. A1ᵇ King James VI. is addressed as Queen Mary's son. A2—A3ª Ad Mariam Stvartam Scotorum Reginam. A3ᵇ—A4ᵇ Sur le tombeau de Marie Stuuart Royne d'Escosse et Douairiere de France. Elegie en laquelle entre-parlent Le Passant et La Mvse. The British Museum copy has 2 blank leaves at beginning with a MS. Title written on one of these: Mariae Stvartae Scotorum Reginae Parentatis Authore [name erased] 1587. The British Museum Catalogue suggests that the tract was printed at Douay. It may be noted that the initials P. M. P. Q. M. which head the tract are the same as those attached to one of the poems in De Jezabelis Angliae Parricidio (No. 152).

Class IX.   *B.M.*

1588

162. Execvtion oder Todt Marien Stuarts Koniginnen aus Schotlandt gewesenen Koniginnen zu Franckreich welche Adi 18. Februarii Anno 1587. Stilo Nouo in Engelandt enthauptet worden ist im Schloss Fodrigham in Nortthamptoschir [Woodcut]. Zu Magdeburgk bey Johan Francken Anno 1588.

4to (7½ × 5¾). A—B in fours. A1ª Title. A1ᵇ Mariæ Scotorum Regniæ Epitaphium. 16 lines same as in No. 155. A2—B4ª Text. B4ᵇ blank.

(*See Facsimile No. XIV.*)

Class IV.   *S.*

163. Apologie ov Defense de l'honorable sentence & tres-iuste execution de defuncte Marie Steuard derniere Royne d'Ecosse. Enrichie de plusieurs exemples par comparaisons & diuerses histoires d'Empereurs, Rois, & Papes ce-deuant aduenues: auec les opinions d'hommes entendus en tel cas . . . Aprez la fin dv liure sont adioustées

les copies des lettres, actes & articles, qui seruent à découuir & à bien verifier la trahison de ladite Royne d'Ecosse &c. à l'encontre de la Royne, de la Noblesse & de l'Estat d'Angleterre. Le tout traduit d'Anglois en François, suiuant l'original imprimé à Londres, par Jean Ouinted, 1587. Vlpian Maxim. Juris executio nullam habet iniuriam. L'execution du droit ne fait tort à persone.
Imprime nouuellement. 1588.

    8vo (6 × 4¼). A--T in eights. A 1-8 Title, Epistle, and two leaves of errata. B—P3 Text, pp. 1-214, without catchwords. The above is a translation of No. 145. It is followed on P4 by a fresh Title: Recueil de certaines reqvestes . . . faicte à la Majesté de la Royne d'Angleterre par tovs les seigneurs . . . à Richmont le 12 & 24 Nov. 1586. Avec les responces faite . . . par sa Majesté . . . Le tout translate de l'original imprimé à Londres par Chris. Barker 1586. P5—T8ᵃ Text, pp. 215-287.

    It may be noticed that this translation follows the text given in copy No. 2 (see Note to No. 145), and does not adopt the version of No. 1.

Class IV.   *B.M. Adv. S.*

164.   Maria Stuarta, Regina Scotiæ, Dotaria Franciæ, Hæres Angliæ et Hyberniæ, Martyr Ecclesie, Innocens à cæde Darleana: Vindice Oberto Barnestapolio. Continet hæc epistola historiam penè totam vitæ, quam Regina Scotiæ egit miserè, sed exegit gloriosè. rationem tituli præfert frons sequentis pagellæ. [Woodcut Printer's mark.] Cum gratia & priuilegio Cæsareæ Maiestatis.

Ingolstadii, ex Officina VVolfgangi Ederi. Anno M.D.LXXXVIII.

    8vo (6⅞ × 3⅞). A—E in eights + F⁴. Title and Preface 6 ll. Text pp. 1-71. On recto of F3 is a colophon. Last leaf blank. The Preface is addressed to Cardinal Allen, and is dated from Venice. The author is Robert Turner of Barnstaple in Devonshire, afterwards Rector of the University of Ingolstadt.

Class VII.   *Adv. Signet. S.*

165.   Hystoria Ecclesiastica del scisma del Reyno de Inglaterra. Enla qual se tratã las cosas mas notables q̃ han sucedido en aquel Reyno tocãtes a neuestra sancta Religion, desde que començo hasta la muerte de la Reyna de Escocia. Recogida de diuersos y graues Autores, por el Padre Pedro de Ribadeneyra, de la Compañia de Iesus. Dirigido al Principe de España Don Felipe nuestro Señor.

En Lisboa. Impressa con licencia de la Sancta Inquisiciõ, y Ordinario: En casa de Antonio Aluarez. Año de 1588.

    8vo (5¼ × 4⅞). ***¹²+ A—Ii in eights. ***1—12 Title, Approbation, Dedication, &c., without pagination or catchwords. A—Ii Text, ll. 1-249, and Table 5 ll., with catchwords.

    Queen Mary is referred to not infrequently, and Cap. 40, fol. 218, is devoted to an account of her imprisonment and execution.

Class IV.   *Signet.*

166.   De la Gverre ouuerte entre le Roy d'Escosse & la Royne d'Angleterre. Et la prinse de la ville de Barruic & ruine par luy faicte en plusieurs endroicts d'Angleterre. [Curious woodcut portrait of King James with a ruff round his neck, head-dress and hair, more like a woman than a man; in oval frame, with motto, D. G. Scotorum Rex IACOBVS STEVARTVS. VI.]

A Paris, Par Hubert Velu, demourant Rue d'Arras 1588. Auec permission.

    8vo (6 × 4). A—B in fours. A1 Title, verso blank. A2—B4ᵃ Discours comme le Roy d'Escosse a declaré la guerre à la Royne d'Angleterre, & prins sur elle la Ville de Barruic, & bruslé dix ou douze lieux de son pays depuis le neufiesme du mois de Nouembre dernier passé iusques a maintenant. Et ce qui s'est passé en icelle, le tout fidelement recueilly tant des lettres escrites d'Escosse que d'Angleterre, par gens d'auctorité. B4ᵇ Royal Arms of France crowned.

    This rare tract, giving false information as to the state of political affairs in Scotland during the period of difficulty which arose after Queen Mary's execution, must have been issued in Paris with the cognisance of the Ministers of the French King, with a view of inducing adhesion to the policy of Spain, where the Armada was being prepared. It insinuates that King James was prepared to give his assistance and countenance to the attack.

Class IV.   *B.M.*

167. La Harangue faicte à la Royne d'Angleterre pour la desmouvoir de n' entreprendre ancune Jurisdiction sur la Royne d'Escosse.

    M.D.LXXXVIII.

    4to (6 × 4). A—C in fours + D². A1 Title, verso blank. A2—D2 Text, pp. 1-28.

    This is the speech of Monsieur de Bellievre, the French Ambassador, which is said to have much exasperated Queen Elizabeth.

    Another impression of this rare tract is to be found with the title: Harangue faicte a la Royne d'Angleterre: Par Monsieur de Bellieure (printer's ornament) M.D.LXXXVIII. 4to (6 × 4). A—C in fours + D². It has a sub-title on A2ᵃ p. 3, which is the same as the full title given above.

Class VIII.   *Huth Library. B.M. S.*

168. Ode svr la Mort de la tres-Chrestienne tres-illvstre tres-constante, Marie Royne d'Escosse, morte pour la Foy, le 18 Feburier, 1587. par la cruauté des Anglois heretiques, ennemys de Dieu. Avec l'oraison Funebre prononcee en Mars, à nostre Dame de Paris, au jour de ses obseques & seruice.

    A Paris chez Guillaume Bichon, rüe S. Jacques a l'enseigne du Bichot. M.D.LXXXVIII. Avec Permission.

    4to (5⅞ × 3¾). A—B in fours. 8 ll. without pagination or catchwords. The Oraison Funebre follows with separate title-page and signatures (see No. 169).

Class VII. IX.   *Signet. S.*

169. Oraison Fvnebre de la tres-Chrestienne, tres-illustre tres-constante, Marie Royne d'Escosse, morte pour la Foy, le 18 Feburier, 1587. par la cruaute des Anglois heretiques ennemys de Dieu. Sur le subiect & discours de celle mesme qui fut faicte en Mars, à Nostre Dame de Paris, au iour de ses obseques & seruice, et lors prononcee par R. P. Messire Renauld de Beaulne, Archeuesque de Bourges, Patriarche d'Aquitaine, Conseiller du Roy en son Conseil Priué, & d'Estat.

    A Paris chez Guillaume Bichon ruë S. Jacques à l'enseigne du Bichot. M.D.LXXXVIII. Avec Permission.

    4to (5⅞ × 3¾). (A—I) in fours, pp. 1-48 without catchwords.

    This is the earliest issue of the account of the funeral service performed in Notre Dame de Paris, under the auspices of the French Court, in honour of Queen Mary. It was reprinted frequently at later dates, generally as a supplement to Adam Blackwood's books, and also by Jebb, Vol. II. p. 671.

Class VII.   *Signet. S.*

170. Harangve Fvnebre svr la Mort de la Royne d'Escosse Traduite d'Escossois en Françoys par N. L. R. P.

8vo (6 × 4½). A—C in fours.
The above Title is printed at the top of first leaf, verso blank. A2 A la Royne. A3—C4a Tradvction Françoise d'vne Harangue funebre, sur la mort de la Royne d'Ecosse, par Reuerend Pere en Dieu M. I. L. C4b blank.
Printed at Paris. The Scottish author appears to be John Lesley, Bishop of Ross, as the Preacher refers to himself as acting in the capacity of an orator or Ambassador more than a Bishop. The French translator is Nicolas Loiseul.
This sermon must not be confounded with the Oraison Funebre (No. 169). It contains many curious notices of the execution of Queen Mary, which Bishop Lesley must have received at second hand. The Queen to whom the translation is addressed is Marie de Medicis.

Class VII. *B.M.*

171. Svmmarivm Rationvm, qvibvs Cancellarivs Angliæ et Prolocvtor Pvckeringius Elizabethæ Angliæ Reginæ persuaserunt occidendam . . . Mariam Stuartam Scotiæ Reginam & Jacobi sexti Scotorum Regis matrem : Vna cvm responsionibvs Reginæ Angliae et sententia mortis : quæ omnia Anglice primvm edita svnt, et Londini a typographo regio impressa, ac deinde varios in linguas translata : His additvm est supplicivm et mors Reginæ Scotiæ, vna cvm svccinctis quibusdam animadversionibus, & confutationibus eorum, quæ ei obiecta sunt. Opera Romoaldi Scoti.
Ingoldstadii, ex officina VVolffgangi Ederi. Anno M.D.LXXXVIII.

8vo (6 × 3¾). A—H in eights I4, Title and pp. 134. A letter to Grynaeus on the Zuinglian Church, having no relation to Queen Mary, occupies pp. 107-133.
Another edition was issued in the same year in 4to, without place of printing and without the letter to Grynaeus.

Class VII. *Adv. (Imperfect). Signet. S.*

172. La Mort de la Royne d'Escosse Dovairiere de France, &c.

12mo (5⅛ × 3). A—G in twelves, pp. 1-168. A1 Title. A2—A3a Au Lecteur. A3b A woodcut of the Crucifixion (Calvaire), which differs in arrangement from that in the 8vo edition of 1588 (No. 173). A4—G12 La Mort, &c.
The copy in the Advocates' Library is the only one observed of the size with this form of the woodcut of a Calvaire. Owing to the title having been torn out, it is impossible to ascertain the date of issue, but it appears probable that it is the first edition. Possibly, however, the very curious edition of the same size (No. 179) may be preferred to that position. The text of all the copies is alike, and it is the same as that noted in Histoire et Martyre (No. 180) as "petit livre de sa Mort."
In one or other form it was certainly issued separately in 1588, prior to the publication of Histoire et Martyre (No. 180). It was written by Adam Blackwood, or some other supporter of Queen Mary, from information furnished by Bourgoing, her physician.

Class VII. *Adv. (imperfect).*

173. La Mort de la Royne d'Escosse, Douairiere de France. Où est contenu le vray discours de la procedure des Angloys à l'Execution d'icelle, la Constante & Royalle resolutiõ de sa maiesté defunte : ses vertueux deportements & derniers propos, ses Funerailles & enterremẽt, d'ou on peut cognoistre la traistre cruauté de l'Heretique Angloys à l'encontre d'vne Royne souueraine, Tres-chrestienne & Catholique, Innocente.

Deus, iniqui insurrexerût super me, & synagoga potentium quaesierunt animam meam, & non proposuerunt te in conspectu suo, Psalm 85. 1588.
<blockquote>8vo (6½ × 4). a—k in eights 1⁴. a1 Title, verso blank. a2—a3ª Au Lecteur. a3ᵇ woodcut of the Crucifixion (Calvaire) with a woman embracing Christ's feet, having at foot: Exaltasti super terram habitationem meam : & pro morte defluente deprecata sum. Eccles. 51. a4—l3 La Mort de la Royne d'Escosse Douairiere de France. Pp. 1-166, without catchwords. l4 blank.
The text of this 8vo edition is identical with that of the preceding number, but the Calvaire differs in design from all the others. It contains no indication of the place of printing.</blockquote>
Class VII.   *Signet. S.*

174. Martyre de la Royne d'Escosse Douairiere de France. Contenant le vray discours des traïsons à elle faictes à la suscitation d'Elizabet Angloise, par le quel les mensonges, calomnies & faulses accusations dressees contre ceste tresuertueuse, trescatholique & tresillustre Princesse sont esclarcies & son innocence aueree. Sont adioustees deux Oraisons funebres, l'vne Latine & l'autre Francoise : & vn liure de Poemes Latins & François. Le tout sur le mesme subiect. Pretiosa in conspectu Domini mors sanctorum eius.
En Anvers Chez Gaspar Fleysben M.D.LXXXVIII.
<blockquote>8vo (6⅜ × 3⅞). a⁴+A—Tt in eights. a1 Title, verso blank. a2—a4 Av Lectevr. A—Tt3 Text, pp. 1-659. Tt4 blank.
The first edition with true place of printing indicated and additional matter added.</blockquote>
Class VII.   *Huth Library. S.*

175. Martyre de la Royne d'Escosse Douairiere de France Contenāt le vray discours des trahisons à elle faictes à la suscitation d'Elizabet Angloise, par lequel les mensonges, calomnies & faulses accusations dressees contre ceste tres-vertueuse, tres-Catholique & tres-illustre Princesse sont esclarcies & son innocence averée. Auec son oraison funebre prononcée en l'Eglise nostre dame de Paris. Pretiosa in conspectu Domini mors sanctorum eius.
A Edimbourg. Chez Jean Nafeild. 1588.
<blockquote>12mo (5⅞ × 3¼). A—Z in twelves, Aa⁶. A1 Title, verso blank. A2—A10ª Preliminary. A10ᵇ—X6ª, pp. 1-472, Text. X6ᵇ Epitaphium Elizabethae. X7ª—Z7ᵇ, pp. 50, Oraison Funebre. Z8—Aa5ª, pp. 51-53, and 16 pp. not numbered, Odes and Sonnets. Aa5ᵇ Aa6 blank.
This is the second edition of No. 144 with the fictitious imprint.</blockquote>
Class VII.   *Adv. S.*

1589

176. Martyre de la Royne d'Ecosse, &c.
A Edimbourg Chez Jean Nafield 1589.
<blockquote>This edition is the same in every respect as No. 175.</blockquote>
Class. VII.   *Signet.*

177. 1589. Est natura hominum nouitatis auida. The Scottish Queens Buriall at Peterborough, vpon Tuesday beeing Lammas day 1587.
London printed by A. J. [Abel Jeffes] for Edwarde Venge, and are to be sold at his shop without Bishops-gate.
<blockquote>12mo (5¼ × 3½). Four leaves. Sign. ☙2 and ☙3 on versos of first and second leaf. 1ª Title,</blockquote>

in a woodcut border, with date at top. 1ᵇ—4ᵇ, pp. 1-7, Text. Pages 5 and 6 are transposed, page 5 being printed on recto of leaf 4 and page 6 on verso of leaf 3.

The copy in the Advocates' Library is believed to be unique. It passed to that collection from the Duke of Roxburgh's library, having formerly been in the possession of William Herbert. It was reprinted by Thomas Pitcairn, Collections relative to the Funerals of Mary Queen of Scots. Edinburgh, 1804. 8vo.

Class VII.   *Adv.*

178.   L'Histoire et Vie de Marie Stvart, Royne d'Escosse d'Oiriere de France, heritiere d'Angleterre & d'Ibernye, en laquelle elle est clairement iustifiee de la mort du Prince d'Arlay son mary.

    Composee en Latin par Obert Barnestapolius, & faicte Françoise, par Gabriel de Gutterry Clunisois. Dediée à Madame de Villeroy, Dame d'honneur de la Royne, Mere du Roy.

    A Paris, chez Guillaume Iulien, à l'enseigne de l'Amitié, pres le college de Cambray, M.D.LXXXIX. Auec l'priuilege du Roy.

    12mo (5½ × 4). a + A—H in twelves + 1⁴. Title and Preface, 12 ll. without pagination. Text, pp. 1-208. No catchwords.

This book is a Translation of No. 164.

Class VII.   *S.*

179.   La Mort de la Royne d'Escosse, Douairiere de France. Où est contenu le vray discours de la procedure des Angloys à l'Execution d'icelle, la constante & Royalle resolution de sa maiesté defuncte : ses vertueux deportemēs & derniers propos, ses Funerailles & enterrement d'ou on peut cognoistre la traistre cruauté de l'Heretique Angloys à l'encontre d'vne Roine souueraine, tres-Chrestienne & Catholique, Innocente.

    Deus, iniqui insurrexerunt super me, & synagoga potentiū quæsierunt animam meam, & non proposuerunt te in conspectu suo. M.D.LXXXIX.

    16mo (4¼ × 3¼). A⁴ + A—O in eights. A1 Title, verso blank. A2—A4ᵃ Au Lecteur. A4ᵇ A Calvaire showing wood nails protruding from the cross with a skull at its base, and a band for the reception of an inscription at the top. On a ribbon which is attached to the vertical part of the cross, is the inscription, In hoc signo vinces. A—O5b the usual Text of La Mort. O6ᵃ Acheve d'imprime ce dernier iour de Decembre Mil cinq cens quatre vingtz & huit. O6ᵇ blank.

    Copies have been examined in the British Museum and the Library of the Society of Antiquaries of Scotland, both of which have been much cut down. As stated in note to No. 172, this edition may be the first issue of the book. It appears to be the production of a different printer from any of the others described above. The Calvaire occurs in all, but in this is of an entirely different design. The title runs exactly with that of No. 173, except that in this copy the words "Psalm. 85." are omitted after the quotation.

    The British Museum copy contains, in addition to the text, four folding woodcuts, which, although pertinent to the positions they occupy, have no direct connection with the text. Each of them is headed by a descriptive rubric, as follows :—

    I. (Placed between pp. 12-13). Comme la Royne D'Escosse Recevt son arrest de Mort par le Grand Prevost de la Royne D'Angleterre.

    II. (Pp. 18-19). Comme la Royne ayent recevs son arrest de Mort svr le soir se mit en prieres av pied de son lict toute la nuit.

III. (Pp. 37-38). Comme le Prevost et Archers vindrent le matin pour mener ladite Royne av svplice, et comment elle fut conduite.

IV. (Pp. 111-112). Comme la Royne Fvt Decapitee. This plate is signed at bottom, A Paris de l'Imprimerie de Pierre Ménier. It resembles very strongly the frontispiece attached to Regnault's Tragedy, which is reproduced in Facsimile No. XIX.

These woodcuts are of extreme rarity, and were at one time supposed to exist in a single copy, but at least other two have survived, one of which is noted in Dr Laing's Sale Cat., Part I., No. 2157.

Class VII. *Lib. Soc. Ant. Scot. B.M.*

180. Histoire et Martyre de la Royne d'Escosse dovariere de France, proche heretiere de la Royne d'Angleterre. Contenant les trahisons à elle faictes par Elizabet Angloise, par où on cognoist les mensonges calomnies et faulses accusations enuers ceste bonne Princesse innocente. [Then follows in very minute Italic letter] Auec un petit liure de sa mort, consernant les figures de son arrest, procedure et malice des Anglois, l'execution d'icelle, leur grande tyrannie, sa constance et gaye resolution de sa maiestie, ses vertus, deportemens & derniers propos: son enterrement faict cognoistre la trahitre cruaute des heretiques Anglois enuers ceste Royne Chrestienne.

Pretiosa in conspectu Domini mors Sanctorum eius.

A Paris pour Guillaume Bichon, Rue Sainct Iaques, au Bichot MDLXXXIX.

16mo ($4\frac{1}{2} \times 3\frac{1}{4}$). $a^4 + $A—Kk in eights Ll^4. a1 Title, verso blank. a2—$a4^b$ Au lecteur. A—$Ll4^b$ The usual Text of the Martyre, pp. 1-425. It ends with the words: Louange & gloire en ce monde & vous rendra côtens & bien heureux en l'autre. $Ll4^b$ an arabesque ornament.

This copy, although intimating on its title the addition of "un petit liure de sa mort," contains only the original text of the Martyre of Adam Blackwood. La Mort de la Royne d'Escosse is the "petit liure" which was no doubt added by the printer Bichon to some of the copies of this edition of the Martyre.

Lowndes states (Manual, Vol. III. p. 150) that, although paged separately, La Mort is really part of this book, but the variety of the separate editions shows that it was added simply as a supplement.

Class VII. *B.M.*

181. Historia de lo Svcedido en Escocia, è Inglaterra en quarenta y quatro años que biuio Maria Estuarda, Reyna de Escocia. Escrita por Antonio de Herrera, criado del Rey nuestro Señor. Dirigida à don Diego Fernandez de Cabrera y Bobadilla, Conde de Chinchon Mayordomo de su Magestad, su Tesorero general de los Reynos de la Corona de Aragon, y de sus Consejos de Aragon, y Italia y Alcayde de los Alcaçares Reales de la cuidad de Segouia. [Woodcut of a hawk on the wrist with motto: Spero Lvcem post Tenebras.]

En Madrid, en casa de Pedro Madrigal Año de 1589. Védese in casa de Iuã de Mōtoya, librero.

8vo ($5\frac{1}{2} \times 4\frac{3}{4}$). ¶$+$A—Y in eights. *1 Title, verso blank. *2—8 Preliminary matter. A—X La Historia del Reyno de Escocia 168 ll. Y1-7 Tabla de los Capitulos. Y8 blank.

Reprinted by Jebb, Vol. II. pp. 329-440.

Class X. *B.M.*

1590

182. Historia de lo Svcedido en Escocia, etc.   Escrita por Antonio Herrera.
Con licencia Impressa en Lisboa por Manuel de Lyra 1590
8vo (5⅛ × 3½).   *+A—X in eights.   *1 Title, verso blank.   *2-8 Preliminary matter.
A—X Text and Table.   In the Licence there is the uncommon stipulation that the Printer of this Edition must first obtain the permission of the Printer of the First Edition.
Class X. *B.M.*

1593

183. Churchyard's Challenge. [Printer's mark, with initials I. W.]
London, Printed by John Wolfe.   1593.
4to (6½ × 5).   Five preliminary leaves (the second, fourth, and fifth signed A2, *, and ** respectively)+B — Nn in fours.   1 Title, verso blank.   2 Dedication to Sir John Wolley Secretary for the Latin tung to the Queenes Maiestie.   3 To the worthiest sorte of People that gently can reade, and iustly can iudge.   4ᵃ Here followes the seuerall matters contained in the booke.   4ᵇ—5 The bookes that I can call to memorie alreadie Printed are these that follow. B1—E1ᵃ pp. 1-25, The Earle of Mvrtons Tragedie once Regent of Scotland, and alwaies of great birth, great wisdome, great wealthe, and verie great power and credite : yet Fortune enuying his estate and noblenes brought him to lose his head on a Skaffold at Edenbrough the second of Iune 1581.   E1—Nn4 pp. 25-278, The remaining pieces composing the volume.
The rarity of this book is well known.
Morton's Tragedy has been reprinted in Churchyard's Chips concerning Scotland ... with a Life of the Author by George Chalmers, F.R.S.S.A.   London, 1817.   8vo.
Class IV. *B.M.*

184. Elizabethæ Reginae Angliae Edictvm   Promulgatum Londini 29. Nouemb. Anni M.D.XCI.   Andreae Philopatri ad idem Edictvm responsio. [A Printer's Mark with motto : Melior post fvnera vita.]
Excvsvm M.D.XCIII.
8vo (6 × 3¾).   A—Z in eights Aaᵃ.   A1 Title, verso blank.   A2ᵃ Argumentum libri.   A2ᵇ Index. A3—A7ᵃ Praefatio ad Edictvm.   A7ᵇ—Y5ᵇ Responsio ad Edictvm, in 5 sections.   Y6—Z5ᵃ Instrvctiones ad Commissarios.   Z5ᵇ—Z8ᵇ Index Libri.   Aa1 Errata, 1 leaf without pagination, followed by two blank leaves.
The portion of the book referring to Queen Mary is at pp. 123-133.   This is one of the works of Robert Parsons the Jesuit.
Class IV. *Adv. S.*

1594

185. Relacion del estado del Reyno de Escocia, en lo tocante à nuestra Religion Catolica. Este año del Señor, de mil y quinientos y nouenta y quatro.
Folio (11½ × 7½).   A in four, with catchwords, but without pagination or place of printing. A1—A4ᵃ Title and text.   A4ᵇ blank.
This curious historical tract, written in support of the Catholic party, relates many important events which occurred in Scotland during the persecution of that party in the reign of James VI. Details of the lives of many of the noblemen and other adherents of that party are given.   A considerable portion is devoted to the earlier history of the country during the Reformation times, and to the history of El Duque de Xatelroy (Duke of Chatelherant) and his family, in which connection the martyrdom of Queen Mary is narrated.
Class X. *S.*

1598

186. Historia Belgica Nostri Potissimvm temporis Belgii sub quatvor Burgundis et todidem Austriacis Principibus coniunctionem & gubernationem breuiter. . . . inscripta A E. Meterano Belga. Cum gratia et priuilegio.

    Folio (12 × 7¾). Engraved Title. Proemium, 3 ll. Text, pp. 1-623. Map and 21 Portraits. The History of Queen Mary occurs pp. 410-416, with a Portrait after De Leu.

    There are several editions of the book in Flemish, French, and German.

Class X.   *S.*

1599

187. ΒΑΣΙΛΙΚΟΝ ΔΩΡΟΝ Devided into Three Bookes. [A small arabesque ornament.] Edinbvrgh Printed By Robert Walde-graue Printer to the Kings Majestie. 1599.

    4to (8 × 6). (A)—X in fours. Printed in large italic letter, with pagination and catchwords.

    The first sheet (A) is unsigned. The other sheets are signed on first leaf, and have Arabic numerals irregularly disposed on the following leaves, in some cases on one leaf, and in others on three leaves of the sheet. (A1) Title, enclosed within a woodent border, having a standing female figure on each side, inscribed respectively: Amor Pacis alumnus, and Pax Infesta malis. Verso blank. (A2) The Dedication of the booke. Sonet. Verso blank. (A3) The Argument of the booke. Sonnet. Verso blank. (A4)—B1ᵃ To Henrie my dearest Sonne and Natvral Svccessor. (Printed in roman letter.) B1ᵇ blank. B2—X4ᵃ Text. At bottom of X4ᵃ The Scottish crowned Shield. X4ᵇ blank.

    The rarity of the first edition of King James' celebrated book is accounted for in the following passage from the author's preface to the revised edition, Edinburgh, 1603, 8vo :—" And therefore for the more secret, and close keeping of them, I onely permitted seauen of them to be printed, the Printer being first sworn for secrecie : and these seauen I dispersed amongst some of my trustiest seruants, to be keeped closelie by them : least in case by the iniquitie, or wearing of time any of them might have been lost, yet some of them might have remained after me as witnesses to my Sonne bothe of the honest integritie of my heart, and of my fatherlie affection and naturall care towards him."

    The "wearing of time" had operated to such an extent when the book was reprinted, in 1887, by Mr Charles Butler, for the Roxburgh Club, that a special notice was appended by the editor, Mr Charles Edmonds, as follows :—" It has been generally believed that only one copy of the *original edition* of the Βασιλικον Δωρον, Edinburgh, 1599, that in the Grenville Collection in the British Museum, has come down to us; but the present writer is in a position to affirm, from his own personal knowledge, that a second copy was in the possession of the Right Hon. Sir David Dundas, of the Temple, London, which, on his decease in 1877, passed by will, with his other books, to the Hon. Charles Howard. On the latter's death it became, we believe, the property of the present Earl of Carlisle."

    It may, however, be stated that unless one of the two copies which have been visible at public auction within the last ten years is the same as that attributed to the possession of the Earl of Carlisle, four of the original seven copies are still in existence.

    A portion of the note by Mr Grenville in his Catalogue may be given as appropriately descriptive of the book :—" Prefixed to it are two sonnets, the first of which, entitled ' The Dedication of the Booke,' is not to be found in the subsequent editions. On comparing this with the subsequent ones, I find that alterations were made in the work. For though all the charges against the Scottish preachers are retained, James found it necessary to drop or to soften some of his most unguarded and harsh expressions, and to give an ambiguous turn to the sentences which had created the greatest offence. For example, in the original he says, ' If my conscience had not resolved me, that all my religion was grounded upon the plaine words of the Scripture, I had never outwardly avowed it, for pleasure or awe of the vaine pride of some seditious Preachours.'" In the edition of

1603, that sentence stands thus: "I had never outwardlie avowed it, for pleasure or awe of any flesh." Other alterations of the text are quoted, and the following, among other sentences, is omitted, speaking of the Islanders of Scotland, "Thinke no other of them all, then as Wolves and Wild Boares."

The original autograph MS. of the book in the Scottish tongue is preserved in the British Museum. The hope may be expressed that the Scottish Text Society will carry out the intention, expressed some years since, of editing this interesting document.

The copy now in my possession is bound in apparently the original limp vellum cover, having ornaments stamped in gold on both sides, and is in fine condition.

Class XI.   *B.M. S.*

1600

188.   Kurtzer bericht Aller gedenckwurdigen sachen, so sich in Engelland in den nechsten hundert Jaren verlauffen, auss D. Niclass Sanders, Eduardo Risthono, und andern mehr Engellandischen Historicis zusamen gezogen. Durch Johann Mayr Frisingensem, Pfarrherrn zu Jartz.

Gedruckt zu München durch Nicolaum Henricum im Jar MDC.

4to (8 × 6). Gothic letter. A—G in fours. Title and 2 ll. of Preface, and 25 numbered ll. of Text.

This book, written in the Catholic interest, gives an outline of Queen Mary's History and Execution (ll. 20-22).

Class XI.   *S.*

189.   A facile Traictise, contenand, first ane infallible reul to discerne trevv from fals religion : Nixt, a declaration of the Nature, Numbre, Vertevv & effects of the sacraments ; togider vvith certaine Prayeres of deuotion. Dedicat to his Sovrain Prince King James the Saxt Be Maister Jhone Hamilton Doctor in Theologie.

The kirk of God, is the piller and sure ground of the veritie. 1 Timoth. 3. Vvha heiris nocht the kirk, lat him be to the as a Pagan and Publican. Math. 13.

At Lovan Imprinted be Laurence Kellam. Anno Dom. MDC.

12mo (5 × 3). *¹²+***+A—S in twelves+T—X in sixes. *1—**6 Title, Dedication, and Prayers. A1—T6, pp. 1-144, Text. V1—X6 A Cathalogue of 167 Hereslies, &c. At end : Excuse, guid reider, the erreurs committit in ye prēting ; considder the difficultie to prent our langage in a strāge countrey. God Keip zovv. Al honor and glore to our liuing and gratious God. Finis.

Queen Mary is referred to in the Dedication and throughout the book.

Class XI.   *Adv. S.*

190.   Les Tragedies d'Ant. de Montchrestien sieur de Vasteuille. Plus une Bergerie et vn Poeme de Susan. A Mon-Seigneur Le Prince de Conde.

A Rouen chez Jean Petit dans la Court du Palais auec priuilege Du Roy.

8vo (6¾ × 3¾). Engraved Title with a Portrait of the Author. L'Escossoise ov Le Desastre. A—F4ᵇ pp. 1-56. First edition without date.

A second edition by the same printer, with the date 1601, has the same title as the above, also engraved, but without the author's portrait. 8vo (5⅞ × 2⅞).

Other editions are :—

A Rouen, chez Jean Osmont. 1604. 8vo (5¼ × 3).
A Nyort pour Jacques Vavltier. 1606. 8vo (6⅛ × 3).
A Rouen Martin de la Motte. 1627. 8vo.

In the issues of 1604 and 1606 the tragedy based on the History of Queen Mary is entitled Tragedie de la Reine d'Escosse, instead of L'Escossoise ov Le Desastre.
Montchrestien is the first author who has dramatised any portion of Queen Mary's history.

Class IX.   *B.M.*

1602

191.   Inscriptiones Historicae Regvm Scotorvm, continvata annorvm serie a Fergusio primo Regni Conditore ad nostra tempora : Joh. Jonstonio Abredonense Scoto, Authore. Praefixus est Gathelvs, sive de Gentis origine Fragmentum An. Melvini.
Addita sunt icones omnium regum nobilis Familiae Stuartorum in aere sculptae.
Amsteldami, Excudebat Cornelius Claessonius Andreae Hartio, bibliopolae Edenburgensi. Anno 1602.

4to (9¼ × 6¾). *1–6+A—K in fours. *1 Title, verso blank. *2ᵃ Dedication to James VI. *2ᵇ—*3 Latin verses by Andrew Melvin, Hadrian Damman à Bystervelt, and John Eclinus. *4–5 Gathelus. *6 Catalogus Regum Scotorum Chronologicus. A—H2 (pp. 1–60) Text. H3—K4 Ten woodcut portraits of the Stuart Kings, Queen Mary, and Queen Anna, consort of King James VI., with Latin verses at foot, printed on recto of each leaf.

The above collation represents the usual form of this book. After the accession of King James to the throne of Great Britain, another issue took place. In the British Museum is a copy (Press mark C. 24 b. 27), which appears to be the copy actually presented to the king on his accession to the English throne. The binding is elaborately ornamented, and has the Royal Arms of Great Britain as a centre piece. The sides are covered with fleur-de-lys. The date on the title-page has been originally printed 1602, but has been neatly altered to 1603. The following dedication, which supersedes that noted above, leads to the supposition that this copy, and possibly others, had been specially prepared at the moment of the king's arrival in England :—Sereniss. et Potentiss. Jacobo Primo, Angliae, Scotiae, Franciae, Hiberniae & Britannicarum Insularum &c. Regi invictissimo. Novum imperium florentissimorum Regnorum fecundissimis auspiciis maxima cum totius Orbis Christiani gratulatione incunti Inscriptiones Has Nobilliss. Regum, Maiorum suorum, perpetuâ serie bis mille annor. succedentium Publicae Laetitiae, et Felicitati Britannicae Symbolum. D. D. C. Q. Le. The leaf containing this dedication, unlike the ordinary form, is blank on verso. It is followed by an unsigned leaf, containing on recto and verso Latin dedicatory poems, by Joseph Scaliger, Janus Dousa Nordovicus Dominus Trochaius, and Daniel Heinsius. The remainder of the book in text and in the portraits corresponds with the ordinary form until the portraits of King James and Queen Anna are reached. The ordinary portrait of King James having a tall hat on his head is cancelled, and another with bare head and the bust in armour is substituted. The ordinary portrait of Queen Anna is replaced by another more pleasing variety. Although the dedication is addressed to King James as First of Great Britain, the portrait is titled James VI. of Scotland.

Copies containing the accession variety of portraits of King James and his Queen, but without the special leaf of Dedication and reverting to the original form, appear to have been issued, one of which is in my collection. These copies contain the leaf with the verses of Scaliger and others.

Class VI.   *B.M. Adv. Signet. S.*

1603

192.   ΒΑΣΙΛΙΚΟΝ ΔΩΡΟΝ. or His Maiesties Instrvctions to his Dearest Sonne, Henry the Prince. [The Royal Arms of Scotland.]
Edinbvrgh Printed by Robert Walde-graue Printer to the Kings Majestie. CIƆ. IƆ. C.III.

8vo (6¼ × 4). Printed in roman letter. A⁸+B+b+bb in fours C—K in eights+L⁴. At blank.

A2 Title, verso blank. A3 The Argvment, Sonnet, verso blank. A4—A8ⁿ To Henry my Dearest Sonne. A8ᵇ blank. B1—bb4ⁿ To the Reader. bb4ᵇ blank. C1—L3 (pp. 1-154) Text, terminating with a woodcut of the Scottish shield. L4 blank.

Class XI.   *B.M. Adv. S.*

193. ΒΑΣΙΛΙΚΟΝ ΔΩΡΟΝ. or His Maiesties Instrvctions to his dearest Sonne Henry the Prince. [The Royal Arms of Scotland.]

At London Imprinted by Felix Kyngston, for John Norton, according to the copie printed at Edenburgh 1603.

8vo (6 × 4).) (+ A—K in eights + L⁴.) (1 blank.) (2 Title, verso blank.) (3 Sonnet, verso blank.) (4—) (7 To Henry, &c.) (8 blank. A1—B8 To the Reader, printed in italic letter, without pagination. C1—L3 (pp. 1-154) Text. L4 blank.

This edition seems to have been printed by Walde-grave, probably in London. The woodcut of the Royal Arms and the type are the same as those used by him in printing King James's book, The True Lawe of Free Monarchies, which bears the imprint London, 1603. The Address to the Reader and the Text correspond page by page with the Edinburgh edition of 1603 (No. 192).

Class XI.   *S.*

194. ΒΑΣΙΛΙΚΟΝ ΔΩΡΟΝ. or His Maiesties Instrvctions to his dearest Sonne Henrie the Prince. [Vautrollier's device with Anchora Spei.]

At London Imprinted by Richard Field, for John Norton, according to the copie printed at Edenburgh. 1603.

8vo (6 × 4). The collation is exactly similar to the edition of John Norton, London, 1603 (No. 193), but the types and initial letters are different. Richard Field was Vautrollier's son-in-law and successor, and used his printer's mark.

Many other editions appeared after the king's accession in addition to those named above, including a Latin translation (John Norton, London, 1604), 8vo ; a French translation (John Holman, 1603-1604), and a Swedish translation (1606).

Class XI.   *S.*

195. L'Oraison Fvnebre de Havlt et Pvissant Monseigneur Reverendissime l'Archeuesque de Glasco, Melort James de Bethunes, Ambassadeur pres la Maiesté tres-Chrestienne, pour Serenissime, tres-puissant, & felicissime le Roy Iacques, premier d'Escosse, d'Angleterre & d'Irlande.

Au faux-bourgs S. Germain lez Paris, par Fleury Bourriquant, demeurant en la ruë Neufue, au coing de la ruë du petit Lyon. 1603.

8vo (6¼ × 4). A—E in fours (pp. 1-39), verso of title and last leaf blank.

The sermon was preached on the 30th April 1603 by Pierre Victor Cayer, Dr Theol., in the Church of St John de Lateran. It contains many allusions to Queen Mary.

Class XI.   *S.*

196. [A trewe Description of the nobill Race of the Stewards &c.]

The only copy which appears to exist, in approximately perfect state, of this Scottish version of the Inscriptions by John Johnston of Aberdeen, printed at Amsterdam for Andro Hart, Edinburgh, 1602 (see No. 191), is to be found in the British Museum, but it unfortunately wants the title. It does no contain the dedication or any of the prefatory matter of the Latin edition, and consists of ten leaves arranged in a peculiar manner as follows :—Recto l. 1, blank, verso Portrait of Robert II. Recto

l. 2, Portrait of Robert III., verso blank. Recto l. 3, blank, verso Portrait of James I. Recto l. 4, Portrait of James II., verso blank. Recto l. 5, blank, verso Portrait of James III. Recto l. 6, Portrait of James IV., verso blank. Recto l. 7, blank, verso Portrait of James V. Recto l. 8, Portrait of Queen Mary, verso blank. Recto l. 9, blank, verso Portrait of James VI. Recto l. 10, Portrait of Queen Anna, verso blank. All leaves without signature or pagination. At the foot of recto of l. 10 is the following colophon :—

Printed in Amsterdam, ad the expensis of Andro Hart, Buikseller in Edinburgh. Anno 1603. Cum privilegio Regiae Maiestatis.

The portraits of the kings and queens are the same as those to be found in the Latin edition, those of James VI. and Queen Anna being of the rarer variety, and underneath each is a succinct account of their lives in the Scottish tongue.

The life of Queen Mary is summarised as follows :—"Marie succeeded to her father James the fyfte in the yeire of the vvarld 5513, In the yeire of Christ 1543, a princesse verteouslie inclined. She married first Francis 2, Daulphine, thereafter King of France, then after his death returning hame to Scotland she married Henric Stevvarde Duke of Albanie & Lord Darley, son to Mathevv Erle of Lennox (a comely Prince, Pronepuoy to Henrie the 7 King of England) to vvhom she bare James the 6. She vvas put to death in England 8. Feb. 1586 after 18 yeires captivitie."

The Scottish forms of words and spelling used in the memoirs of the sovereigns, and especially in that of Queen Mary, contrast in a curious manner with the Latin verses appended to the portraits in the original edition. The date of Mary's execution, it will be observed, is given in the old style as 1586, and is probably one of the latest uses of that form in Scotland. After the year 1600 the 1st January became the first day of a new year instead of 25th March. The date of the dedication to King James of the Latin Inscriptiones is 1600, although the book was not printed until 1602.

An imperfect copy, with only six of the portraits, occurred in Laing's Sale, Part I., No. 3453. The title is there given as follows :—A Trewe Description of the nobill Race of the Stewards : succedinge Lineallie to the Crown of Scotland unto this Day. Amsterdam for Andro Hart. N.D. Another edition, with the title Vera Descriptio Augustissimae Stewartorum Familiae, also occurred in the Laing Sale. Part I., No. 3452.

Class XI.   *B.M.*

1605

197. Specvlvm Tragicvm. Regvm, Principvm, & Magnatum superioris sœculi celebriorum ruinas exitusque calamitosas breviter complectens : In quo & iudicia divina & imbecillitas humana insignibus exemplis declarantur. Editio quarta, cùm aliàs, tum & Baronis Montinii historiolâ suo loco insertâ, auctior.

Accessit etiam, memorabilium humilioris fortunæ, intra Speculi tempus, calamitatum Decas ; & Parallela tragica. Auctore I. D.

Lvgdvni Batavorvm, Ex officina Ludovici Elzeverij. cIɔ . Iɔ . cv.

8vo (5⅝ × 3½). A—R in eights. A1 Title, verso blank. A2 Dedication to George Gilpin by the author, John Dickenson. A3—A4ᵃ Joannis Dickensoni ad Lectorem candidum Admonitio. A4ᵇ Idem Joanni Candleri suo, 24 lines of elegiac verse. A5—M7ᵃ Text (pp. 9-189). M7ᵇ—R3 Epilogue Disticha, Decas Tragica, Parallela Tragica (pp. 190-262). R4ᵃ Errata. R4ᵇ—R7ᵃ Index. R7ᵇ—R8 blank.

Succinct accounts of Darnley, Bothwell, Rizzio, Queen Mary, Moray and the other Scottish Regents are given at pp. 94-99. Among the Disticha is the following on Bothwell :—

    Si crimen fuerit genuisse, parentibus ullis,
      Crimen erat magnum te genuisse, tuis.

Other editions of this book were published by Louis Elzevir in 1602, 1603, 1605, in 8vo, and in 1611, 12mo. The edition described above is of considerable rarity.

Class VII.   *S.*

198. Af-beeldinge der Coninghinne Elyzabeth: des Conincks Jacobi vi. der Coniginne Annae syner wrouwe: ende Henrici Frederici des Princen van Wallia. Met een corte beschrijvinghe haeter Stammen, als oock haerer aencoemste, tot de Croone van Engelandt, ende een vehael der voornaemster dinghen by haer wtghericht. Wt vercheyden historien vergadert / ende in druck wegheghveven / door W. B. Lief-hebber der Historien.

T'Aernhem, by Jan Janszoon, Boecvercooper woonende in den Beshagen Bybel.
4to (7¼ × 5½). A—E in fours. The Genealogical register is without pagination. Lives of Elizabeth and James, pp. 1-32.
This compilation seems to be drawn from Camden and other English authorities. It contains numerous notices of Queen Mary, and a short account of the principal events of her life.

Class XI. *S.*

199. La Terza Parte del Tesoro Politico, Nella quale si contengono Relationi, Instruttioni, Trattati, & Discorsi, non meno dotti, & curiosi, che vtili, per conseguire la perfetta cognitione della Ragione di Stato.

8vo (6 × 3⅞). S. l. et. a.; but in MS. at bottom of title: Turnoni. 1605. Title and Index 4 pp. Text pp. 1-606. At p. 522, Narratione dello stato della Regina di Scotia, & del Prencipe suo figliuolo. Nella quale si contengono le persecutioni e prigionia d'essa Regina con la Morte del Re Henrico suo Marito, & altri trauagliosi accidenti occorsi in esso Regno.

This treatise is printed anonymously, but is the composition of Francesco Marcaldi, a Florentine. This 16th century author wrote historical notices of many of the sovereigns of his time, and of the Republics of Venice and Genoa. (See *Bibliotica Manoseritta Farsetti*, Par. 2, p. 201.) His account of Scotland in the Reign of Queen Mary was issued by him at various times with separate dedications to different patrons. Three copies of his autograph MS. are in my possession; one dated at Siena, 8th Feb. 1580; a second from Bologna, 15th December 1581; a third from Cremona, 21st January 1583. Another copy is mentioned in the Catalogue of the Capilupi MSS. as having been dedicated to Alessandro Capulupi from Mantova, 14th December 1582. Among the Laing MSS. in the Library of the University of Edinburgh two other copies occur, one dated from Luca, 24th January 1580, and the other from Firenze, 6th December 1578. An autograph note of Dr Laing's states that he had seen another copy from Venetia, 8th March 1580. Bishop Nicolson (Scottish Historical Library, London, 1702, p. 165; 8vo), mentions that a copy had been "communicated to him by the famous and truly honourable J. Evelyn Esq. It gives only a very short Account of this unfortunate Princess's Life and Troubles, from her birth to the 36th year of her Life and Reign; where the Manuscript breaks off, this copy being incomplete. However it appears that there is not much wanting: For the Dedication is from Venice 29. of May 1581, and the last Chapter is: Il presente Stato di Scotia A.D. 1578." The Treatise printed in this book and the subsequent edition of 1612 has not hitherto been recognised as the work of Marcaldi.

Class VII. *B.M. Edin. Univ. (in MS.) S. (in MS.)*

1607

200. A Historie contayning the Warres, Treaties, Marriages, and other occurrents betweene England and Scotland, from King William the Conqueror, vntill the happy Vnion of them both in our gratious King James. With a briefe declaration of the first Inhabitants of this Island: And what seuerall Nations haue sithence settled them-selues therein one after another. [Woodcut.]

Imprinted at London by G. Eld. 1607.
4to (7¼ × 5¼). A—Bb in eights Cc4. A1 blank. A2 Title, verso blank. A3-4 Dedication to

A HISTORIE CON-
tayning the VVarres, Treaties, Marriages, *and other occurrents betweene*
England and Scotland, from King William the
Conqueror, vntill the happy Vnion of them
both in our gratious King IAMES.

With a briefe declaration of the first Inhabitants of this
Iland : And what feuerall Nations haue fithence fet-
led them-felues therein one after an other:

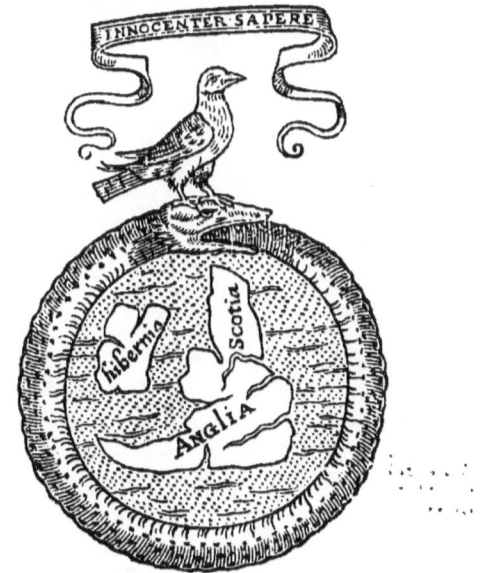

Imprinted at London by G. *Eld.* 1607.

Edin. Bibl. Soc.—*Queen Mary Literature.* Facsimile No. XV. See No. 200, page 69.

Prince Henry, signed by the Author. A5-7 To the Reader, signed by the Author (Edward Ayscu), and dated from Cotham in Lincolnshire, 24th March 1606. A8 blank. B—Cc4 Text, pp. 1-396.

(See Facsimile No. XV.)

Class XI.   *B.M. S.*

1608

201.   Illvstrivm Mvliervm, et illvstrivm litteris virorvm Elogia, a Jvlio Caesare Capacio Neapolitanæ vrbi à Secretis conscripta.
Neapoli Apud Io. Iacobum Carlinum, & Constantinum Vitalem. 1608.
4to (8¾ × 6¾). A—Bbb in fours. Title, Dedication, and Text: pp. 1-387. Imprimatur and Colophon on verso of last leaf.
The Life of Queen Mary appears at p. 131, and is terminated by two Latin Sonnets.
Class VI. XI.   *S.*

202.   Sanctarum Precationvm Prooemia, sev mavis, ejaculationes animæ ad orandum se præparantis. Per Adam. Blacvodævm Regis apud Pictones in præsidali curia Consiliarium.
Augustoriti Pictonum. Ex officina Iuliani Thorelli, Typographi Vniuersitatis. 1608.
8vo (5¼ × 3¼). ¶⁴+¶¶²+a—c in eights+d⁴. ¶1—¶¶2 Title, Dedication and one blank leaf. a—d4 Text. Dedicated to James Betoun, Archbishop of Glasgow.
Poem on the flight of Queen Mary into England is at p. 39.
Class VI.   *Adv.*

1609

203.   Varii generis Poematia. Per Adam. Blacvodævm in Præsidali Pictonum consessu, & in Metropolitano decurionum collegio Cōsiliarium.
Pictavis, Ex officina libraria Ivliani Thorelli Academiæ typographi. 1609.
8vo (5½ × 3¼). A⁸+B⁴+A—E in eights+F⁴+A—B in eights+C⁶. A—B4 Title and Pref. 12 leaves, one blank. A—F4 Text: pp. 1-86. At page 81, Ode, E Gallico illustrissimæ Scotorum Gallorumque (quā dotariam vocant) reginæ, followed by some Anagrams on the Queen's name. A—C5, pp. 1-42: A Letter of James VI., dated Paris Prid id. Junii 1606, prefacing a Poem addressed to James on his succession to the English throne, with several references to Queen Mary. C6 Errata for the whole volume.
Class VI.   *Adv.*

1610

204.   ΒΑΣΙΛΙΚΟΝ ΔΩΡΟΝ sive Commentarivs Exigeticvs in Serenissimi Magnæ Britanniæ Regis Jacobi Praefationem Monitoriam; et in Apologiam pro Iuramento fidelitatis; Avctore Iacobo Gretsero Societatis Iesv, Sacræ Theologiæ in Academia Ingolstadiensi Professore.
Anno M.DC.X. Ingolstadii Ex Typographeio Adami Sartorii.
4to (7½ × 6). *+A—Z+a—p in fours. A1 Title, verso blank. *1-4 Mariæ Stvartæ Gallorvm ac Scotorvm olim Reginae; Jacobi Magnæ Britanniæ Regis Matri; nvnc caeli indigenae; Epistola Dedicatoria. A2-4 Praefatio ad Lectorem (pp. 3-8). B1 Index capitum (pp. 9-10). B2 Approbationes (pp. 11-12). B3—k1ᵇ Text (pp. 13-258). k2—p4⁴ Index and errata. p4ᵇ blank.
This book, although bearing the same general title as King James' work, is a sharp attack on him and the Protestants by the Jesuit Gretsen. The dedication to "Mary in Heaven" is singular.
Queen Mary is referred to frequently in some parts of the book.
Class IV. V. XI.   *S.*

205. A Catalogve of the Kings of Scotland. Together with their seuerall Armes, Wiues, and Issue.
London M.DC.X.
Folio (9 × 6¾). ¶ + ¶¶ + ¶¶¶ in sixes, with pagination 1–36, inclusive of title. ¶1ª Title, within a woodcut border. ¶1ᵇ Life of Malcolm Canmore, &c. The life of Queen Mary is to be found at pp. 33–35.
Class XI.   *B.M.*

1612

206. The abridgement or Summarie of the Scots Chronicles, with a short description of their originall, from the comming of Gathelvs their first Progenitor out of Græcia into Egypt. And their comming into Portingall and Spaine, and of their Kings and Gouernours in Spaine, Ireland and Albion, now called Scotland, (howbeit the whole number are not extant) with a true Chronologie of all their Kings. Their Reignes, Deaths and Burials, from Fergvsivs the first King of Scotland, vntill his Royal Maiestie, now happily Raigning ouer all Great Brittaine and Ireland, and all the Isles to them appertaining. With a true description and diuision of the whole Realme of Scotland, and of the principall Cities, Townes, Abbies, Fortes, Castles, Towers and Riuers, and of the commodities in euery part thereof, and of the Isles in generall, with a memoriall of the most rare and wonderfull things in Scotland. By John Monipennie.
Printed at Brittaines Bursse by John Budge. 1612.
4to (7½ × 5¾). A² + B—N in fours + O². A1 Title, verso blank. A2 Dedication to the most High and Mightie Monarch, James, &c. B—O2 Text (pp. 1–100).
See the Edinburgh edition in 8vo (No. 229).
Class X.   *Adv. S.*

207. Del Tesoro Politico La Parte Terza e Qvarta nelle quale &c. Con Indice.
Helenopoli Impensis Joannis Theobaldi Schönwetteri. 1612.
4to (8½ × 6½). *⁴ Title and Arguments. Text, pp. 1–471.
See No. 199, First edition, 1605, as to the Narratione dello stato della Regina di Scotia, &c., which is to be found at p. 223 of this edition.
Class VII.   *B.M.*   *Edin. University (in MS.)*   *S. (in MS.)*

1615

208. Annales Rervm Anglicarvm et Hibernicarvm Regnante Elizabetha, ad Annvm Salvtis M.D.LXXXIX. Gvilielmo Camdeno Avthore.
Londini, Typis Guilielmi Stansbij, Impensis Simonis Watersoni, ad insigne Coronae in Coemeterio Paulino. M.DC.XV.
Folio (11 × 7¼). A—Vvv in fours. A1 Title, verso blank. A2—A4ᵇ Lectori. B—C4ª Apparatus. C4ᵇ blank, pp. 1–16. D—Sss2ª, pp. 17–499, Text. Sss2ᵇ blank. Sss3—Vvv4 Index, without pagination.
The copy in the British Museum, from which the collation is taken, belonged to Charles II., and has his crown and usual cypher in the corners of the red morocco binding.
The second part, which was not published until 1627, after the deaths of King James and Camden, is by the same printers, and is included in the above volume, but it has no reference to Queen Mary.
Class X.   *B.M.*   *Signet.*

1619

209. Reverendissime in Christo Patris, Patricii Adamsoni, Sancti-Andreae in Scotia Archiepiscopi dignissimi ac doctissimi, Poemata sacra, cum aliis opusculis. Studio ac industria Tho. Volvseni J. C. Expolita & Recognita. [Printer's Mark.] Londini apud Ioannem Billivm Anno M.D.CXIX.

<blockquote>
4to (7½ × 5½). a—c in fours + ¶², followed by the different works, with signatures as noted below. a 1 Title, with royal arms of Great Britain on verso. a2ª—c4ª Dedication, &c. c4ᵇ blank. ¶1 De authoris. ¶2 Quae in hoc volumine continentur. a1—d4 Prologus in Jobum, &c. B—O3, pp. 1-102, Jobus sive de constantia lib. O4 blank. P1—S2 Threnorum Jeremiæ Libellus, with title dated 1618. T1—Dd2, pp. 1-57, Apocalypsis, with title dated 1618. A1ª Title: Serenissimi ac nobilissimi, Scotiæ, Angliæ, Franciæ, & Hybernicæ Principis, Henrici Stvardi Illustrissimi Herois ac Mariæ Reginæ amplissimae filii Genethliacum. A Patricio Adamsono Scoto. Poeta ornatissimo Parisiis conscriptum & ibidem typis audaciùs commissum, 25 Junii, sexto à partu die. 1566. A1ᵇ Royal arms of Great Britain. A2 Dedication to Charles, Prince of Wales, &c., dated : Edinoduno pridie Cal. Augusti 1617, and signed Thos. Volvsenus. A3—B2 Text. B—L2 (B3 and B4 duplicated) Catechismus Latino Carmine Redditus, with title dated 1618. L3—M4 De Papistarum ineptiis, with title dated 1618. N1—S2 Confessio Fidei, with title dated 1618. S3 blank. S4—Aa2 Epigrammata, &c. * Leaf of errata to the whole volume.

Queen Mary is frequently mentioned in various parts of these works. The prior edition of Adamson's Genethliacum, which is referred to in this title and in the general list of Adamson's works as having been printed by him at Paris in 1566, has never come under my observation. Is it possible that the news of the birth of the Prince could have reached Paris in six days?

Genethliacum was introduced by Arthur Johnston as the opening poem in his collection, "Deliciae Poetarum Scotorum, 1637" (No. 232).
</blockquote>

Class VI.   *B.M. Adv. S.*

1621

210. Les Memoires de Messire Michel de Castelnau Seignevr de Mavvissiere. Paris. 1621.

<blockquote>
4to. See No. 261 for the more complete edition.
</blockquote>

Class XI.

211. Les Recherches de la France D'Estienne Pasqvier Conseiller et Advocat general du Roy en la Chambre des Comptes de Paris. Avgmentees en ceste derniere edition de trois liures entiers, outres plusieurs Chapitres entrelassez en chacun des autres Liures, tirez de la Bibliotheque de l'Autheur. [Royal Arms of France.]

A Paris, chez Laurens Somius, ruë Sainct Iacques au Coq, & Compas d'or. M.DC.XXI. Avec Privilege dv Roy.

<blockquote>
Folio (14½ × 9). Title and Table 10 ll., with portrait of Pasquier on verso of last. Text, pp. 1-1019. Table, 38 ll. In livre sixieme Chap. xv. is to be found De la Mort de Marie Sthuart Royne d'Escosse veufue en premieres nopces de François second de nom Roy de France. Pasquier excuses himself from passing from France to England, because he speaks of a Princess, widow of one of the Kings of France. He says, " L'Histoire du Connétable de Sainct Pol a engendré dedans mon ame vn pesle-mesle de depet & compassion, Despit en le voyant en sa bonne fortune trop oublieuse de son devoir. Compassion quant apres tant de grandeurs, dont elle etait comble, je vois la fin estee aboutie à vn malheureux escharfaut. Mais en celle que je discourray maintenant, il me semble n'y auoir que pleurs : & parauanture se trouuera il homme qui en la lisant ne pardonnera à ses yeux." The narrative of Pasquier is apparently drawn from Black-
</blockquote>

wood's Martyre de la Royne d'Escosse (No. 144). After extolling the Queen's constancy in her religion and misfortune, he says, " Quoy faisant elle triompha non seulement de la mort, ains de la Royne mesme d'Angleterre & ensiuelit d'vne mesme main tous les bruits sinistres dont les maluieillans s'estoient preualus encontr'elle. De moy comme nos pensees sont libres, je ne fais aucune doute, que tout ce qu'on mist en la bouche de ceste Dame auant sa decés ne soit veritable : et pour ceste cause voyant ces durs traitemens exercez sur elle, je croyais que le son de ces cloches seroit vn tauxin, et les feux vn flambeav de guerre qui s'espandroit quelque iour par toute l'Angleterre : toutefois le tems ma depuis enseigné que jetois un tres-mauuais faizeur d'Almanachs."

The first edition of Les Recherches de l'asquier was published in Paris, 1596, but it contains no reference to Queen Mary, except a notice of her marriage to the Dauphin.

Another edition, a reprint of that of 1621. Paris chez Pierre Menard, 1643. Folio.

Class X. *B.M.*

1623

212. Les Oevvres de Pierre de Ronsard Gentilhomme Vandosmois Prince de Poetes François, Reueues et augmentees et illustrees de Commentaires et remarques.

A Paris, chez Nicolas Bvon, ruë St Jacques à l'enseigne St Claude et de l'Homme Sauuage. Auec priuilege du Roy. M.DC.XXIII.

Folio (16½ × 11). 2 vols. The above title is within an engraved emblematical border. Guiltier fecit. The second vol. has a separate title with Bvon's printer's mark, but the pagination runs through both volumes. Introductory matter 7 ll. Pp. 1-1728 followed by 6 ll. of table. Both volumes are ornamented with ten portraits of the kings of France (including Francis II.) and celebrated characters of Ronsard's period, and very voluminous notes and criticisms by Marcassus and others.

Le Premier Livre des Poemes de P. de Ronsard. Dediez a Tres-illvstre et Tres-Vertevse Princesse Marie Stvart, Royne d'Escosse, occurs at pp. 1171-1230. A frontispiece portrait, Tho. de Leu F. et ex., with the legend Marie Stewart Reyne de Fran et Descosse, has the following verses underneath :—

Et les belles beautez, et les grandeur plus grandes
Sont pleines de dangers, et de malheurs divers :
Ce sont Buttes a Maux : Qui n'en croira mes vers
Viene voir ceste Reyne et lise ses legendes.

The opening sonnet and six of the succeeding poems are addressed to the Queen, and were probably forwarded to Scotland by Ronsard shortly after her return from France.

The poems of Ronsard have been printed in France in very numerous editions (see Brunet, Manuel du Libraire, Vol. IV. p. 1374). The edition of 1623 has been included in this list as the most beautiful among the number, and because it embraces the celebrated portrait of Queen Mary by T. de Leu in a fine state, as well as that of Francis II. by the same engraver.

Class II. V. VI. *B.M. Adv. Signet.*

1624

213. Vita Mariæ Stvartæ Scotiæ Reginæ. Dotariæ, Galliæ. Angliæ & Hiberniæ Hoeredis, Scriptori Georgio Conræo Scoto. Ad Vrbanvm VIII Pont. Max.

Wircebvrgi, Apud Stephanum Fleischmann. M.DC. XXIV. Superiorum permissu.

8vo (6 × 3¾). A—I in eights. With catchwords, but no pagination. A1 Title, verso blank. A2—A5ᵇ Dedication to Pope Urban VIII. dated Romæ ex comitatis Illustrissimi Nepotis tui Cardinalis Barberini Scotiæ Protectoris A. d. IX. Kalend. Aprilis Anni M.D.C.XXIV. Portrait on verso of a leaf without signature, in square frame, having the arms of Scotland, England,

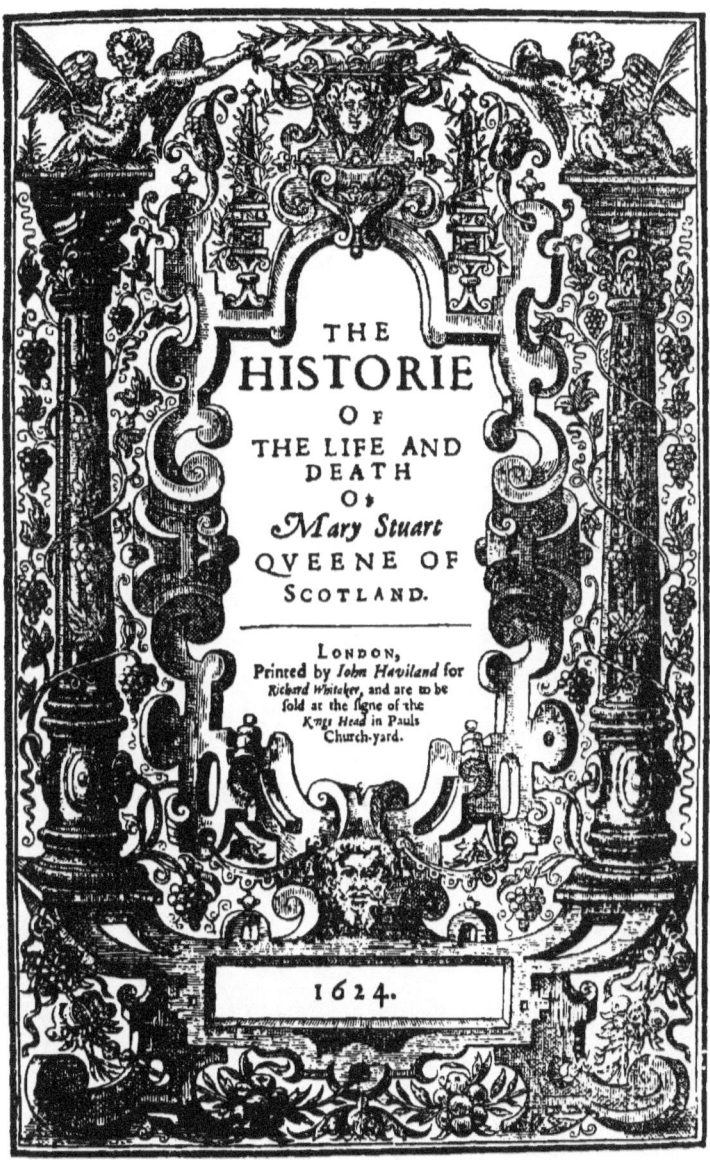

Edin. Bibl. Soc.—Queen Mary Literature. Facsimile No. XVII. See No. 215, page 73.
Reduced: size of original 9¼ × 5⅛ inches.

France, and Ireland in the corners, and an oval band with the inscription, MARIA STVARTA Regina. At foot the following inscription, MARIA SCOTIÆ et Galliæ de Facto, de Iure, Angliæ et Hyberniæ, Regina. A suis deturgata in Angliam refugii causa descendens cognatæ Elizabethæ tum regnantis perfidia, Senatusq; Anglici inuidia, post 19, captiuitatis annos religionis ergo, capite obtruncala martyrem consummauit Anno Aetatis Regniq. 45. Ano. 1587. I. Leipold sculp. A6—I7^b Text, ending on fourth line from top of page. The remainder of the page contains a Latin poem addressed to G. Connaeus by Cardinal Barberini. I8^a Apostrophe ad Mariam Stuartam Martyrem, and the Imprimatur. I8^b blank.

The portrait of Queen Mary, placed between the dedication and the text, is of extreme rarity and esteemed for its high quality. This, the first edition of George Cone's Life of Queen Mary, is of great rarity. (See No. 214.)

Class VII.   *S.*

214. Vita Mariae Stvartae Scotiae Reginae, Dotariæ Galliæ, Angliæ & Hibernie Hæredis. Scriptore Georgio Connaeo Scoto. Ad Urbanvm VIII. Pont. Max.
Romae, Apud Ioannem Paulum Gellium. MDCXXIV. Svperiorvm Permissv.

12mo (5½ × 3). †⁴ + A—G in twelves + H⁴. †1 Title, verso blank. †2—†7^a Dedication to Pope Urban VIII., dated Romæ ex cometatu Illustrissimi Nepotis tui Cardinalis Barberini Scotiæ Protectoris A. d. IX. Kal. Aprilis Anni MDCXXIV. †7^b Imprimatur. †8^b Portrait of Queen Mary within emblematical border, having the motto : Una pro Multa, at the top, and an oval frame with the title Regina Maria Stvarta. Suspended from the frame are the crowns of Scotland, France, England, and Ireland. At the bottom the text, Ne Dimittas legem matris tuae ut addatur gratia capiti tuo et torques collo tuo. Pro. 2. A1—II6^b Text, having the following colophon : Romæ, ex Typographia Andreæ Phæi MDCXXIV. pp. 1-180. II7^a Errata. II7^b—H8 blank. Catchwords. Printed in roman letter, with the letters and other documents quoted in italic.

This edition is of more common occurrence than that of Wireeburgh (No. 213). The typographical execution is inferior, but with the exception of the omission in this edition of the Latin poems found at the end of the other, the matter is identical. This book is reprinted by P. Jebb (De vita et rebus Gestis Mariae, London, 1725, Folio, Vol. II. p. 1.) from this edition, as the Latin verses referred to above do not appear in the reprint.

Class VII.   *Adv. S.*

215. The Historie of the Life and Death of Mary Stuart Queene of Scotland.
London, Printed by John Haviland for Richard Whitaker, and are to be sold at the signe of the Kings Head in Pauls Church-yard. 1624.

Folio (12½ × 7⅜). A⁶ + B—Hh in fours Ii⁶. A1^a blank. A1^b Frontispiece : portrait of Queen Mary, R. Elstrack sculpsit (*see Facsimile No. XVI.*) A2^a Title, within woodcut border (*see reduced Facsimile No. XVII.*) A2^b blank. A3 To the King's most Excellent Maiestie. The Epistle Dedicatory, signed by Wil. Strangvage. A4—A6 The Preface. B—Ii5 Text. Ii6 blank, pp. 1-250, printed within ruled lines, with catchwords.

The collation given above is common to the two forms in which this book was issued. It has been the custom of bibliographers to catalogue this edition as the production of Wil. Strangauge, and to refer to the second edition of 1636 (No. 231) as having been issued in the name of W. Udall. Some copies are, however, to be found in every respect similar to this of 1624, with the single exception of the name of W. Udall being appended to the Epistle Dedicatory instead of that of Wil. Strangvage. Examples in this state are to be found in the Huth Library, the Signet Library, and in my collection; but while the Stranguage variety is not very frequently to be met with, the Udall is of great rarity.

K

Le Long (Bibliotheque Historique de la France, folio, Paris, 1769, 4 vols., Vol. II. p. 652) has noted copies of both forms; but not having read the books, he has entered them as separate works, with the same title, one by Stranguage, the other by Udall.

The double signature is not the only peculiarity to be noted. It has hitherto been assumed that the work was an original one, and the first English History of the Life of Queen Mary, as the following passage from the Epistle Dedicatory amply warrants:—" For these reasons I presumed to present vnto your Highnesse this Treatise of the life and death of your Royal Mother, the Lady Mary Stvart Queene of Scotland; A History most fit for this your Meridian of Greate Britaine, and yet neuer published in the English tongue before."

A careful examination of the text shows that instead of being an original composition, every paragraph, from the beginning to the end, is a literal translation from the Latin of William Camden's Annales Rerum Anglicarum et Hibernicarum Regnante Elizabetha. The opening passage is to be found in the edition, London, 1615, folio, at p. 41, and the closing passage at p. 469; or in the Elzevir Edition, Lugd. Bort., 1675, 8vo, p. 30 and p. 542 respectively.

The method pursued by the translator, whatever may have been his real name, is marked by considerable ingenuity and skill. He has extracted from Camden all the passages bearing on the history of Queen Mary, and, where necessary, he has added a few simple connecting words to link the sentences.

Camden's Annals were not translated into English until 1625 (No. 217), and then from a French translation, and this was followed in 1630 (No. 226) by another direct from the Latin.

The text of the Stranguage-Udall book differs from both in the rendering of the passages employed.

It may be a subject for speculation whether the book was prepared under the auspices of Camden himself. At the moment of its publication he was no longer in life, as, after some months of feeble health, he died on 9th November 1623. The original edition of the first portion of the Annals, which contains all the matter connected with the history of Queen Mary, was published in London in 1615 (No. 208). This book appeared under the sanction of a warrant from King James to Camden and Sir Robert Cotton to print and publish it. As stated in the warrant, the king had perused the sheets, and, it has been alleged, had corrected many portions pertaining to his mother's history. The limits of this note do not permit a detail of the controversy which Camden and Isaac Casaubon waged with De Thou on the former's change of opinions regarding the disputed points in Queen Mary's life, or to recapitulate the charges of partiality alleged against him (see Thuanus Historia sui temporis, Londini, folio, 7 vols., Vols. I. and VII., for the correspondence). It appears not to be improbable that, although Camden did not live to see the Life and Death of Queen Mary published, he must have been privy to the translation. The tenor of the Epistle Dedicatory to the King bears the mark of composition by a man of position, rather than an unknown or pseudonymous author, and if not written it may at least have been inspired by the true author of the history, which it presented in a new form. The more curious puzzle is why the name of the apparent author should have been changed after the commencement of the issue. From the continuance of the name of Udall on the edition of 1636, it seems certain that the name of Stranguage was used on the earlier copies, and was a pseudonym, which was abandoned on ascertaining the success of the book. Who was Udall? Camden, in 1575, became second master at Westminster School, while Nicolas Udall, the well-known author, was the head master, to which position Camden himself succeeded in 1593. It is suggested that W. Udall may have been a son or relative of Nicolas Udall, whose acquaintance Camden had made at Westminster, and whom he employed to make the translation and compile the book. On Camden's death, Udall, afraid to risk the publication in his own name of a book treating on what was still so delicate a subject, published it under an assumed name, which, after a not unfavourable reception by the ruling powers of the earlier copies, was changed to his own.

Class VII.   B.M. (Stranguage).   Signet (Udall).   Adv. (Stranguage)   S. Udall and [Stranguage.

1625

216.   Annales Rervm Anglicarvm, et Hibernicarvm, Regnante Elizabetha Autore Gvil. Camdeno. Prima Pars emendatior, altera nunc prima in lucem edita.
Lug. Batavorvm Ex Officina Elzeveriana cıɔ ıɔc xxv.

>8vo (7 × 4¾). *+**+A—Kkk in eights. *1 Engraved Title. *2-8 Ad Lectorem, portrait of Queen Elizabeth on verso of eighth leaf, recto blank. **—Kkk Text (Pp. 1-855) and Index.

Class XI.   *S.*

217.   Annales. The True & Royall History of the famous Empresse Elizabeth Queene of England France and Ireland &c. True faith's defendresse of Diuine renowne and happy Memory. Wherein all such memorable things as happened during hir blessed raigne, with such acts and Treaties as past betwixt hir Ma.tie and Scotland, France, Spaine, Italy, Germany, Poland, Sweden, Denmark, Russia, and the Netherlands, are exactly described.

London printed for Benjamin Fisher and are to be sould at the Talbot in Pater Noster Rowe 1625.

>4to (8½ × 6¼). Frontispiece and Title without sign. 46 leaves with irregular signatures, Dedications and other preliminary matter. B—Kkk+B—Gg+Aaaa—Eeee in fours+Ffff² Text. The title-page and portrait are engraved by Vaughan.
>
>A translation from a French version of Camden's Annals by Abraham Darcie, who signs the Dedication to Prince Charles and other prefatory matter. The continuation of this book by Thomas Browne, London, 1629, has no special reference to Queen Mary. (See No. 226.)

Class XI.   *B.M.   Adv.   S.*

1627

218.   A Thankfvll Remembrance of Gods Mercy. In an Historicall Collection of the great and mercifull Deliverances of the Church and State of England, since the Gospel beganne here to flourish, from the beginning of Queene Elizabeth. Collected by Geo. Carleton, Doctor of Divinity and Bishop of Chichester. The Third Edition revised and enlarged. Psalm iii. 2. The works of the Lord are great, and ought to bee sought out of all them that love Him.

London, Printed by M. Flesher for Robert Mylbourne and Humphrey Robinson at the signe of the three Pigeons in Pauls Churchyard—1627.

>4to (7 × 5¼). A—Oo in fours+Pp². A1a an engraved short Title with emblematical ornaments, a portrait of Queen Elizabeth, entitled Deborah, on the right, and another of King James, entitled Salomon, on the left; with a frontispiece portrait of the author, Bishop Carleton. A1b blank. A2 full title as above, verso blank. A 3-4. The Epistle dedicatorie to Charles Prince of Great Britain, &c. B1—Pp2a, pp. 1-291. Text within ruled lines. Pp2b blank.
>
>There are numerous curious woodcuts illustrating episodes of the history of the period. Queen Mary is very frequently mentioned, but any account of her tragical death is carefully omitted.
>
>The first edition of this book was issued in 1624, with engraved as well as printed title-page. A second, revised and enlarged, in 1625. The above collation is from the third edition. A fourth was published in 1630. The four editions are to be found in the British Museum.

Class XI.   *B.M.   Adv. (2nd Ed.)   Signet (4th Ed.)   S. (3rd Ed.)*

219. Corona Tragica. Vida y Mverte de la Serenissima Reyna de Escocia Maria Estvarda A nvestro S.S.^{mo} Padre Vrbano VIII. P.M. Por Lope Felix de Vega Carpio Procurador Fiscal de la Camara Apostolica, y Capellan de San Segundo en la santa Iglesia de Auila. Versa est en luctum cithara mea. Con Privilegio.
En Madrid por la viuda de Luis Sanchez, Impressora del Reyno. Año M.DC.XXVII. A costa de Alonso Perez mercader de libros.

<small>4to (8 × 6). ¶ + A—P in eights + Q⁶. ¶1-7 Preliminary. ¶8 blank, followed by a portrait of Queen Mary on separate leaf. A—Q⁶ Text and subsidiary poems.</small>

Class IX. *Adv. Signet. S.*

220. Maria Stvarta Regina Scotiæ Dotaria Franciæ, Hæres Angliæ et Hiberniæ; Martyr Ecclesiæ, Innocens à cæde Darleana : Vindice Oberto Barnestapolio. Continet hæc Epistola historiam penè totam vitae, quam Regina Scotiæ egit miserè, sed exegit gloriosè, rationem tituli præfert frons sequentis pagellæ.
Coloniæ sumptibus Petri Henningii, Bibliopolæ Coloniensis Anno M.DC.XXVII.

<small>8vo (6½ × 3⅞). aa—bb in eights + cc⁶. Title, with address to the Reader on verso, and 2 ll. preliminary matter. Text pp. 1-68. Approbatio on recto of last leaf.
This is the second edition of No. 164.</small>

Class VII. *S.*

221. Svmmarivm Rationvm qvibvs Cancellarivs Angliæ et Prolocvtor Pvckeringius Elizabethæ Angliæ Reginæ persuaserunt occidendam esse serenissimam Principem Mariam Stuartam Scotiæ Reginam & Jacobi Sexti Scotorum Regis matrem : Vna cvm Responsionibvs Reginæ Angliæ et Sententia mortis. Quæ omnia anglice primvm edita svnt, et Londini a Typographo Regio impressa, ac deinde varias in linguas translata : His additvm est supplicivm & mors Reginae Scotiae, vna cum succinctis quibusdam animaduersionibus & confutationibus eorum, quae ei objecta sunt. Opera Romoaldi Scoti.
Coloniæ sumptibus Petri Henningii Bibliopolæ Coloniensis Anno M.DC.XXVII.

<small>8vo (6½ × 3⅞). a—g in eights. Title and pp. 1-109.
Pp. 85-109 contain a letter to Grynaeus regarding the Zuinglian Church, which has no reference to Queen Mary. This is the second edition of No. 171, and is usually found bound with the above number.</small>

Class VII. *S.*

1628

222. La Reina di Scotia Tragedia di Federigo della Valle al sommo Pontefice, et Sig. nostro Vrbano VIII.
In Milano per gli heredi di Melchior Malatesta Stampatori Regij, e Ducali. MDCXXVIII.

<small>4to (7¾ × 6). *² + A—N in fours. Text, pp. 1-102. The last three pages are misprinted 200-201-202. Last leaf blank.</small>

Class IX. *S.*

223. Georgii Conæi de dvplici statv Religionis apvd Scotos Libri duo. Ad illvstriss^{mvm} Principem Franciscvm S. R. E. Card. Barberinvm Magnæ Brittaniæ Protectorem. [Printer's mark overshadowed by a Cardinal's hat in red.]

Romæ, Typis Vaticanis. M.D.C.XXVIII. Svperiorvm Permissv.

4to (8¼ × 6¼). a⁶+A—Z in fours. a1 Title, verso blank. a2-6 Dedication, Ad lectorem, with Privilege and Errata on verso of last leaf. A—Y Text (pp. 1-176). Z1-4 Index.

Class IX. *Adv. Signet. S.*

Rerum Anglicarum Henrico VIII. Edvvardo VI. et Maria regnantibus, Annales. Londini Apud Ioannem Billivm Typographum Regium. M.DC.XXVIII.

4to (7¼ × 5½). ⅞+A—Hh in fours. ⁂1 Title, verso blank. ⁂2 Dedication to Charles 1., Majestatis vestræ humillimus sacellanus F. II. (*Francis Godwin, Bishop of Hereford*). §3-4 Ad lectorem. A1—IIh3 Annales, pp. 1-246. IIh4 Colophon, verso blank.

The initial letters of the chapters form the words, Franciscus Godwinus Laudavensis Episcopus hos conscripsit.

The first reference to Queen Mary is at p. 136, where it is stated that immediately the death of James V. was known in England, the question of marrying the infant Scottish Queen to Prince Edward was mooted, but it was uncertain from whom the idea sprung. Many pages following are almost entirely occupied with an account of Scottish affairs and schemes for the prosecution of the marriage treaty. Allusions to Queen Mary occur in other portions of these Annals.

Class XI. *Adv. B.M.*

Vera et Sincera Historia Schismatis Anglicani, De eius Origine ac Progressu : Tribus libris fideliter conscripta, ab R. D. Nicolao Sandero Anglo, Doct : Theologo ; aucta per Edvardvm Rishtonvm. Nunc postremum Appendice ex R. P. Petri Ribadeneiræ libris, aucta & castigatius edita.

Coloniæ Agrippinæ Apud Petrvm Henningivm sub signo Cuniculi Anno MDCXX.VIII.

8vo (6 × 3¾). *+A—Ii in eights. *1 Title, verso blank. *2—*4ᵃ Rishthonus Lectori. *4ᵇ—*5ᵇ Præfatio Avthoris. *6—*8 Approbatio, Argumentum et Index Martyrum. A1—Aa1 Text and Index. Aa2—Ii8 Appendix Ribadeneiræ.

Class XI. *S.*

1630

The Historie of the most Renowned and Victorious Princesse Elizabeth late Queene of England. Contayning all the Important and Remarkeable Passages of State both at Home and Abroad, during her Long and Prosperous raigne. Composed by way of Annals. Neuer heretofore so Faithfully and fully published in English.

London, Printed by Benjamin Fisher and are to be sold at his shop in Aldersgate streete at the signe of the Talbot. MDCXXX.

Folio (11 × 7). Frontispiece portrait of Queen Elizabeth, without engraver's name, and Title, unsigned, verso blank. A⁴+B²+B—Ggggg in fours. A—B2ᵇ To the Reader, signed R. N., *i.e.*, Robert Norton, the translator. B1ᵃ—B3 The Author to the Reader. B4—C4 The Introduction. D—Eeee Text. Ffff—Ggggg3 Index. Last leaf blank. Each book has separate pagination.

This is the first translation into English of Camden's Annals from the original Latin, that of A. Darcie (No. 217) being drawn from the French translation of P. de Bellegent. (R. Field, Londres, 1624. 4to). Another edition of this translation was issued by T. Harper for B. Fisher. London, 1635. Folio.

Class XI. *B.M.*

1631

227. Davidis Camerarii Scoti de Scotorvm Fortitvdine, Doctrina, & Pietate, ac de ortu & progressu hæresis in Regnis Scotiæ & Angliæ. Libri Qvatvor. Nvnc primvm in lvcem editi.

Parisiis, sumptibus Petri Baillet, viâ Jacobæâ, sub Gallo & Leone repente. M.DC.XXXI. Cvm privilegio Regis.

 4to (9 × 6¾). Title, Dedication to Charles I., and Index, 10 ll. unsigned. A—Nn in fours +O². Text (pp. 1-288), Privilege and Errata. Index capitum.

Class XI.   *Adv. Signet. S.*

1633

228. Maria Regina di Scotia. Poema Heroico del P. Prior D. Bassiano Gatti Monaco di S. Girolamo alla Santita di N. S. Vrbano VIII.

In Bologna per Nicolo Tebaldini. 1633. Con Licenzia di Superiori.

 4to (8½ × 6½). a+A—X in fours+2 ll. unsigned. a1ª Woodcut Title, verso blank. a2 Dedication. a3—a4ª Poems in honour of Mary, one signed by Rubert Bodius Scotus Doct., and another by Thomas Camerarius Scotus. a4ᵇ Priviledges. A—X (pp. 1-176) Text. 2 ll. unsigned Table.

 The title (*see Facsimile No. XVIII.*) is placed underneath a very curious emblematical picture of the Queen's execution, surmounted by the arms of Pope Urban VIII.

Class IX.   *B.M. S.*

229. The Abridgement or Svmmarie of the Scots Chronicles, with a short description of their originall, from the comming of Gathelus, their first Progenitour, out of Græcia into Egypt. And their comming into Portingall and Spaine . . . with a true Chronologie of all their Kings. Their Reignes, Deaths, and Burials, from Fergusius, the first King of Scotland, vntill his Royall Maiestie now happily raigning over all Great Britaine and Ireland, and all the Iles to them appertaining . . . . . Latelie corrected and augmented.

Edinbvrgh. Printed by I. W. for Iohn Wood. 1633.

 8vo (5½ × 3¾). A—Q in eights+R⁶, without pagination. A1 Title. Sybillae on verso. A2 Dedication to King James by John Monipennie. A3—R6 Text.

 See the 4to edition (No. 206).

Class XI.   *Adv. Signet. S.*

1635

230. Motivos Para Favorecer La Religion Catolica en la nacion Escocesa. Escritos por H. S.

 Folio (11¼ × 7½). 2 ll. without signature, pagination, date, or place of printing.

 This tract, printed in 1635, as may be gathered from the text, is written in favour of the Scottish Roman Catholics. It passes in review the principal events in the history of the country, inclusive of the death of Queen Mary. It very pointedly eulogises among Scottish historians, poets, jurists, and philosophers, George Buchanan, Adam Blackwood, Napier of Merchiston, John Barclay, the author of Argenis, and the Catholics Gordon, Hay, Crighton, Tyrie, &c.

 It further cites the names of two Scotsmen, Colonels Gordon and Lesley, who had in the preceding year performed prodigies of valour in the Low Countries.

Class XI.   *S.*

MARIA REGINA DI SCOTIA
POEMA HEROICO DEL P. PRIOR D. BASSIANO GATTI
MONACO DI S. GIROLAMO
ALLA SANTITA DI N.S. VRBANO VIII.

Edin. Bibl. Soc.—Queen Mary Literature. Facsimile No. XX. See No. 233, page 79.

1636

231. The Historie of the Life and Death of Mary Stuart Queene of Scotland.
London Printed by John Haviland, and are to be sold by William Sheares in Britaines Burse at the Signe of the Harrow. 1636.

12mo (5¾ × 3¾). A—X in twelves + Y⁶. Portrait, two Titles and Epistle Dedicatorie to King James VI. (signed W. Vdall) 3 ll. The Preface 6 ll. without pagination. Text pp. 1-493.

The above title is preceded by one within an engraved border (Will. Marshall sculpsit 1636) with frontispiece portrait of the Queen, and imprint: London Printed for Will: Sheares at the Signe of the Harrow in the New Exchange.

A reprint of the Folio printed in 1624 under the names of W. Strangvage and W. Udall (No. 215).

Class VII.   *S.*

1637

232. Delitiae Poetarvm Scotorvm hujus aevi illustrivm. [The Sphere with motto: Indefessus Agendo.]
Amsterdami Apud Johannem Blaev. CIƆ IƆ CXXXVII.

2 vols. 12mo (4½ × 2¾). Vol. I. pp. 1-699. Vol. II. pp. 1-573, and one leaf Catalogue, verso blank.

This collection, edited by Arthur Johnston, contains poems by Adamson, Anderson, Craig, and others, referring to Queen Mary. It is dedicated to John Scot of Scotstarvet. The privilege is signed by John [Adamson] Archbishop of St Andrews.

Class VI.   *Adv.*   *S.*

1639

233. Marie Stvard Reyne d'Ecosse Tragedie de Monsieur Regnavlt. [Printer's mark with the punning motto: Heureux qui naist ainsi.]
A Paris, chez Tovssainct Qvinet, au Palais, dans la petite Salle sous la montée de la Cour des Aydes. MDCXXXIX. Avec privilege dv Roy.

4to (8¾ × 6¾). [A—B?] + A—M in fours + N² (2 sheets are signed D). The printed Title is preceded by an engraved one (*see Facsimile No. XIX.*) A1ª Title, verso blank. A2—[B4] Dedication to Cardinal Richelieu, Sonnets, &c. A—N2ª, pp. 1-107, Text. N2ᵇ blank.

In the copy described the eight preliminary leaves are mounted, and the signatures are therefore uncertain.

Another edition was issued in the same year by the same printer, in 12mo (5 × 3), with a reduced copy of the engraved title (*see Facsimile No. XX.*)

Class IX.   *Adv.*   *S.*

1642

234. Roberti Johnstoni Scoto-Britanni Historiarvm Libri Duo. Continentes Rerum Britannicarum vicinarumque Regionum historias maximè memorabiles. Sunt praeter hos adhuc xx libri, qui Typographo nondum in manus venêre.
Amstelodami typis Judoci Broersz. Anno. CIƆIƆCXLII.

12mo (4¾ × 2¾). Title, Dedication to Charles I., &c. 12 ll. Book I. pp. 1-273. Book II. pp. 1-224.

Another edition—Amstelodami 1655. Folio. (See the English translation, No. 240.)

Class X   *Adv.*   *S.*

1643

235. Histoire de France depvis Faramond jusqv'a maintenant . . . Avec les Portraits au natvrel des Roys des Reynes & des Dauphins tirez de leurs Chartes Effigies, & autres anciens originaux ; ou de leurs veritables copies conseruées dans les plus curieux Cabinets de l'Europe. . . . Par F. G. dv Mezeray. A Paris chez Mathiev Gvillemot, ruë Sainct Jacques au coin de la ruë da la Parchuinerie. M.DC.XLIII. Avec Privilege dv Roy.

Folio (16½ × 11). 3 vols. The printed Title is preceded by an engraved one. The second vol. has an independent engraved title and sub-title, dated 1646. The third vol. a sub-title, dated 1651. The earliest notice of Queen Mary is in Vol. II., in the reign of Henri II., giving an account of her marriage to the Dauphin. In the same vol., in the reign of her husband, Francois II., passages describe her assumption of the Royal Arms of England on the death of Mary of England, and her subsequent renunciation of this position, and some attention is given to the French expedition into Scotland in 1543 and the general politics of the country, specially as to the rise of Protestantism. After the death of Francis, the author devotes a chapter to an abridged life of Mary until her death, which is accompanied by a very fine and pleasing engraved portrait, in the robes and crown of a Queen of France, in a circular frame, with the inscription, MARIA STVARTA REG. FRAN. ET SCOT FRANCISCI II. REGIS VXOR., and the motto, Nvnqvam nisi Rectam, in the corners. On shield below the portrait, Marie Stvart Espovse dv Roy François II., with the following verses underneath :—

> L'Avevgle passion d'vne Reyne puissante
> Fit passer celle-cy du Throne à l'Echafaut ;
> La coupable icy bas condamna l'innocente,
> Elle ne pût eviter la Justice d'enhaut.

Facsimiles are given of the obverse and reverse of all the medals and coins issued by Mary and Francis in France. One of these, assumed at the time of their marriage as a device, has two globes, separated by a naked sword pointed to the sky, covered by a crown with a double riband motto, Unus non sufficit orbis, intended to represent their possession of two kingdoms. There are two engravings of Francis—one as Dauphin, the other as King.

Class XI. *B.M.*

1644

236. The Historie of the Reformation of the Church of Scotland ; containing five Books : Together with some Treatises conducing to the History. Published by Authority. Jerem. 5. 1. 2 Cor. 13. 8.

London Printed by John Raworth, for George Thomason and Octavian Pullen, and are to be sold at the signe of the Rose in Pauls Church-Yard. M.DCXLIV.

Folio (11 × 7½). *+**+a—g in fours+h⁶ Prefatory matter. B—Lll in fours, pp. 1–460, History. Mmm—Cccc3, pp. 1–121, containing several of Knox's Sermons.

By John Knox, edited by D. B. [David Buchanan]. The first issued edition following the suppressed and incomplete one by Vautrollier of 1586-87. (See No. 130.)

This edition was reprinted in 4to, Edin. 1644.

Class X. *Adv. S.*

237. Adami Blacvodæi in Cvria Praesidiali Pictonvm et Vrbis in decurionum Collegio Regis Consiliarij Opera Omnia.

Parisiis, Apud Sebastianvm Cramoisy, Regis ac Regine Regentis Architypographum et Gabrielem Cramoisy viâ Iacobæâ, sub Ciconiis. M.DC.XLIV. Cum Priuilegio Regis Christianissimi.

 4to (8½ × 7). a+e+i+o+u+A—EEeee in fours. a1 Title, verso blank. a2 Elenchus operum. a3ᵃ blank. a3ᵇ Portrait of A. Blackwood by Joan. Picart. a4—u4 Life of Blackwood, Epitaph, &c. A—EEeee, pp. 1-735 Blackwood's works. Index. Last two ll. blank.

Class IV. VI. XI.   *Adv. S.*

238. The History of the Houses of Douglas and Angus. Written by Master David Hume of Godscroft.

 Edinburgh Printed by Evan Tyler, Printer to the Kings most Excellent Majestie. 1644.

 Folio (11½ × 7½). Title, blank on verso, and two unsigned leaves of preliminary matter + A—Lll in fours. A—B2 The Preface. B3—Lll3 (pp. 1-440) Text. Lll4 blank. Some copies have the dates 1643 and 1648 respectively in the two parts.

 Another edition with the title, A General History of Scotland, &c. London. Simon Miller 1657. Folio.

Class XI.   *Adv. Signet. S.*

1646

239. Maria Stuart of Gemartelde Majesteit. [Portrait of the Queen with emblem of united Thistle, Lily, and Rose, and motto: Myn harte kenner zit om hooghe].

 Te Kevlen in d'oude druckerye. 1646.

 4to (8 × 6). A—I in fours, without pagination, but with catchwords.

 This tragedy is the work of J. van den Vondel, who has been described as the Dutch Shakespeare. It is dedicated to the Prince Palatine, King of Bavaria, the husband of Princess Elizabeth, Queen Mary's granddaughter. At the end there is a Dutch translation of a portion of Camden's *Annals* regarding Queen Mary, and two Latin Epitaphs, one being that placed by King James on the Queen's tomb in Westminster Abbey.

 This tragedy is also to be found in collected editions of Van den Vondel's works. Amsterdam. 4to.

Class VI. IX. XI.   *S.*

240. The Historie of Scotland, during the Minority of King Iames. Written in Latine by Robert Johnston. Done into English by T. M.

 London by W. Wilson, for Abel Roper, &c. 1646.

 12mo (5½ × 3). Title and Introduction 6 ll. Text B—G in twelves, last leaf blank. Imprimatur Na: Brent Jan 5 1645 is on G11.

 This is the English translation of No. 234.

Class X.   *S.*

1647

241. Het Leeven van Maria Stuart Koninginne van Schotlant.

 Uyt verscheyde treslijke, soo Roomsche, als andere Schrijvers by een versamelt, door L. V. Bos.

 t'Amsterdam, Gedrukt by Jacob Lescaille. Voor Gerret van Thye Boeckverkooper in de Langebrugsteeg in de gekroonde Bybel, in't jaer 1647.

 4to (7¾ × 5½). A—I in fours. A1 Title, verso blank. A2 Voorereden aen den Leesin, signed L. V. Bos. A3—I4 Text, pp. 5-72. Pagination runs from title, with catchwords.

The author of this Life of Queen Mary, Lambert van den Bos, poet and historian, wrote also under the name of L. Sylvia Amstelodamensis, and in English as Lambert Wood, Gent. This name is sometimes found as Van den Bosch.

Class VII. *B.M.* *Edin. Univ.*

242. La Gallerie des Femmes Fortes. par le P. Pierre Le Moyne de la Compagnie de Iesus. A Paris, chez Antoine de Sommaville, au Palais en la Salle des Merciers, à l'Escu de France. MDCXLVII. Avec privilege du Roy.

Folio (15 × 10¼). Title (printed in red and black) and Prelim. 35 ll., with vowel signatures. A—Ddd in fours, Text (pp. 1-378). Poem and Table, 10 ll. unpaged.

Historie de Marie Stvart is at p. 351, with a large engraved portrait (Vigron inuenit, Mariette excud.) The Queen's execution is shown in the background, and a quotation from Thuanus is at the bottom. See the Elzevir Edition, 1660 (No. 262).

Class VII. *Adv.*

1648

243. The manifold Practises and Attempts of the Hamiltons, and particularly of the present Duke of Hamilton Now Generall of the Scottish Army to get the Crown of Scotland. Discovered in an intercepted Letter written from a Malignant here in London to his friend in Scotland. The letter is directed thus on the back :

For the much Honoured, 21. 53. 7. 10. 19. 72. 67. 40.

Printed at London, in the year 1648.

4to (7¼ × 5½). A—C in fours. A1 Title, verso blank. A—C4ª Text. C4ᵇ blank. Pp. 3-23 with catchwords.

This tract and No. 244 form, respectively, a virulent attack on the Hamilton family, and a defence of their position during the troublous times of the Revolution in 1648. Both tracts deal considerably in detail with the history of Queen Mary, especially in reference to her connection with the Hamilton family and its alleged pretensions to the Crown. They each contain curious passages in reference to many episodes of the Queen's history. Buchanan is named as the author of all the calumnies regarding the Queen "in his *Dialogus De Jure Regni apud Scotos*, his *Detectio* and *History*, as also by the charge which the Earls of Murray, Morton, and others gave in to Queen Elizabeth against Queen Mary, and as King James declares plainly in his *Basilikon Doron.*" A passage may be quoted from No. 244, p. 6, in reference to the murder of Darnley : "When the King was thus removed and so the Crown brought a degree nearer to the house of *Hamilton*, it seemed to them very probable (as it was indeed) that *Bothuel* should destroy the young king, and not suffer him to live to revenge his Father's death, and prejudge the children of *Bothuel* with the Queen in the succession to the Crown, and if the King were destroyed, they hoped that the Queen and *Bothuel* would be so hateful to the people for the murther of her husband and her sonne, that they would have easie accesse to the Crown, or otherwise that they might kil *Bothuel;* in which case they were in hope the Queen should marry John Hamilton the Duke's Sonne, whom she entertained, often with merry looks and chearful countenance. But the King being preserved and the Queen keeped in *Loch-Lern* by command of the Parliament, the Hamiltons took another course. . . ." This statement is replied to in No. 244, p. 5 : "And for his eldest son the Earl of Arran, he was known to be distracted, and died so without marriage, and the Lord *John* the second son, this Duke's Grand-father, never was a suitor to the Queen that I can read in any but this Pamphleter, though I cannot see, that it had been a crime in either to have been suitors, more than it was for the Lord *Darneley* to marry her."

A copy of this tract is in the Advocates' Library, but the reply, No. 244, does not appear to find a place there.

Class XI. *Adv. S.*

244. The Lyer laid open in a Letter, first Written to a Friend in the Country, at his desire, for his private satisfaction, and now Printed for the Publick, Touching a late Pamphlet, intituled, The Manifold Practises and Attempts of the Hamiltons: And Particularly, of the present Duke of Hamilton, (Now Generall of the Scottish Army) to get the Crown of Scotland.
London, Printed in the Yeer, 1648.

  4to ($7\frac{1}{4} \times 5\frac{1}{2}$). A—B in fours. A1 Title, verso blank. A2—B4 Text, pp. 3-16, with catchwords. See No. 243.

Class XI.   *S.*

245. Historia di Maria Stvarda Regina di Francia, e di Scotia. Nel P. Nicolò Causino della Compagnia di Giesù. Portata dal Francese nell' Italiano dal P. Carlo Antonio Berardi dell' istessa Compagnia.
In Bologna, MDCXLVIII. per Carlo Zenero. Con licenza de' Superiori.

  12mo ($5\frac{1}{4} \times 3\frac{3}{4}$). A—G in twelves + II⁵. Text, pages 9-173, and five pages of table. A4 should probably contain a Dedication, but it does not occur in the copy from which the collation is taken. On recto of leaf preceding title is a short title, Historia di Maria Stvarda Regina de Francia, e di Scotia.
  This is a translation of the Life of Mary in Nicholas Causin's La Cour Sainte.

Class VII.   *S.*

1649

246. Jacob van Oorts Stuarts Ongeluckige Heerschappye, ofte Kort verhael van alle d'ongelucken en rampsaligheden het Doorluchtigh Huys van Stuart over-komen, sints Robbert, d'eerste uyt desen Huyse, Koningh van Schotlandt, &c., &c.
Tot Dordrecht, voor Abraham Andriessz: Boeck-verkooper. A°. 1649.

  8vo (6 × 4). *+A—N in eights+O⁴. *1-8 Title and prefatory matter. A—M6ᵃ Text, &c., pp. 1-187. M6ᵇ—O4ᵇ Table, &c., without pagination.
  Contains a portrait of Queen Mary, after De Leu.

Class VII.   *Adv. S.*

1650

247. Historia di Maria Stvarda Regina di Francia, e di Scotia. del Padre Nicolo Cavsino della Compagnia de Giesù. Portata del Francese nell' Italiano Dal Padre Carlo Antonio Berardi dell' istessa Compagnia. Consacrata all' Illustriss. & Excellentiss. Signora Moresina Moresini Minio. [Printer's Mark, a crown, sword, and sceptre.]
In Venetia per Domen. Lovisa à Rialto, in Ruga d'Oresi sotto il Portico. Con licenza de' Superiori.

  12mo ($5\frac{1}{4} \times 3\frac{1}{4}$). A—E in twelves. Title and one leaf of dedication. Historia, pp. 5-120.
  The British Museum Catalogue suggests 1650 as year of publication. See Bologna edition of 1648. (No. 245.)

Class VII.   *B.M.*

1651

248. A Detection of the Actions of Mary Queen of Scots, concerning the Murder of her Husband, and her Conspiracie, Adulterie, and pretended Marriage with the Earl

Bothwel. And a Defence of the true Lords maintainers of the Kings Maiesties Action and Authoritie. Written in Latine by G. Buchanan. Translated into Scotch. And now made English [A Thistle]. Printed in the year 1651.

12mo (5½ × 3). A—E in twelves + F⁹. A1ᵇ Frontispiece Portrait of Queen Mary. A2ᵃ Title, verso blank. A3—F9ᵃ Text, pp. 1-133. F9ᵇ The address, Now judge Englishmen if it be good to change Queens, &c.

The frontispiece portrait is of a rare form not noticed elsewhere. The Queen holds a Crucifix in her right hand. It is flanked by the crowned Royal Arms of the four kingdoms, with the legend, Maria Scot. Gal. Angl. Iber. Regina. Although included in the title, the book, when complete, does not contain A Defence of the Lords, &c.

This is the first edition of the English translation, which was reprinted in 1689 (No. 283).

Class IV.   *S.*

1652

249. The Divine Catastrophe of the Kingly Family of the House of Stuarts: or a short History of the Rise, Reign, and Ruine Thereof. Wherein the most secret and Chamber-abominations of the two last Kings are discovered, Divine Justice in King Charles his overthrow vindicated, and the Parliaments proceedings against him clearly justified, By Sir Edward Peyton Knight and Baronet, a diligent observer of Those Times.

London, Printed for Giles Calvert, at the black Spread-Eagle at the West-end of Pauls. 1652.

8vo (5½ × 3½). A⁴ + B—K in eights + L⁴. A1 blank, A2 Title, verso blank. A3—A4 To the Supreme Authoritie of this Nation, Assembled in this present Parliament. B—L3 Text, pp. 1-149, with catchwords; pp. 143-144 are omitted. L4 blank.

This scandalous libel, containing probably more false statements than any other contemporary book, includes a so-called sketch of Queen Mary's history. It is a tissue of falsehood from beginning to end. The work was printed in Sir Anthony Weldon's Court and Character of King James, written and taken by Sir A. W., being an Eye and Eare Witness. London, 1650, 12mo; an equally villanous book. For this reason the authorship of this work has been attributed to Weldon. It was again reprinted in 1731, London, 8vo, but the impression was seized and the printer arrested, by order of the Government.

Class XI.   *Adv. Signet. S.*

250. Compendi Historici del Conte Alfonso Loschi Vicentino Academico Insensato, Olimpico, e Risiorito, il Riacceso. Consacrato alla Maesta' Christianissima da Lvigi Qvartodecimo Re di Francia, e di Navarra.

In Venetia MDCLII. Appresso Gio: Pietri Pinelli. Con licenza de' Svperiori, et Privileggio.

Folio (13 × 9). a1 Title, verso blank. a2 Dedication. a3-4 Preliminary matter. Genealogical Table one folding leaf, engraved. A—Kk (pp. 1-360) Text, 4 ll. Index, &c. Table of errata. The book contains 14 engraved Genealogical tables.

The portion regarding Queen Mary is found at pp. 217-233.

There is another edition: Bologna, 1654, 4to, in Advocates' Library.

Class XI.   *S.*

1655] 85

251. Het Vorstelyck Treur-Toonneel, of Op-en Onder-gangh der Grooten. Begrypende omtrent hondert jaren, van 1500. tot 1600. toe.
Uyt verscheyde Schryvers en Talen versamelt, Door L. v. Bos.
Geçiert met kunstige Afbeeldingen der voornaemste persoonen, seer konstigh naer 't leven en koper ghesneden.
't Amsterdam, By Nicolaes van Ravesteyn op S. Anthonis Marckt 1652.

> 8vo (5¾ × 3¾). ⁂ 1-8 Engraved Frontispiece with short Title on shield, and 7 ll. of Preliminary matter and Table. A—Fff in eights + Ggg⁴, last blank, Text (pp. 1-838), and 18 portraits. At p. 745 (Treatise No. 48) Hendrich en Maria Stuart Konninge en Koningen van Schotland, with an engraving of Queen Mary after De Leu. The history is drawn from De Thou.

Class X. *S.*

1655

252. The Compleat Ambassador: or two Treaties of the intended marriage of Qu: Elizabeth of glorious memory; comprised in Letters of negotiation of Sir Francis Walsingham, her Resident in France. Together with the answers of the Lord Burleigh, the Earl of Leicester, Sir Tho: Smith and others . . . Faithfully Collected by the truly Honourable Sir Dudly Digges Knight, late Master of the Rolls.
London: Printed by Tho. Newcomb, for Gabriel Bodell &c. 1655.

> Folio (12½ × 7¾). Engraved Frontispiece of Queen Elizabeth on her Throne, supported by Lord Burleigh and Sir Francis Walsingham. Title, verso blank. To the Reader, two leaves unsigned. a1-4 A Table of all the Letters contained in this book. B—Iii in fours + Kkk², pp. 1-441, Text. Table 3 ll.
> Queen Mary is referred to very frequently throughout the correspondence and in the Preface.

Class XI. *Adv. Signet. S.*

253. The History of Scotland from the year 1423 until the year 1542. containing the Lives and Reigns of James the I. the II. the III. the IV. the V. with several Memorials of State during the Reigns of James VI. & Charls I. By William Drummond of Hauthornden. With a prefatory Introduction by Mr Hall of Grays-Inn.
London by Henry Hills for Rich. Tomlins and himself, and are to be sold at their houses near Py-Corner. MDCLV.

> Folio (10¾ × 7). Title, verso blank. Preface 9 ll. irregularly signed. B—I'p in fours. Text: pp. 1-292, and 1 leaf blank. Portraits by Gaywood of the author and the five Jameses.
> At the end are familiar epistles, among which is one to Ben Johnson regarding Queen Mary.
> The more common edition of this book is the second, 1684, 8vo (*Adv.*)

Class X. *S.*

254. The History of the Church of Scotland Beginning the year of our Lord 203, and continued to the end of the Reign of King James the VI. of ever blessed memory. Wherein are described The Progress of Christianity The Perfections and interruptions of it; The Foundations of Churches . . . The Reformation of Religion and the frequent Disturbances of that Nation by Wars, Conspiracies Tumults Schism. Together with great variety of other matters Written both Ecclesiasticall and Politicall by that Grave and Reverend Prelate, and wice Churchman John Spotswood Lord

Archbishop of St Andrews and Privy Counsellor to King Charles I. that most Religious and blessed Prince. . . .
London, Printed by J. Flesher for R. Royston at the Angel in Ivie-lane. M.DC.LV.

Folio (12½ × 7¾). A—Bbb in sixes + pp. 1-54 unsigned. A1ᵃ blank. A1ᵇ Frontispiece, portrait of Spotswood, W. Hollar fecit. A2ᵃ Title, verso blank. A3—A4 Introduction and author's life. A5—A6 Portrait of Charles I. and the author's dedication to him. B—Bbb Text. Pp. 1-54 Index.
The life of Queen Mary is dealt with in great detail. The book was reprinted thrice during the seventeenth century, and afterwards by the Bannatyne Club and the Spottiswoode Society.
The British Museum copy belonged to Charles II.

Class X.   *B.M.*

1656

255. A compleat History of the Lives and Reigns of Mary Queen of Scotland and of her Son & Successor, James the Sixth, King of Scotland; And (after Queen Elizabeth) King of Great Britain, France, and Ireland, The First, (of ever blessed memory). Reconciling several opinions In Testimony of Her, and confuting others, in vindication of Him, against two scandalous Authors; I The Court and Character of King James II The History of Great Britain &c. &c.
Faithfully performed By William Sanderson, Esq.
London Printed for Humphrey Moseley &c., and are to be sold in Pauls Church-yard, at Py Corner and on Lud-Gate-Hill. MDCLVI.

Folio (10¾ × 7). A⁴ + a⁴ + b² + B—Iiii in fours + Kkkk². A1 Title, verso blank. A2—62 Proeme, Index, &c. to the first part. B—Nn2, pp. 1-262, Text. Nn3 Title: The Reigne and Death of King James of Great Brittain, France and Ireland, the First &c. The Second Part. London, Printed by Henry Hills, 1655; followed by six leaves containing the Proeme, Index, &c., to the second part. N4—Kkkk1 Text. Kkkk2 blank. A portrait of Queen Mary faces the first title, and one of King James that of the second part.

Class X.   *Adv. Signet. S.*

256. Observations upon some particular Persons and Passages, in a Book lately made publick; intituled, A Compleat History of the Lives and Reignes of Mary Queen of Scotland, and of Her Son James, The Sixth of Scotland, and the First of England, France and Ireland.
Written by a Lover of the Truth.
              Mat. 7. 5. First cast out the beam . . .
              Ecclus. 4. 25-26. In no wise speak against the truth . . .
London, Printed by Ga. Bedell and Tho. Collins at the middle-Temple Gate, Fleet Street, 1656.

4to (7¾ × 5¾). Title on unsigned leaf, verso blank. A—C in fours. Text, pp. 1-21.
The author was Carew Raleigh, son of Sir Walter Raleigh.
The portion of this book which refers to Queen Mary is at p. 4. It regards the allegation that Queen Elizabeth wished to have Queen Mary poisoned by Paulet and Drury. Raleigh affirms that this is a scandal on that excellent Princess. He says that Queen Mary's death proceeded from the Scots themselves, and quotes Lord Gray's speech: [Mor]tua non mordet.

Class IV.   *Adv.*

257. An Answer to a Scurrilous Pamplet, Intitvled, Observations upon a Compleat History of the Lives and Reignes of Mary Queen of Scotland and of her son King James, of Great Britain, France and Ireland the Sixth. The Libeller without a name set out by G. Bedell and T. Collins two Booksellers: But the History Vindicated by the Author William Sanderson Esq.

London, Printed for the Author, and are to be sold by George Sawbridge and Richard Tomlin. 1656.

4to (7¼ × 5¼). Title, verso blank. A—D in fours. a1 To the Reader. A2—D Text, with catchwords, but without pagination.

Sanderson reaffirms his position in reply to Raleigh. He says, "all authors herein, English, Scotish, Latine, French, Spanish, do intimate a cunning unwilling willingness in Queen Elizabeth, to stain her honour in the blood of the Queen of Scots, her kinswoman and next to succeed to this crown; and desirous to be rid of her one way or another she treats with Davison, out and in what to do."

Class IV. *Adv.*

1657

258. Historical Collections of Ecclesiastick Affairs in Scotland and Politick related to them, Including the Murder of the Cardinal of St Andrews, And the beheading of their Queen Mary in England. By Ri. Watson. Sanguis sanguinem tetigit. Hosea Chap. 4. ver. 2. By swearing, and lying, and killing, and stealing, and committing adultery they break out, And bloud toucheth bloud.

London, Printed by G. D. for John Garfield, and are to be sold at his Shop at the sign of the Rolling-Presse for Pictures, near the Royal Exchange in Cornhill over against Popes-head-alley. 1657.

8vo (5⅞ × 3⅞). A—O in eights + P⁴. A1 blank. A2 Title, verso blank. A3—8 Dedication. B—P3 Text, pp. 1-210. P4 List of books sold by Garfield.

Class VII. *Adv. Signet. S.*

1658

259. Historical Memoires on the Reigns of Queen Elizabeth, and King James.

London: Printed by J. Grismond, and are to be sold by T. Robinson Bookseller in Oxon. 1658.

12mo (5⅞ × 3¼). A—M in twelves + N⁴. A1 Frontispiece Portrait of Queen Elizabeth. A2 Title, verso blank. A3—5 The Epistle. A6 Separate Title for the Memoirs of Queen Elizabeth. A7—12 To the Reader, &c. B1—F6 Text pp. 1-108. F7—N6 (with a frontispiece portrait of James), Traditionall Memoyres on the Raigne of King James. It was reprinted with an introduction and notes by Sir Walter Scott.

This book is by Francis Osborne. Secret History of the Court of James I., Edin., 8vo, 2 vols., 1811.

Class XI. *Adv. S.*

1659

260. Examen Historicum: Or a Discovery and Examination of the Mistakes, Falsities, & Defects in some Modern Histories. Occasioned by the Partiality and Inadvertencies of their severall Authours. In two Books. Tacit. in vit. Iul. Agric. & Horat. de Arte Poet. &c.

London, printed for Henry Seile and Richard Royston, and are to be sold over against S. Dunstans Church in Fleetstreet, and at the Angel in Ivy-Lane 1659.

8vo (7¼ × 4½). Part I., with separate Title, is an examination of Thomas Fuller's Church History of Britain. Part II., with separate Title, contains (pp. 1-202) some Advertisements on these following Histories:—
1. The compleat History of Mary Queen of Scots & of her Son & successor, King James the Sixth.
2. The History of the Reign & death of King James of Great Britain, France & Ireland, the first.
3. The compleat History of the Life & Reign of King Charls, from his cradle to his Grave.

This is followed by An Appendix to the Advertisements on Mr Sanderson's Histories in answer to some Passages in a scurrulous Pamphlet called A 'Post-Haste, A reply, &c. Ovid Metam. Lib. I. The pagination of this portion continues to p. 208, but is followed by eleven leaves without numbers.

The author of this work is Peter Heylin.

Class XI. S.

1660

261. Les Memoires de Messire Michel de Castelnav, Seignevr de Mavvissiere. Illustrez et avgmentez de plvsievrs Commentaires & Manuscrits, tant Lettres Instructions Traittez qu' autres Pieces Secrettes & Originalles seruants à donner la verité de l'Histoire des Regnes de François II. Charles IX. & Henry III. & de la Regence & du Gouuernement de Catherine de Medicis, &c. &c. Par J. Le Labovrevr. Conseiller et Aumosnier du Roy, Prieur de Juvigné. [Lamy's Printer's Mark.]

A Paris chez Pierre Lamy, au Palais, au second Pillier de la Grande Salle, au Grand Cesar. MDC.LX. Avec Privilege dv Roy.

Folio (16 × 10), 2 vols. Vol. I. Title, verso blank. Very beautiful engraved portrait of Mareschal Le Marquis de Castelnau (Nanteiul ad viu. faciebat 1658). Dedication of Le Laboureur and Preface 7 ll. Engraved Portrait of Michel de Castelnau (De la Roussiere delin. et sculp.) Life of M. de Castelnau, &c., with privilege on verso of last leaf. Livre I.-VII. of Memoirs pp. 1-269. Additions de Le Laboureur pp. 275-907. Table 5 ll. Vol. II. Repetition of Title and of Marquis de Castelnau's Portrait. Additions of Le Laboureur pp. 1-909. Genealogies de plusieurs maisons allices à celle de Castelnau 1 leaf and pp. 1-125. Table 6 ll.

In addition to the History of Queen Mary in the Memoirs, Le Laboureur devotes large attention to her life in his Additions.

Class VII. XI. S.

262. La Gallerie des Femmes Fortes par le P. Pierre Le Moyne de la Compagnie de Jesvs.

A Leiden chez Jean Elsevier, et A Paris chez Charles Angot ruë St Jacques. M.DC.LX. Auec Priuilege du Roy.

12mo (5⅛ × 3). * + ** + *** + A—T in twelves + V¹⁹. Engraved Title, Title, Dedication, Preface, &c. Text pp. 1-452, followed by Table. Each Life is accompanied by a Portrait. That of Queen Mary is of an unusual type. There is a distant view of the Execution in the background. Underneath are the words, Marie Stuart Augustus Thuanus Lib. 86.

There are several re-impressions of this edition dated from Paris.

Class VII. S.

1664

263. La Covr Sainte dv R. Pere Nicolas Cavssin de la Compagnie de Iesvs mise en vn bel ordre, avec vne notable augmentation des Vies des Personnes Illustres de la Cour tant du vieil que du nouueau Testament. Et avgmentée en cette derniere Edition de la vie de l'Autheur, & de diverses Histoires.

A Paris chez Denis Bechet, Rue Saint Jacques, au Compas d'Or et à l'Escu au Soleil. MDCLXIIII. Avec privilege, et approbation.

Folio (15 × 9½). 2 vols. Volume I., with Portrait of the Author, pp. 1-558. Volume II., pp. 1-607. The Life of Queen Mary, with a Portrait, pp. 287-317.

Class VII. *Adv.*

1669

264. Propugnaculum Catholicae Veritatis, Libris X. Constrvctvm, in duásque Partes divisum. Pars Prima Historica in quinque libros secta. Opus plane novum, utile lectuque perjucundum, (ut ex sequenti rerum contentarum brevi Elencho colligere fas est) In gratiam veritatis indagatorum, ac confusionem in malo obstinatorum, nunc primò editum, & in lucem publicatum, Authore R. P. F. Antonio Brvodino, Tuomoniensi Hiberno, Ordin: Minor: Strict: Observ: Reform: Lectore jubilato; Almae Provinciae Bohemiae Definitore habituali, nec non Conventús Pragensûs B. V. ad Nives Actuali Guardiano.

Pragae, Typis Universitatis Carolo-Ferdinandeae, in Collegio Societ: Jesu ad S. Clementem. Anno M.DC.LXIX.

4to (7½ × 5¾). Title, dedication, indices, and errata 40 ll. Text pp. 1-1100. Index 6 ll. Chapters XV-XIX of Book III. are devoted to a History of Heresy in Scotland, the events of Queen Mary's reign, and her personal history. The Summary of Chapter XV. begins thus:—Gallicus morbus Scotos infecit, mortuô Rege.

Class IV. *Signet.*

1675

265. Marie Stvart Reyne d'Escosse. Nouvelle Historique.

A Paris chez Louis Billaine, au second Pillier de la grande Salle du Palais, au Grand Cesar. 1675. Avec Privilege dv Roy.

12mo (6 × 3¾). In 3 parts, each having separate sign. and pagination.

The authorship is attributed to Pierre le Pesant Sieur De Boisguilbert, Lieutenant-General au Baillage de Rouen.

Class VII. *Adv. S.*

266. Joannis Bisselii è Societate Jesu, Aetatis nostrae gestorum eminentium Medulla Historica. Septennium II. ab Anno M.DC.VIII usque ad Annum M.DC.XIV.

Ambergae apud Joannem Burger 1675.

8vo (6¼ × 5¾). Medulla, 2 Titles, pp. 1-511, and a Portrait of Q. Mary at p. 465. Appendix and Title, &c., pp. 1-362, and a Portrait of Queen Mary at p. 248.

Preceding the above title is an engraved one with vignette emblems referring to the persons treated of in the book. One of these represents the head of Queen Mary on a charger, with the inscription, Maria Stuarta R. Sc. Following this book, as an appendix, is:—Mariæ Stuartæ Viventis ; ac Morientis Acta. Ambergae apud Joannem Burgen 1675.

The removal of the Queen's remains to Westminster by King James in 1614 called forth this Treatise.

Class XI.   *Signet. S.*

267.   De Origine Moribus & rebus gestis Scotorum, &c., &c. Authore Joanne Leslæo Episcopo Rossense : Romæ 1578. Nunc denuo recens. Anno Domini 1675.

4to (7½ × 6). A—Iiii in fours. Pp. 1–453. List of Kings and Index.

This Edition does not contain the Map of Scotland ; and the portraits of the Kings and Queen Mary are of inferior execution to those of the first Edition (No. 100). The Portrait of King Donald I. is printed upside down.

Class X.   *Adv. S.*

1677

268.   The History of the Church and State of Scotland, Beginning the Year of our Lord 203, and continued to the end of the Reign of King James the VI. of ever blessed Memory. In seven Books, Wherein are described, The Progress of Christianity, The Persecutions and Interruptions of it, The Foundation of Churches, The Erecting of Bishopricks, The Building and Endowing Monasteries and other Religious Places, The Succession of Bishops in their Sees, The Reformation of Religion, And the frequent Disturbances of that Nation by Wars, Conspiracies, Tumults, Schisms. . . . Written by that Grave and Reverend Prelate and wise Counsellor. J. Spotswood Lord Archbishop of S. Andrews, and Privy Counsellor to King Charles the First, that most Religious and Blessed Prince and Martyr. . . . The Fourth Edition corrected, whereunto is added a Large Appendix.

London Printed for R. Royston, Bookseller to his Most Sacred Majesty. MDCLXXVII.

Folio (12½ × 8). A + a + B—Zz in sixes + Aaa⁴ + Bbb⁴ + Ccc² + A—G in fours. A1 Portrait of Spottiswood. A2 Title, verso blank. A3—a6 Preliminary. B—Aaa⁴ Text. Bbb1—Ccc2 Table, &c. A1—G4 Appendix. Portrait of King Charles I. (See No. 254.)

Class X.   *Adv.*

1678

269.   The True History of the Church of Scotland from the beginning of the Reformation, unto the end of the Reigne of King James VI. Wherein besides some touches of the Civil state and Alteration of Affaires, in their due order ; there is not only a series of the Assemblies. . . . Written by that learned and laborious Servant of Christ Mr David Calderwood. At the Appointment of the General Assembly, by whom his labours herein were several times revised and examined, and at length approved for the Press.

Printed in the year M.DC.LXXVIII.

Folio (11¾ × 6¼). Title, verso blank, and 2 ll. of Address to the Reader. Text, pp. 1–838. Errata and Index, 8 ll. Printed in Holland.

The Wodrow Society published, under the editorship of the Rev. Thomas Thomson, a new edition of Calderwood's History, drawn from the author's MSS. preserved in the British Museum. Edinburgh, 8 vols. 8vo.

Class X.   *B.M. Adv. Signet.*

270. The Holy Court in Five Tomes. The First treating of motives, which should excite men of Quality to Christian Perfection : The Second of the Prelate, Souldier, Statesman and Lady: The Third of Maxims of Christianity against Prophaness, Divided into Three Parts, viz. Divinity, Government of this Life, and State of the other World : . . . The Fifth containing the Lives of the most Famous and Illustrious Courtiers ; taken both out of the Old and New Testament, and other Modern Authors. Written in French by Nicholas Caussin, Translated into English by Sir T. H. and others. The Fourth Edition.

London printed for John Williams Bookseller at the Crowne in St Pauls Churchyard. 1678.

> Folio (14⅞ × 8⅞). An engraved short Title, followed by the above printed one. 12 ll. Titles and preliminaries. Text pp. 1–855. Table 7 ll.
> The Life of Queen Mary, preceded by a portrait, is at pp. 811–835.
> The preceding editions of the English version of La Cour Sainte did not include the Life of Queen Mary. The Translation is dedicated to Queen Henrietta Maria, and the copy from which the collation is taken was formerly in the possession of King Charles I., and has his cypher and crown impressed on the binding.

Class VII.   *S.*

1680

271. The True History of the Church of Scotland. From the beginning of the Reformation Unto the end of the Reign of King James VI. beginning 1560 and ending 1625. By Mr David Calderwood Author of Altare Damascenum.

Printed in the year 1680.

> Folio (12 × 7½). Title, verso blank. Letter to the Reader, 3 ll. Text, pp. 1–838. Errata, p. 839. Printed in Holland.
> Another edition was issued in 1704. Folio. (See No. 269.)

Class X.   *B.M.*

272. Q. D. V. B. Causas Amissæ Majestatis odium & Contemptum Mariæ Stuartæ, Scotorum olim Reginæ. In congressu disputantium exponent, Præses M. Gaspar Henricus Graun, Strignicens. Misn. & Respondens Cornelius Henricus Lindnerus Lommaciens. Misn. D. XIII. Octobr. Anno MDCLXXX. H. L. Q. S.

Wittenbergæ Imprimebat Mathæus Henchelius. Acad. Typogr.

> 4to (7¾ × 6). A—B in fours, without pagination.

Class IV.   *S.*

273. De Jure Regni apud Scotos. or a Dialogue, concerning the due Privilege of Government in the Kingdom of Scotland, Betwixt George Buchanan and Thomas Maitland, by the said George Buchanan, and translated out of the Original Latine into English. By Philalethes.

Printed in the year 1680.

> 12mo (5¼ × 4). A—F in twelves. A1 Title, verso blank. A2–3 The Translator to the Reader. A4–5 Epistle to the King. A6—F12 A dialogue, &c., pp. 1–134.

Class IV.   *Adv. S.*

1681

274. A Brief Account of His Sacred Majestie's Descent In a true Line Male, From King Ethodius the First, who began to Reign Anno Christi, 162. Written in a Letter to a Friend, Anno 1681. Sæpè tibi Pater est, sæpè legendus avus. [A crowned Thistle.]
Edinburgh, Printed by the Heirs of Andrew Anderson, Printer to His most Sacred Majesty, Anno Dom. M.DC.LXXXI.

Folio (12 × 7). A—I in twos. A1^a Title. A1^b The Printer to the Reader, and errata. A2—H1 Text. H2—I2^a Latin verses. I2^b blank.
The line of descent is worked out through Lord Darnley. Queen Mary and Darnley are the subjects of some of the Latin verses.

Class VI. XI.   *Adv. S.*

275. A brief History of the Life of Mary Queen of Scots, and the Occasions that brought Her, and Thomas Duke of Norfolk, to their Tragical Ends. Shewing the hopes the Papists then had of a Popish Successor in England ; and their Plots to accomplish them. With a full account of the Tryals of that Queen, and the said Duke. As also the Trial of Philip Howard, Earl of Arundel. From the Papers of a Secretary of Sir Francis Walsingham. Now published by a Person of Quality.
London Printed for Tho. Cockerill at the sign of the Three Legs in the Poultrey over against the Stocks-Market. 1681.

Folio (12 × 8). Title, verso blank. A—S in twos, pp. 1–67.
The Secretary was William Walsingham, brother of Sir Francis.

Class VI.   *S.*

1682

276. La Reggia delle Vedove Sacre del Padre Maestro Girolamo Ercolani Padovano de' Predicatori. Diuisa in due Parti. Consacrata all Ill. & Ecc. Sig La Signora Principessa D. Teresa Pamfili Cybo Principessa di Carrara, &c.
In Bologna M.DC.LXXXII, per Gioseffo Longhi.

8vo (6½ × 4¼). 2 vols., 562 and 583 pp. respectively.
The above title is preceded by another short one within an elaborate woodcut border.
The History of Queen Mary is to be found in Vol. II., pp. 289–417. It is prefaced by a curious woodcut representing the Execution of the Queen, who is on the scaffold bearing a crucifix and rosary, accompanied by two female attendants and the executioner. The text is drawn principally from Camden.

Class XI.   *S.*

1683

277. Memoires of the Family of the Stuarts, and the Remarkable Providences of God towards them ; In An Historical Account of the Lives of those His Majesty's Progenitors of that Name, that were Kings of Scotland.

Fallitur egregio quisquis sub principe credit
Servitium : Nusquam libertas gratior extat
Quam sub rege pio . . . Claudianus.

London, Printed by J. Wallis for Walter Kettleby, at the Bishops-Head in St Pauls Church-yard, 1683.

> 8vo (7½ × 4½). A⁴+b⁴+B—M in eights. A1 Blank. A2ᵃ Title, verso blank. A3—b4 Preface. B—M8ᵃ Text, pp. 1-185. M8ᵇ blank. The Life of Queen Mary is at pp. 117-185.
> The author was John Watson, M.A., a Scotsman, in his youth "a preacher" in the Canongate, Edinburgh, and afterwards Rector of Kirby-Cave, in Norfolk. He died suddenly on returning there from London, whither he had proceeded to congratulate Charles II. on his restoration.

Class XI.   *Adv. S.*

278.   The Memoirs of Sir James Melvil of Hal-hill: containing An Impartial Account of the most remarkable Affairs of State during the last Age, not mention'd by other Historians: more particularly Relating to the Kingdoms of England and Scotland, under the Reigns of Queen Elizabeth, Mary Queen of Scots, and King James. In all which Transactions the Author was Personally and Publickly concern'd. Now published from the Original Manuscript. By George Scott, Gent.

London, Printed by E. H. for Robert Boulter at the Turks-Head in Cornhill, against the Royal-Exchange, 1683.

> Folio (12 × 7¼). a—b+B—Gg in fours. a1—b4 Title and prefatory matter. B—Gg Text (pp. 1-204) and 14 ll. of Table, without pagination.
> These Memoirs were again edited by Mr Thomas Thomson for the Bannatyne Club, Edinburgh, 1827, 4to, and for the Maitland Club, Edinburgh, 1833, 4to.

Class X.   *Adv. S.*

1684

279.   The Island Queens: Or, the Death of Mary, Queen of Scotland, a Tragedy. Publish'd only in Defence of the Author and the Play, against some mistaken Censures, occasion'd by its being prohibited the Stage. Vis Consili expers mole ruit sua &c. Horace Lib. 3 Ode 3. By Jo. Banks.

London Printed for R. Bentley, in Russel Street, in Covent Garden, 1684.

> 4to (8½ × 6½). Title, verso blank + A² + B—K in fours. A1-2 Dedication to the Dutchess of Norfolk. B—K3 Text. K4 blank.
> The dedication is curious, showing that the Play was not allowed to be acted. It was reprinted in 1704 under the title of The Albion Queens.

Class IX.   *S.*

1685

280.   Medulla Historiæ Scoticæ. Being a Comprehensive History of the Lives and Reigns of the Kings of Scotland, from Fergus the first, to our Gracious Sovereign Charles the Second. Containing the most remarkable Transactions . . . To which is added A breif account of the Present State of Scotland, the Names of the Nobility, and Principal Ministers of Church and State, the Laws Criminal: A description of that Engine with which Malefactors are Tortured, called the Boot.

London, Printed for Randal Taylor, near Stationers Hall, 1685.

> 12mo (6 × 3½). Frontispiece, portrait of James Duke of York (James II.) Title, verso blank. Dedication, signed W. A. (William Alexander), 1 leaf. Preliminary 4 ll. List of Kings 1 leaf. Text, pp. 233.
> Queen Mary's Reign is entered as that of Henry Stewart and Mary Stewart.

Class XI.   *Adv. (Imperfect). S.*

1686

281. Teatro de Perepezie Poema Eroico Descritto dal P. Abbate D. Angelo Maria Lenti Ascolano, della Congregazione Oliuetana. Nella trauagliosa vita, e lagrimeuol morte di Maria Stuarda, Regina di Francia, e di Scozia. Dedicato con profondissimo ossequio al Merito segnalato Dell' Eminentiss. e Reuerendiss. Signor Cardinale D. Benedetto Pamfilii. [A rude but curious woodcut of Europa and the Bull.]
 In Napoli, per Carlo Porsile 1686.
> 8vo (6¼ × 4). A—Z in eights. Preliminary matter 8 ll. Text, pp. 15-366 and one leaf of errata. A woodcut frontispiece with a very curious but fanciful drawing of the Queen's Execution and a portrait of Cardinal Pamphili.
> The facts of the History are drawn from Causin and Sanderson.

Class IX. *S.*

282. The History of the Church of Peterburgh: wherein the most remarkable Things concerning that Place, from the First Foundation thereof: With other Passages of History, not unworthy Publick View, are represented. By Symon Gunton, late Prebendary of that Church. Illustrated with Sculptures. And set forth by Symon Patrick, D.D. now Dean of the same.
 London Printed for Richard Chiswell, at the Rose and Crown in S. Paul's Church-Yard, MDCLXXXVI.
> Folio (14 × 8¾). First leaf, recto blank, verso Imprimatur. Engraved Frontispiece. Title, verso blank, and Preface 2 ll. B—Uu in fours Xx⁶, Text, pp. 1-348.
> The account of the Execution and Funeral of Queen Mary, at which Richard Howland, Dean of Peterburgh, officiated, is at pp. 73-81.
> It is reprinted in Pitcairn's Collections relative to the Funerals of Mary Queen of Scots. Edinburgh, 1804, 8vo.

Class XI. *Adv. S.*

1689

283. A Detection of the Actions of Mary Queen of Scots, concerning the Murther of Her Husband, and her Conspiracy, Adultery, & pretended Marriage with the Earl Bothwel. And a Defence of the True Lords, Maintainers of the King's Majesties Action and Authority. Written in Latin by G. Buchanan. Translated into Scotch. And now made English.
 London, Printed, and are to be sold by Richard Janeway, on Queen's Head-Ally, near Pater Noster Row. 1689.
> 4to (8 × 5¾). *²+B—K in fours+L². Title and Prefatory 2 ll. Text, pp. 1-76.

Class IV. *Adv. S.*

284. De Jure Regni apud Scotos. or, a Dialogue, concerning the due Priviledge of Government in the Kingdom of Scotland. Betwixt George Buchanan and Thomas Maitland, by the said George Buchanan. Translated out of the Original Latine into English. by Philalethes.
 London, Printed for Richard Baldwin. 1689.
> 4to (8 × 5¾). A²+B—K in fours. Title and 2 ll. Prefatory. Text, pp. 1-70.

Class IV. *Adv. S.*

1690

285. Allegations In behalf of the High and Mighty Princess the Lady Mary, now Queen of Scots, against the Opinions and Books set forth in the Part and Favour of the Lady Katherine and the rest of the Issues of the French Queen touching the Succession of the Crown. Written in the time of Queen Elizabeth.
London, Printed by J. D. in the year 1690.

    Folio (12 × 7). A—E in twos, pp. 1-19. A1 Title, verso blank. A2^a The Publisher to the Reader. A2^b The Author to the Reader. B—E2^a Text. E2^b blank.
    This book, although issued separately, originally formed part of the Appendix to the Fundamental Constitution of the English Government by William Attwood. London, 1690, Folio.

Class IV.   *Edin. Univ.*   *S.*

1693

286. Historia o vero Vita de Elizabetta Regina d'Inghilterra. detta per Sopranome la Comediante Politica. scritta da Gregorio Leti. Arrichita di molte Figure.
Amsterdamo, appresso Abramo Wolfgang. 1693.

    8vo (6 × 3½). 2 vols. Each vol. has an engraved Title, with portrait of Queen Elizabeth. Vol. I., Dedication, &c., 12 ll. Historia pp. 1-552. Index 12 ll., with 37 Portraits. Vol. II., pp. 1-586. Index 6 ll., 16 Portraits and 2 Plans.
    The references to Queen Mary's life occur in Vol. I. at several places. Her portrait is at p. 488. In Vol. II. is a lengthy account of her trial and execution. A French translation of this book is in the Advocates' Library. 2 vols. 12mo, Amsterdam, 1703.

Class V. VI.   *S.*

1699

287. Memoires de Messire Pierre de Bourdeille, Seigneur de Brantome, Contenant Les Vies de Dames Illustres de France de son temps [The sphere].
A Leyde chez Jean Sambix le Jeune, à la Sphere. M.DC.XCIX.

    12mo (5¼ × 3). Title, verso blank. *2 Au Lecteur. *3 Contenu de ce Volume. A—Q in twelves. Text pp. 1-348.
    Discours Troisiesme, de la Reyne d'Escosse, jadis Reyne de nostre France: pp. 107-165.
    Brunet (*Manuel du Libraire*, Vol. I., p. 1211) mentions an edition, 9 vols. 12mo, Leyde, Jean Sambix, 1665-6, but no copy has come under my observation.

Class VII.   *B.M.*

288. A Relation of the Death of David Rizzi, Chief Favorite to Mary Stuart Queen of Scotland; who was killed in the Apartment of the said Queen on the 9th of March 1565. Written by the Lord Ruthen one of the principal Persons concerned in that Action. Published from an Original Manuscript. Together with an account of David Rizzi, faithfully translated from Geo. Buchanan's History of Scotland.
London, Printed for A. Baldwin in Warwick-lane. 1699.

    8vo (7 × 4¼). A—C in eights+D². A1 Title, verso blank. Text pp. 3-51, with catchwords.
    This tract was reprinted in *Scotia Rediviva* (1826), Vol. I. p. 327, and in a 4to edition, London, Triphook, 1815.

Class VII.   *Signet.*   *S.*

1700

289.   Mary Queen, of Scots Dowary, when married to the Douphine of France.
    4to (7¾ × 5¾).   6 leaves.   Title and pp. 3-11.
   The Text is an Epithalamium upon the marriage of Mary Queen of Scots to the Dauphin of France, afterwards Francis the Second, which commences as follows:—
   What sudden heat inspires my lab'ring Mind?
   Why Phoebus, long a Stranger now so kind?
   Parnassus grove which had forbore to sing
   Does with revived Io Pæans ring.
   The tract is without place or date.   The British Museum Catalogue suggests 1700.

Class IX.   *B.M.*

INDEX TO TITLES.

The figures refer to the numbers of the books.

Abridgement . . . of the Scots Chronicles: Monipennie 206, 229
Act of Privy Council, 12 June, 1567 . . 51
Actis . . . of Parliament. 1565 . . 36
Actis Of Parliament. 1568 . . . 56
Acts . . . maid in Parliamentis. 1566 . 45
Ad Persecutores Anglos. *c.* 1584 . . 126
Adamson (P.) Poemata sacra. 1619 . . 209
Admonitioun direct to the trew Lordes. M. G. B. 1571 (two editions) . . 70, 71
Advorte Hospes. (1587) 161
Af-beeldinge der Coninghinne Elyzabeth. (1605) 198
Allegations against the Surmisid Title of the Quine of Scotts. 1565. . . . 37
Allegations in behalf of the . . . Lady Mary. 1690 285
Allen (Cardinal). Ad Persecutores Anglos. *c.* 1584 126
—— A Defence of the English Catholics . 126
Apologie ou Defense de l'honorable sentence . . . de defuncte Marie Steuard. 1588 163
Appellation of John Knoxe. 1558 . . 20
Ayscu (E.) A Historie contayning the Warres. 1607 200

Ballat declaring the Nobill and gude inclinatioun of our King: Sempill. 1567 . 52
Banks (J.) The Island Queens. 1684 . 279
Barnestapolius (O.) *See* Turner (R.) .
Βασιλικον Δωρον 187, 192-194
Βασιλικον Δωρον: Gretsen. 1610 . . 204
Beaugué (Ian de). L'Histoire De La Guerre D'Escosse. 1556. 9
Bellay (J. du). Entreprise du Roy-Daulphin. 1559 25
—— Poematum Libri quatuor. 1558 . . 10
—— Tumulus Henrici Secundi. 1559 . 26
Belleforest (F. de). *See* L'Innocence de . . . Marie Royne d'Escosse. 1572 . . 85
Bellièvre (P. de). La Harangue faicte à la Royne d'Angleterre. 1588 . . . 167
Bernard (J.) Discours des plus memorables faicts. (1579) 106

Beza (T.) and G. Buchanan. Latin Poems. 1569 60
Bishoppis lyfe and testament: Sempill. 1571 68
Bisselius (J.) Aetatis nostrae gestorum. 1675 266
Bizzari (P.) Varia opuscula. 1565 . . 39
Blackwood (A.) Adversus Georgii Buchanani Dialogum. 1581 117
—— Martyre de la Royne d'Escosse 144, 174-176, 180
—— Opera Omnia. 1644 . . . 237
—— Sanctarum Precationum Prooemia. 1608 202
—— Varii generis Poematia. 1609 . 203
Boisguilbert (Sieur de). Marie Stuart Reyne d'Escosse. 1675 265
Bos (L. van). Het Leeven van Maria Stuart. 1647 241
—— Het Vorstelyck Treur-Toonneel. 1652 251
Brantôme (Seigneur de). Memoires. 1699 287
Brief Account of His Sacred Majestie's Descent. 1681 274
Brief History of the Life of Mary Queen of Scots. 1681 275
Broadsides 48-55, 57, 64-66, 68, 78, 134, 154, 156
Bruodinus (A.) Propugnaculum Catholicae Veritatis. 1669 264
Buchanan (G.) A Detection 75, 76, 80, 81, 248, 283
—— Ane Admonitioun. 1571 . . 70, 71
—— De Jure Regni . 109, 111, 113, 114, 122
—— De Jure Regni, translated into English 273, 284
—— De Maria Scotorum Regina. (1571) . 75
—— Histoire de Marie Royne d'Escosse. 1572 82
—— Poetae eximij Franciscanus. (1566) . 43
—— Psalmorum Davidis paraphrasis poetica. (1564) 35
—— Rerum Scoticarum Historia . 121, 122
—— *See* Beza (T.) and
—— *See* Copie of a letter . . . concernyng the . . . detection. (1572) . . 84
Burne (Nicol). The Disputation concerning the controversit headdis of Religion. 1581 120
By de Coninginne De waerachtighe Copie van de proclamatie. (1586) . . 135

Calderwood (D.) History of the Church of Scotland 269, 271

INDEX TO TITLES.

Camden (W.) Annales . . . 208, 216
—— The same (English translation) . 217, 226
Camerarius (D.) De Scotorum Fortitudine. 1631 227
Capacio (J. C.) Illustrium Mulierum. 1608 201
Carleton (G.) A Thankfull Remembrance. 1627 218
Castelnau, Michel de, Memoires de . 210, 261
Catalogue of the Kings of Scotland. 1610 . 205
Catharinæ Mediceæ . . . vitæ. 1575 . . 95
Causin (N.) Historia di Maria Stuarda 245, 247
—— La Cour Sainte. 1664 . . . 263
—— The Holy Court. 1678 . . . 270
Cayer (P. V.) L'Oraison Funebre de . . . l'Archevesque de Glasco. 1603 . . 195
Censure of a loyall Subiect. 1587 . . 141
Chambers (D.) Discours de la Legitime Succession des Femmes. 1579 . . . 109
—— Histoire Abbregee de tous les Roys. 1579 107
—— La Recerche des Singularitez . . . concernant l'estat d'Escosse. 1579 . . 108
Churchyard (T.) A generall rehearsall of Warres. (1579) 105
—— Firste parte of Churchyardes Chippes. 1575 94
Churchyard's Challenge. 1593 . . 183
Cockburn (P.) In Dominicam Orationem. 1555 8
Compassionevole et Memorabil Caso della morte della Regina di Scotia. 1587 151, 152
Complaynt of Scotland. (1549) . . 6
Complaynt of Scotland: Sempill. (1567) . 48
Cone (G.) De duplici statu Religionis. 1628 223
—— Vita Mariæ Stuartæ. 1624 . . 213, 214
Copie d'une Lettre de la Royne d'Escosse. 1572 86
Copie of a Letter: Elder. (1555) . . 7
Copie of a letter . . . concernyng the credit of the late published detection. (1572) . 84
Copie of a Letter to . . . the Earle of Leycester. 1586 131
Copye wan eenen brief aen den E. den Grave van Leycester. 1587 . . . 143
Craig (T.) Henrici . . . et Marie . . . Epithalamium. 1565 38
Crompton (R.) A short declaration of the ende of Traytors. 1587 . . . 140
—— Copye wan eenen brief aen den E. den Grave van Leycester. 1587 . . 143
—— The Copie of a Letter to . . . the Earle of Leycester. 1586 . . . 131

De Iezabelis Angliæ Parricidio. (1587) . 153
De Justitia Britannica. 1584 . . . 125
De la Guerre ouverte entre le Roy d'Escosse & la Royne d'Angleterre. 1588 . . 166
De Maria Scotorum Regina. (1571) . . 75
Deeclaratioun of the Lordis iust quarrell: Sempill. 1567 55
Defence of the English Catholics . . . 126
Defence of the Honorable sentence and execution of the Queene of Scots. (1587) . 145
Defence of the honour of the . . . Queene of Scotlande: Lesley. 1569 . . . 62
—— The same. 1571 73
Del Tesoro Politico: Marcaldi. 1612 . . 207
Delitiae Poetarum Scotorum. 1637 . . 232
Della Valle (F.) La Reina di Scotia Tragedia. 1628 222
Diallog betuix honour gude Fame, and the Authour: Sempill. 1570 . . . 63
Dialogi ab Eusebio Philadelpho. 1574 . 88
Dickenson (J.) Speculum Tragicum. 1605 197
Digges (Sir D.) The Compleat Ambassador. 1665 252
Discours de la Mort de . . . Marie Stouard. (1587) 160
Discours des Troubles nouvellement advenus au Royaume d'Angleterre . . . 47, 67
Discours du Grand et Magnifique Triumphe. 1558 15-17
Discours Merveilleux de la vie . . . de Catherine de Medicis. 1575 . . . 96
Discours Moral de la Paix. 1559 . . 27
Discourse touching the pretended match betwene the Duke of Norfolke and the Queene of Scottes. (1569) . . . 61
Discoverie of a Gaping Gulf: Stubbs. 1579 104
Discoverie of the treasons . . . by Francis Throckemorton. 1584 124
Disputation concerning the controversit headdis of Religion. 1581 . . . 120
Drummond (W.) History of Scotland. 1655 253

Effect of the declaration made . . . by M. Recorder of London. (1571) . . 72
Elder (J.) Copie of a letter. (1555) . . 7
Elegie sur le despart de la Royne Marie. 1561 31
Elizabethæ Reginae Angliae Edictum . . . Andreae Philopatri . . . responsio. 1593 184
Epistle or exhortation to unitie and peace. (1548) 4
Epistola exhortatoria ad pacem. 1548 . 4
Epitome of the Title . . . to the Sovereigntie of Scotlande. 1548 3

INDEX TO TITLES.

Ercolani (G.) La Reggia delle Vedove sacre.
1682 276
Ex Cujusdam commentariis Historiarum. 1558 19
Examen Historicum : Heylin. 1659 . . 260
Execution oder Todt Marien Stuart . 157, 162
Exhortacion to the Scottes. 1547 . . 2
Exhortatioun to the Lordis : Sempill. 1567 54
Expedicion in Scotlande, The late. 1544 . 1
Expedicion into Scotlande : Patten. 1548 . 5

Frarin (P.) An Oration against the Unlaw-
full Insurrections. 1566 . . . 46
Fulke (W.) An Apologie . . . against the
railing declamation of Peter Frarine. 1586 133
Fulwell (U.) The Flower of Fame. 1575 . 93

Gatti (Bassiano). Maria Regina di Scotia. 1633 228
Godwin (F.) Rerum Anglicarum . . .
Annales. 1628 224
Grafton (R.) A Chronicle at large. 1569 . 59
Graun (G. H.) Q. D. V. B. Causas . . .
Mariæ Stuartæ. 1680 272
Gretson (J.) Βασιλικον Δωρον. 1610 . 204
Guillonius (R.) Nuptiale Carmen. 1558 . 11
Gunton (S.) The History of the Church of
Peterburgh. 1686 282

Hamilton (J.) A facile Traictise. 1600 . 189
—— Ane Catholik and facile Traictise. 1581 118
Hamiltons, The manifold Practises . . . of
the. 1648 . . . . . 243, 244
Harangue de Tresnoble . . . Marie D'estuart.
1563 34
Harangue faicte à la Royne d'Angleterre. 1588 167
Harangue Funebre sur la Mort de la Royne
d'Escosse. (1588) 170
Herrera (A. de). Historia de lo Sucedido en
Escocia 181, 182
Heylin (P.) Examen Historicum. 1659 . 260
Histoire de Marie Royne d'Escosse. 1572 . 82
Histoire et Martyre de la Royne d'Escosse. 1589 180
Historia Belgica. (1598) 186
Historical Memoires on the Reigns of Queen
Elizabeth, and King James. 1658 . 259
Historie of . . . Princesse Elizabeth : Cam-
den. 1630 226
Historie of the Life and Death of Mary
Stuart 215, 231
Holinshed (R.) Chronicles. 1577 . . 99
Hospitalius (M.) Galliarum Cancellarii
Epistolarum. 1585 128

Hume (D.) History of the Houses of Douglas
and Angus. 1644 238

In Francisci . . . et Mariæ . . . Nuptias.
1558 13
Innocence de . . . Marie Royne d'Escosse.
1572 85
Johnston (J.) A trewe Description of the
nobill Race of the Stewards. 1603 . 196
—— Inscriptiones Historicae Regum Scotorum.
1602 191
Johnston (R.) Historiarum Libri Duo. 1642 234
—— Historie of Scotland. 1646 . . 240

Kempe (W.) A Dutiful Invective. 1587 . 139
Knox (J.) A Sermon. 1566 . . . 42
—— History of the Reformation . . 130, 236
—— The Appellation . . . from the cruell
. . . sentence. 1558 20
—— The First Blast of the Trumpet. 1558 21
Kurtzer Auszzug. 1566 44
Kurtzer unnd gründtlicher bericht. 1587 . 158
Kyffin (M.) A Defence of the Honorable
sentence and execution of the Queene of
Scots. (1587) 145
—— Apologie ou Defense de l'honorable
sentence . . . de defuncte Marie Steuard.
1588 163

Laing (J.) De vita et moribus . . . Hæreti-
corum. 1581 119
—— De vita et moribus Theodori Bezae. 1585 127
Lamentation of Lady Scotland : Sempill. 1572 77
La Planche (R. de). See Lisle (F. de)
La Tapie (J. de). Chantz Royaulx. 1558 . 14
Le Laboureur (J.) Les Memoires de Messire
Michel de Castelnau. 1660 . . . 261
Le Moyne (P.) La Gallerie des Femmes
Fortes 242, 262
Lesley (J.) A defence of the honour of the
. . . Queene of Scotlande. 1569 . 62
—— A Treatise concerning the Defence of
the Honour of . . . Marie Queene of
Scotland. 1571 73
—— A Treatise Touching the Right . . . of
. . . Marie, Queene of Scotland . 74, 123
—— Ad Nobilitatem Populumq. Scoticum. 1578 101
—— De Illustrium Foeminarum. 1580 . 116
—— De Origine Moribus 100, 267
—— De Titulo et Jure . . . Mariæ Scotorum
Reginæ. 1580 115

INDEX TO TITLES.

Lesley (J.) Declaration del Titulo . . . Maria Reyna de Escoçia. (1587) . . . 138
—— Du Droict et Tiltre de . . . Marie Royne d'Escosse. (1587) 137
—— Harangue Funebre sur la Mort de la Royne d'Escosse. (1588) . . . 170
—— Libri Duo. 1574 91
—— Pro libertate impetranda Oratio. 1574 . 92
Leti (G.) Historia o vero Vita de Elizabetta. 1693 286
Lettera di Sartorio Loscho. 1587 . . 146
Lisle (F. de). La Legende de Charles Cardinal de Lorraine 97, 112
—— A Legendarie . . . of Charles Cardinal of Lorraine. 1577 98
Loschi (A.) Compendi Historici. 1652 . 250
Lyer laid open. 1648 244

Manifold Practices . . . of the Hamiltons. 1648 . . . . 243, 244
Manolesso (E. M.) Historia Nova. 1572 . 79
Marcaldi (F.) Del Tesoro Politico. 1612 . 207
—— La Terza Parte del Tesoro Politico. (1605) 199
Maria Stuart of Gemartelde Majesteit. 1646 239
Maria Stuarta . . . Vindice Oberto Barnestapolio. 1588 164
Mariæ Scotorum Reginæ Epitaphium. (1587) 156
Mariae Stuartae Scotorum Reginae Principis Catholicae. 1587 159
Marie der Konigin . . . eigentliche Bildtnuss. (1587) 154
Marie Stuart Reyne d'Escosse. 1675 . . 265
Martyre de la Royne: Blackwood 144, 174-176, 180
Mary Queen of Scots Dowary. (1700) . 289
Mayr (J.) Kurtzer bericht. 1600 . . 188
Medulla Historiæ Scoticæ. 1685 . . 280
Melvil, Sir James, Memoirs of. 1683 . 278
Memoires de l'Estat de France. 1578 . 103
Memoires of the Family of the Stuarts. 1683 277
Mercerius (J.) Dialogus in . . . Nuptias. 1558 18
Mezeray (F. G. du). Histoire de France. 1643 235
Monipennie (J.) Scots Chronicles . 206, 229
Montchrestien (A. de). Tragedies . . 190
Mort de la Royne d'Escosse . 172, 173, 179
Motivos Para Favorecer La Religion Catolica. (1635) 230

New ballat set out be ane Fugitue Scottisman: Sempill. 1572 78
Norton (T.) To the Quenes Maiesties poore deceived Subiectes. 1569 . . . 58

Observations upon . . . A Compleat History. 1656 256
Ode sur la Mort de . . . Marie Royne d'Escosse. 1588 168
Oort (J. van). Stuarts Ongeluckige Heerschappye. 1649 246
Oraison Funebre de . . . l'Archevesque de Glasco. 1603 195
Oraison Funebre de . . . Marie Royne d'Escosse. 1588 169
Oraison funebre es Obseques de . . . Princesse, Marie. 1561 30
Ordoure and Doctrine of the Generall Fast. 1574 90
Ordres Tenuz à la reception . . . du . . . Francois II. & de la Roine, en la ville d'Orleans. (1560) 29
Osborne (F.) Historical Memoires. (1658) 259

Paix, faicte entre . . . Henry II. 1559 . 24
Parry, William, Declaration of the horrible Treasons by. (1585) 129
Parsons (R.) Elizabethæ Reginae Angliae Edictum . . . responsio. 1593 . . 184
Pasquier (Estienne). Recherches. 1621 . 211
Patten (W.) Expedicion into Scotlande. 1548 5
Perlin (Estienne). Description des Royaulmes d'Angleterre et d'Escosse. 1558 . . 22
Peyton (Sir E.) The Divine Catastrophe. 1652 249
Philadelphus (E.) Dialogi. 1574 . . 88
—— La Reveille-Matin. 1574 . . . 89
Philippes (Morgan). *See* Lesley (J.)
Poysonit Schot: Sempill. 1570 . . 64
Proclamation, 11th June, 1567 . . . 50
—— 26th June, 1567 49
—— 7th May, 1568 57
—— 4th Dec., 1586 . . . 134, 135, 143
Proditionis ab aliquot Scotiæ Perduellibus. 1566 40
Promtuarii Iconum. 1578 102

Raleigh (C.) Observations upon . . . A Compleat History. 1656 . . . 256
Regents tragedie: Sempill. 1570 . . 65
Regnault ( ). Marie Stuard, Tragedie. 1639 233
Relacion del estado del Reyno de Escocia. 1594 185
Relation of the death of David Rizzi. 1699 288
Rerum Anglicarum . . . Annales. 1628 . 224
Reveille-Matin des Francois. Philadelphe. 1574 89
Ribadeneyra (P. de). Hystoria Ecclesiastica. 1588 165

INDEX TO TITLES.

Ronsard (P. de). Elegie sur le despart de la Royne Marie. 1561 31
—— Oeuvres. 1623 212

Salutem in Christo. 1571 69
Sanders (N.) Vera . . . Historia Schismatis. 1628 225
Sanderson (W.) A compleat History of the Lives and Reigns. 1656 . . . 255
—— An Answer to a Scurrilous Pamplet. 1656 257
Scott (G.) The Memoirs of Sir James Melvil. 1683 278
Scottish Queens Buriall at Peterborough. 1589 177
Scotus (Romoaldus). Summarium Rationum 171, 221
Sempill (R.) Ane deeclaratioun of the Lordis iust quarrell. 1567 55
—— Ane Exhortatioun to the Lordis. 1567 54
—— Ane new ballat. 1572 . . . 78
—— Ane Tragedie. 1570 63
—— Ballat declaring the Nobill and gude inclinatioun of our King. 1567 . . 52
—— Testament and tragedie of umquhile King Henrie Stewart. 1567 . . . 53
—— The Bishoppis lyfe and testament. 1571 68
—— The Complaynt of Scotland. (1567) . 48
—— The Lamentation of Lady Scotland. 1572 77
—— The Poysonit Schot. 1570 . . . 64
—— The Regents tragedie. 1570 . . 65
—— The spur to the Lordis. 1570 . . 66
Short Discourse . . . of all the late pretended Treasons. (1586) 132
Somerset (Duke of). Epistle or exhortation. 1548 4
Speculum Tragicum : Dickenson. 1605 . 197
Spotswood (J.) History of the Church of Scotland 254, 268
Spur to the Lordis : Sempill. 1570 . . 66
Stranguage (W.) See Historie . . 215, 231
Stubbs (J.) The Discoverie of a Gaping Gulf. 1579 104
Symeoni (G.) Epitalamio. 1559 . . 23

Tapie (J. de la). See La Tapie (J. de)
Teatro de Perepezie Poema. 1686 . . 281
Terza Parte del Tesoro Politico : Marcaldi. (1605) 199

Testament and tragedie of umquhile King Henrie Stewart : Sempill. 1567 . . 53
Theatrum Crudelitatum Hæreticorum : Verstegan. 1587 155
Three Partes of Commentaries . . . of the Civill warres of Fraunce. *Trans.* by Timme. 1574 87
Throckemorton, Francis, Discoverie of the treasons by. 1584 124
Timme (T.) *trans.* The Three Partes of Commentaries . . . of the Civill warres of Fraunce. 1574 87
Tragedie in form of ane Diallog : Sempill. 1570 63
Treatise of Treasons. 1572 . . . 83
Triomphes faictz a l'entrée du Roy a Chenonceau. 1559 28
True and plaine declaration of the horrible Treasons, practised by William Parry. (1585) 129
Turnebus (A.) Epithalamium. 1558 . . 12
Turner (R.) L'Histoire et Vie de Marie Stuart. 1589 178
—— Maria Stuarta, Regina Scotiæ . 164, 220

Udall (W.) *See* Historie . . 215, 231

Vega (Lope F. de). Corona Tragica. 1627 219
Vera, e compita Relazione del . . . Regina 147-149
Vera Relatione del . . . Regina. 1587 . 150
Verstegan (N.) Theatrum Crudelitatum Hæreticorum. 1587 . . . 155
Vincentius Lirinensis . . . of the catholik fayth. 1563 33
Vondel (J. van den). Maria Stuart. 1646 . 239

Waerachtich verhael. 1587 . . . 136
Walsingham (W.) *See* A brief History . . . of Mary Queen of Scots. 1681 . . 275
Warachtich verhael van seeckere requesten. 1587 142
Watson (J.) Memoires of the Family of the Stuarts. 1683 277
Watson (R.) Historical Collections. 1657 . 258
Whetstone (G.) The Censure of a loyall Subiect. 1587 141
Winzet (N.) Certane Tractatis. 1562 . 32
—— Translation of Vincentius Lirinensis . . . of the catholik fayth. 1563 . . 33
Wood (Lambert). *See* Bos (L. van.)

LIST OF FACSIMILES.

Title-page. Arms of Queen Mary, from Lesley's History. 1578 . No. 101
- I. Title-page of An exhortacion to the Scottes. 1547 . . No. 2
- II. Title-page of An Epitome of the title. 1548 . . No. 3
- III. Title-page of An Epistle or exhortacion, to vnitie & peace. 1548 No. 4
- IV. Title-page of Perlin's Description des Royavlmes. 1558 . No. 22
- V. Title-page of Les Ordres tenvz à la reception . . . du . . . Francois II. & de la Roine. 1560 . . . . . No. 29
- VI. Title-page of Allegations against the Svrmisid Title of the Quine of Scotts. 1565 . . . . No. 37
- VII. Last page of the same.
- VIII. Title-page of Lesley's A defence of the honour of the Quene of Scotlande. 1569 . . . . No. 62
- IX. Title-page of Sempill's Ane Tragedie in forme of ane Diallog. 1570 . . . . No. 63
- X. Genealogical tree of the Scottish Kings, from Lesley's History. 1578 . . . . No. 101
- XI. Portraits of Queen Mary and James VI., from the same.
- XII. Title-page of Lesley's Declaration del Titvlo. 1587 . . No. 138
- XIII. Execution of Queen Mary, from Verstegan's Theatrvm Crudelitatum Hæreticorum. 1587 . . . . . . No. 155
- XIV. Title-page of Execvtion oder Todt Marien Stuarts. 1588 . No. 162
- XV. Title-page of Ayscu's Historie. 1607 . . . . . No. 200
- XVI. Portrait of Queen Mary, from The Historie of . . . Mary Stuart. 1624 . . . . No. 215
- XVII. Title-page of the same.
- XVIII. Title-page of Gatti's Maria Regina di Scotia. 1633 . . No. 228
- XIX. Engraved title-page of Regnault's Marie Stvard. 1639. 4to. . No. 233
- XX. The same. 12mo edition.

www.ingramcontent.com/pod-product-compliance
Lightning Source LLC
Chambersburg PA
CBHW030342170426
43202CB00010B/1212